Mosaic Madness

THE POVERTY AND POTENTIAL OF LIFE IN CANADA

REGINALD W. BIBBY

To Delphine and Karen,
two special sisters
who have given far more
than they have taken

First published in 1990 by
Stoddart Publishing Co. Limited
34 Lesmill Road
Toronto, Canada
M3B 2T6
Second printing April 1991

Canadian Cataloguing in Publication Data
Bibby, Reginald W. (Reginald Wayne), 1943-
Mosaic madness

ISBN 0-7737-5399-0

1. Multiculturalism - Canada.* 2. Canada - Social conditions - 1945- . I. Title.

FC104.B52 1990 305'.8'00971 C90-094769-1
F1035.A1B52 1990

Indexing, Heather L. Ebbs
Typeset by Jay Tee Graphics Ltd.
Printed and bound in Canada

The author gratefully acknowledges the permission of Gallup Canada Inc. to use data in tables included in this book, as well as Edward B. Marks Music Co. for permission to use lyrics from the song "Two Out of Three Ain't Bad" (Jim Steinman) © 1977 — Edward B. Marks Music Co. Used by permission. All rights reserved.

CONTENTS

PREFACE

THIS BOOK IS AN EFFORT to interpret the times. We don't lack information these days. Compliments of the media and education, we have data and ideas coming out of our ears. But it's another thing to understand what it all means. Our preoccupation with things specific and our frequent lack of historical perspective can add up to our knowing much about little, and little about much.

Those of you who are familiar with my work know that I have given considerable energy to generating information. Central to my research have been the Project Canada national surveys, carried out every five years since 1975. Complementing these adult surveys have been the Project Teen Canada national youth surveys, conducted in 1984 and 1987 with Don Posterski.

Such data collection has been motivated by what I call "a chipmunk mentality." Like the chipmunk who comes out of the tree trunk, runs along the branch, and stands on its hind legs, trying to figure out what's going on, I am first and foremost curious about life. Frankly, I'm not all that interested in methods and theory — or even sociology itself; but I am interested in finding out "how the world works." To the extent that data and methods and sociology and whatever can help in the chipmunk quest, I find them valuable.

This book should therefore come as no surprise. It represents an effort to draw on the information available concerning our past and present to "make sense" of what is going on. Those of you who are more interested than I in theoretical discourse and data analysis will perhaps be disappointed. Our interests are not the same. Not that the book lacks theory or data.

My debt to others is enormous. The framework for analyzing Canadian life was stimulated by two primary sources — Robert Bellah and his famous "et als" (Richard Madsen, William Sullivan, Ann Swidler, and Steve Tipton) in the book *Habits of the*

Heart, and Allan Bloom in *The Closing of the American Mind*. Inadvertently, these Americans have provided critiques more appropriate to Canada than to the United States.

The effort to span so much of Canadian life would never have been possible without my being able to draw heavily on the superb contributions of many writers and scholars. Among them are Howard Palmer (intergroup relations), Doris Anderson (women), Kevin Christiano (Pierre Trudeau), Seymour Lipset (Canadian-American comparisons), and the superb analyses of Canadian spheres of life compiled by James Curtis and Lorne Tepperman. The Gallup organization has been compiling a treasury of Canadian attitudes through their surveys dating back to the 1940s; I am extremely grateful to Gallup Canada, Inc., for permitting me to reproduce some of their findings. The data being generated by Statistics Canada, of course, continues to be indispensable to an understanding of Canadian life; I appreciate being allowed to make use of "Statscan" material, including findings released through its excellent publication, *Canadian Social Trends*.

I will be making considerable use of two concepts. The first is individualism, by which I mean the tendency to stress the individual over the group. The second is relativism, the inclination to see the merits of behavior and ideas not as universal or "absolute" but as varying with individuals and their environments, and, in the end, as being equally valid because they are *chosen*. While both concepts have their origins with academics, my interest is in the extent to which they have wandered from their ivory-tower birthplaces and have been out playing with average Canadians. Most people probably aren't clear on the presence of the two wayward concepts and would be hard pressed to define either. Similar to how they operate appliances and VCRs, they don't understand them, but just use them.

Let me anticipate three problems that may be raised. First, concerning concepts, some readers may say that my use of the two tradition-laden terms is too loose. I would stress that for me a definition only tries to capture the essence of a concept. If what I am describing does not match or cover the full range of what some choose to call individualism or relativism, then I probably need to give my concepts different labels. My interest lies not with the two symbols but with two significant patterns in Canadian life. I don't want the thesis to be lost over a definitional squabble.

Second, concerning data, other readers may charge me with spreading myself too thin by exploring the extent to which the two themes have touched the various spheres of Canadian society, past and present. I would encourage them to focus on my thesis, treating my use of history and what is taking place interpersonally and institutionally as modest illustrative attempts to examine the thesis. Of course there is much more to be said historically, interpersonally, and institutionally. The information available in each area is formidable and, to any researcher, more than a little intimidating. I have sampled material, not so that it can stand as an end in itself, but for the purpose of exploring my argument. I hope those with expertise in the diverse areas that the book addresses will not merely ask me to add more data, but will ask themselves how well the thesis fits the information as they know it.

Third, concerning consistency, some will say that while I am critical of the excesses of relativism, I myself do not offer absolute answers when addressing topics like family life, sexuality, and religion. They are right. My problem with relativisim is not that it is never appropriate. Clearly, some things *are* relative. My concern is that relativism taken to excess blinds us to the exploration of the merits of ideas and behavior. What I am arguing for, therefore, is the pursuit of accuracy and the best. Through such quests we will be able to gain understanding as to what kinds of behavior and which ideas are relative to well-being and "truth," versus being "better" and "best."

In the past, some people ruled out exploration on the basis that they already had all the absolute answers. In the present, many are ruling out exploration on the basis that they already have all the relativistic answers. Both approaches are equally closed-minded. More seriously, neither works. There are times when the person operating with absolutes encounters situations in which solutions *are not* clear-cut. There are also times when relativistically minded people find themselves facing varied situations where the solutions *are* clear-cut.

What I am offering is both description and methodological prescription. Most of the answers will be found in the future.

The book has been a substantial undertaking. I thank Don Posterski for sharing the initial dream, and many people for enduring my demanding schedule, notably my parents and Reggie, Dave, and Russ. I sincerely thank Donald G. Bastian of Stoddart Publishing who, once again, as with *The Emerging Generation* and *Fragmented Gods*, has brought his insights and talent, humor and friendship to this project.

I love life, and believe that the best in life is found through combining our heads and our hearts. My hope is that *Mosaic Madness* will stimulate thought and stir emotions, leading Canadians to pursue with improved clarity that which is possible.

Mosaic Madness

INTRODUCTION

THE 1990s ARE A TIME of startling changes worldwide. Late 1989 saw the dismantling of the Eastern bloc, with Poland, Hungary, Czechoslovakia, East Germany, and Romania severing their ties with Communism and declaring their autonomy. The Soviet Union, on the heels of its unexpected 1989 policies of economic reform (*perestroika*) and critiquing of the old (*glasnost*), announced in early 1990 the end of its single-party system. China may well be the next Communist giant to regroup. In Latin America, Panamanian dictator Manuel Noriega was ousted in favor of a democratic government, while Daniel Ortega was handed a stunning upset in an unprecedented free election in Nicaragua. Other countries, including El Salvador, could soon follow. In South Africa, Nelson Mandela emerged after twenty-seven years of political captivity and declared that apartheid would soon be a thing of the past. The Middle East perhaps will be the next place where the curtain will rise on the unforeseen.

The pervasive theme in these dramatic political developments is that of *freedom*. At the collective level, people are saying that they want the freedom to govern themselves, to develop their economies, to enhance their overall quality of life. Closely tied to the theme of freedom is the theme of *the individual*. At the personal level, men and women are saying that they want to be free from oppressive regimes, free to express themselves, free to work, to worship, to travel, to share in what their nations and the world have to offer, free to become everything that they as individuals are capable of being.

Closely tied to the themes of freedom and the individual is a third important emphasis — *pluralism*. Sheer diversity, nationally and globally, makes pluralism a descriptive term: we have many "pluralistic" societies; internationally, we have a "pluralistic" planet. As a policy, pluralism contributes to collective and personal freedom by legitimizing diversity. It resolves the question of how different individuals who want to be free can live in community. Pluralism diplomatically and optimistically declares that the whole is best served by the contribution of varied parts.

Nationwide and worldwide, such a policy translates into an emphasis on coexistence, versus conquest or assimilation. Pluralism's call for tolerance and respect frequently takes the form of statements about human rights. Expressed nationally, it means that Californians are expected to coexist on U.S. turf with Mexican Americans, that ethnic groups in the Soviet Union no longer need to pretend that they don't exist, that Blacks and Whites in South Africa can live as equals in an integrated society, that minority-group members in Canada no longer need to change their names and cultures if they want to "fit in." Expressed globally, it means that war and domination of societies no longer are appropriate. Cultural obliteration in the form of both intolerance and alleged enlightening is likewise an unacceptable violation of the norms of planetary pluralism. Customs and languages, worldviews and religions, are not to be tampered with.

The three themes of freedom, the individual, and pluralism are joined by a fourth centrally important characteristic — *relativism*. The free expression of the individual and groups is made possible only by suspending value judgments about how people live. *Truth* and *best* are not listed in the pluralism dictionary. The only truth is that everything is relative. "Cultural relativism" is accepted as a given; those who dare to assert that their culture is best are dubbed ethnocentric; those who dare to assert that they have the truth are labeled bigots. Truth has been replaced by personal viewpoint.

Many observers are heralding these significant worldwide developments as indications of a new era in world history. What lies ahead, they say, are unprecedented peace and affluence. Social forecasters John Naisbitt and Patricia Aburdene, for example, maintain that "the great unifying theme at the conclusion of the twentieth century is the triumph of the individual. Threatened by totalitarianism for much of this century," say the two authors, "individuals are meeting the millennium more powerful than ever before."[1] As for the future, they write: "On the threshold of the millennium . . . we possess the tools and the capacity to build utopia here and now. . . . Within the hearts and minds of humanity, there has been a commitment to life, to the utopian quest for peace and prosperity for all, which today we can clearly visualize."[2]

Our planet is indeed moving toward worldwide freedom, led by the emancipated individual. That freedom is being made possible by pluralism and relativism. It all sounds progressive, for many exciting, and for the likes of Naisbitt and Aburdene a cause for celebration.

But hold on everybody — the victory party is premature. Since the 1960s, one country has been leading the world in advocating freedom through pluralism and relativism. It has been carrying out something of a unique experiment in trying to be a multinational society, enshrining coexistence and tolerance. The preliminary results are beginning to appear. The news is not that good.

Societies on the verge of implementing pluralistic ideals would do well to take a good look at this important case example. The country? *Canada.*

1

Our Predicament

On an ordinary September night in 1988, a far from ordinary event took place. A man from Canada did something no other human had previously done. He blazed down a track in Korea in the fastest time ever, and a nation enjoyed a rare moment of collective ecstasy as he leaned over and accepted the gold. The fact that he was assisted by a banned drug soon transformed jubilant celebration into painful disappointment and anger. Millions who had passionately cheered now passionately chided. Some reminded the critics that any young man might well have broken under the pressure of such gigantic national expectations. In the end, Ben Johnson seems to have done what was best for Ben Johnson. And a nation walked away. Did Ben Johnson have any obligation to Canada? Did Canada have any obligation to Ben Johnson? Was it wrong for him to break the rules? Was it wrong to have any rules? Was it wrong only because he got caught?

In Victoria just a few weeks earlier, Canada's largest Protestant denomination acknowledged that sexual orientation should not be a barrier to full participation in the Church. Practicing homosexuals could be ordained as Christian ministers. While some applauded the United Church decision as prophetic, large numbers of members and adherents felt betrayed, and some threatened to leave. The controversy continues into the 1990s. If individual faith is tied to religious community, what happens when one's group does not represent one's views? Is the individual led by God? Is the group led by God? Is no one led by God? Is truth just an outdated illusion, replaced in our time by personal preference?

Canadians were no better prepared to respond to an international controversy that erupted in early 1989 after an author attacked a major religion and found himself condemned to die. It was an unlikely matchup — Salman Rushdie vs. Ayatollah Khomeini — with a worldwide audience looking on. Is ultimate good found in being open to unlimited expression, or are there times when such expression is purchased at the price of others' pain, and therefore must be denied? Does freedom of expression include the freedom to assail what some cherish or, in turn, to assail the assailer . . . and then to assail the assailer of the assailer? Is there no limit to such a regression of individual rights, some boundary that preserves what is socially important?

Then there was the turban controversy. In 1989, the federal Solicitor General announced that the face of the RCMP would be altered to better reflect the changing nature of Canadian society. Variations to the uniform would be considered; Sikhs might be allowed to wear turbans. A great outcry was heard, particularly from western Canada. Some people, including the Prime Minister, saw the protest as blatant racism. Others maintained that the changes represented the dismantling of one of the cherished symbols of Canadian life. In a pluralistic society, is it possible to have *any* collective symbols that do not offend the cultural inclinations of some? Is it possible to have consensus on anything at a national level? Does the invitation to come to Canada carry an expectation that accommodations will be made to our culture? Are we expecting more of ourselves than other people would expect of us in their countries?

The June 1990 failure to ratify the Meech Lake accord renewed speculation that Quebec would abandon its traditional place in Canada. After three years of doomsday proclamations and mounting anxiety, Canadians were left, not with a positive outcome, but with more uncertainty than ever about the country's future. Is such ongoing strain really necessary? Can Quebec and the rest of Canada not decide what is best for each other? When will Quebec decide what it wants from Canada? When will the rest of Canada respect Quebec's wishes and get on with life? How long must we live in such political limbo, giving our resources and energies to such debilitating "nation-building"?

Incidents and issues such as these are a reflection of a crisis in social life that Canadians are experiencing from coast to coast. It's more than Meech Lake; together or apart, Canada and Quebec will continue to experience the crisis. It's more than Free Trade or the GST. It's more than federalism or regionalism, racism or sexism. It's almost Canadian sacrilege to say it, but still it needs to be said: the crisis stems from the unintended consequences of the policy that is our pride and joy — *pluralism*.

The Heralded Mosaic

Faced with the problem of creating a society in which people of varied linguistic and cultural backgrounds can live together, Canadians have decided to convert a demographic reality into a national virtue. We have decreed that what is descriptively obvious should be prescriptively valued. Canada, we have concluded, will be a multinational society, a multicultural mosaic of people from varied backgrounds who will have the freedom to live as they see fit.

FREEDOM FOR EVERYONE

In this country, there will be no pressure, as there is in some other countries — notably the United States — to discard one's cultural past, and conform to the dominant culture. The name of the Canadian cultural game is not *melting* but *mosaic*. Our premier spokesman for a multinational Canada, Pierre Elliott Trudeau, eloquently expressed things this way: "Canada . . . is a human place, a sanctuary of sanity in an increasingly troubled world. We need not search further for our identity. These traits of tolerance and courtesy and respect for our environment and one another provide it. I suggest that a superior form of identity would be difficult to find."[1] The central goal of Canadian life has become harmonious coexistence, the central means equality and justice. We aspire to accept and respect the ideas and lifestyles of one another, to be equitable and fair. Beyond mere platitudes, Canada has enshrined good intentions in bilingual and multicultural policies, along with a Charter of Rights and Freedoms.

In Canada, we decry any signs of racism or bigotry, exploitation or abuse. We have written laws into our criminal code that prohibit the willful promotion of hatred against any identifiable group. Our social scientists — going back at least to Carleton University's John Porter and his *Vertical Mosaic* of 1965 — have given preeminent attention to issues of equality and justice as they affect minorities, women, the poor, and others. The media instill in us the primacy of such issues by consistently treating charges of racism or unfair treatment as front-page news.

Few events have more dramatically disclosed the importance that Canada officially gives to equality than the national soul-searching that followed the tragic slaying of fourteen young women at the University of Montreal in December 1989. As Canadians, we have aspired to coexistence; there is no place here for disrespect, let alone hatred. The charges of rampant sexism and misogyny in the aftermath of Montreal left the nation dazed. What was being attacked was not our Achilles heel but our heart. Peaceful coexistence has been our national dream. In Montreal, that dream was interrupted by a nightmare.

Canada might not be among the world's elite nations, especially when we compare ourselves with our giant cousin to the south. But we like to believe that we have one special thing going for us — our mosaic. Joe Clark's oft-cited phrase sums up our self-image: "We are a community of communities." Such an endorsement of pluralism, we have believed, gives us a social system and a social outlook that is right for the day. As two York University sociologists, Linda Hunter and Judith Posner, put it, "Canada as a whole presents a neutral, affable face that distinguishes the country, for example, from its more exuberant and aggressive neighbor. . . . Canada's gentler cultural presence may be ahead of its time."[2]

There we have it: a country comprised of diversified groups that together comprise a mosaic — except there's more. Our emphasis on *individual* freedom means that, beyond the cultural groups that comprise the national mosaic, we also have individual mosaic pieces within each group. If the prophet Ezekiel saw "wheels within wheels" as he looked toward the heavens, those looking toward Canada today see "mosaics within mosaics."

Our mosaics have not stopped with the sphere of intergroup relations. Pluralism at the group and individual levels has become part of the Canadian psyche. Some time ago it left its cultural cradle. The pluralism infant has been growing up in the past three decades. It has been traveling across the country, visiting our moral, religious, family, educational, and political spheres. We now have not only a cultural mosaic but also a moral mosaic, a meaning system mosaic, a family structure mosaic, a sexual mosaic. And that's just the shortlist. Pluralism has come to pervade Canadian minds and Canadian institutions.

Everywhere it has traveled, pluralism has left behind its familiar emphases — tolerance, respect, appreciation for diversity, the insistence that individuals must be free to think and to behave according to their consciences. The result is that ours has become a society in which everything seems possible.

IMPROVING ON TRUTH

Pluralism translates into emancipated groups and emancipated individuals. Indispensable to such a posture is the accompanying declaration that all viewpoints are equally valid and that all pursuits are equally noble.

Such legitimization of diverse choice has been provided by the widespread acceptance of *relativism*. Absolutists assert that truth transcends cultures and individuals. In contrast, relativists assert that viewpoints reflect the social and intellectual settings from which people come. "Truth" is socially constructed. Consequently, the origin of ideas is not mysterious; ideas can be traced back to social locations.

The emphasis on relativism grew out of the laudable desire of nineteenth-century social scientists to describe foreign cultures in the cultures' own terms. Marriage and sexual practices in Polynesia, for instance, should be described in Polynesian terms, rather than in terms that flow from Western assumptions and practices. Many philosophers made similar efforts. Ethical relativism, for example, recognizes that fundamental differences in ethical views and practices fall along cultural lines, with no one position necessarily transcending all cultures.

In Canada, pluralism articulates the pathway to group and

individual freedom. But relativism plays the important role of providing the rationale for freedom of thought and behavior. If pluralism is the pitcher, relativism is the center-fielder. Relativism pronounces that it is appropriate and ideal that a culture encourage a wide variety of views and lifestyles. Pluralism establishes choices; relativism declares the choices valid.

It all sounds reasonable and logical, maybe even a shade ingenious. The picture that emerges, according to sociologist Carol Agòcs, is one of Canadian culture as an intricate tapestry of many hues, woven from the strands of many cultures.[3] At its best, Canada stands as a model to the world, a nation that can be a home to people of all nations and cultures, a microcosm of the harmony and peace that are possible when cultural diversity is tolerated and respected.

But then again, not a few times in history the unsound has been mistaken for the profound.

Too Much of a Good Thing

Social life has always required a balance between the individual and the group. It also has required a balance between encouraging choice and insisting on the careful evaluation of choices in order to determine which positions are better, best, and true.

Since the 1960s, Canada has been encouraging the freedom of groups and individuals without simultaneously laying down cultural expectations. Canada has also been encouraging the expression of viewpoints without simultaneously insisting on the importance of evaluating the merits of those viewpoints. During the past thirty years, colorful collages of mosaics have been forming throughout Canadian life. Our expectation has been that fragments of the mosaic will somehow add up to a healthy and cohesive society. It is not at all clear why we should expect such an outcome.

To encourage individual mosaic fragments may well result in the production of individual mosaic fragments — and not much more. The multiculturalism assumption — that a positive sense of one's group will lead to tolerance and respect of other groups — has not received strong support, notes McGill University sociologist Morton Weinfeld. The evidence, he says, "suggests a kind of ethnocentric effect, so that greater preoccupation with one's own group makes one more distant from and antipathetic to others."[4]

The evaluation research, however, has just begun. The official enshrinement of pluralism is a fairly recent development, dating back only to 1969 in the case of bilingualism, 1971 for multiculturalism, and 1982 for the Charter of Rights and Freedoms. The truth of the matter is that we know very little about the effects of pluralism on our culture as a whole. We also don't have the luxury of being able to look to other countries to get some sneak previews of how things will turn out. While other societies may be pluralistic in the sense that they are culturally diverse, virtually no other country actually declares itself "multicultural." England, for example, is culturally varied, but people are expected to be "English" — however culturally inflated that concept may be. Similarly, the United States is culturally diverse, but there has been a historical sense that people who come to America become Americans, regardless of how much they may value the cultures of their homelands. Demographer Myron Weiner comments that societies are rarely open to the arrival of persons with racial or ethnic characteristics different from their own.[5] Consequently it is no exaggeration to say that Canada is a world leader in enshrining multinationalism and multiculturalism. "In a sense," says sociologist Roderic Beaujot of the University of Western Ontario, "Canada is trying something unique and needs to ensure that this continues to be a successful experiment."[6]

The early returns for pluralism's impact on life in this country are just now starting to come in. The preliminary results indicate that pluralism is having some significant, unanticipated consequences. For starters, our rights are outdistancing our rules. Armed with our new Charter, groups and individuals are insisting that they are entitled to the right to equal expression, participation, and prosperity. Racial minorities, women, the elderly, and the disabled are working hard to combat inequities. Individuals are invoking the Charter as they square off on every topic imaginable — abortion, homosexuality, knowingly transmitting AIDS, euthanasia, blood transfusions, the spreading of hatred, crosses in Remembrance Day celebrations, Sunday shopping, religion in the schools, female participation in sports, the wearing of turbans, membership in private clubs, age- and gender-based insurance rates, mandatory breathalyzer tests, mandatory wearing of seat belts, displaying excessive tattoos, being drunk in a public place, gun controls, opposition to all-White male regiments, and on and on.

As George Bain put it, in his nationally syndicated column of June 16, 1990: " . . . Canadians have a lamentably limited capacity to see a national interest broader than the membership list of the occupational, economic, cultural, ethnic, gender, environmental, or other groups with which they identify in spirit if not formally."

Given our emphasis on equality and justice, it's fair enough that we Canadians insist on our rights. However, when our own rights conflict with another person's rights — as is increasingly the case — we obviously have a problem. Something has to give. Unfortunately, pluralism Canadian-style is showing a limited ability to provide a way out.

RESOLVING CONFLICTING RIGHTS

One possibility is for both of us to give a little and seek a solution where we both win, where we both get as much as is socially possible of what we want. In popular parlance, the goal is a win-win outcome. But the current Canadian obsession with group and individual rights doesn't seem to include the inclination to give up much of anything. People seem to want a total victory, "a blow-out." Many Canadians come precariously close to equating "win-win" with the forfeiting of integrity, "win-lose" with the triumph of right.

The abortion debate is a case in point. Both sides have shown little sign of being willing to settle for anything less than a shutout of the opposition. Nothing short of a win-lose situation will do. For politicians, the abortion debate is a no-win issue because everyone wants a win-lose outcome, including many politicians themselves. Following the May 1990 Commons' passing of the new abortion legislation, Justice Minister Kim Campbell told reporters, "We have found some common ground." But anti-abortionist Liberal Don Boudria said, "If the government thinks this issue is going to go away, it is mistaken." Pro-abortionist Dawn Black of the NDP predicted that women would "continue to struggle" until they are "fully equal, participating citizens in this country."[7]

Future historians will note with interest that we applauded a Charter of Rights and Freedoms but had no counterbalancing Charter of Social Responsibility. As long as we ourselves won, we frequently were content to blank our opponents.

CRISIS? WHAT CRISIS?

	% Agreeing					
	NAT	BC	PR	ONT	QUE	ATL
In general, the Charter is a good thing for Canada.	81	76	79	82	89	80
The Charter of Rights will strengthen Canadian national identity.	63	58	62	59	66	71
The idea that everyone has a right to their own opinion is being carried too far these days.	38	34	35	32	48	40

SOURCE: *Charter Survey*, York University, 1987.

If win-win is out of the question, a second logical way to resolve conflicting rights might be to introduce an outside standard to determine which position is the more correct or appropriate. The problem here however is that relativism has decreed that all viewpoints have equal value.

No one viewpoint is superior to or more accurate than another; no one lifestyle is more valid than another. To live by the sword of relativism, which sanctioned collective and individual pluralism, may also be to die by it.

In Canada, truth has become little more than personal opinion. "It's all relative," declare Canadians from British Columbia to Newfoundland. Consequently, we aren't sure how to respond to Ben Johnson, to homosexuals who want to be ordained, to writers whose works upset others, to the desire to preserve valued cultural symbols. Relativism has slain moral consensus. It has stripped us of our ethical and moral guidelines, leaving us with no authoritative instruments with which to measure social life. Our standards for evaluating ideas and behavior have been restricted to our local cultural and religious domains. Those same historians who never found our charter of social responsibility will further note that we were a country that was a champion of choice, that we triumphantly discarded the idea that there are better and best choices in favor of worshipping choice as an end in itself.

A CAUSE FOR PAUSE

If we don't resolve our difficulties by pursuing a win-win solution or by using an outside ethical standard, the remaining recourse is the courthouse. And, in case no one has noticed, that's where we are increasingly ending up. As we approach the new century, we find ourselves playing a disorganized social game. We are stressing individual rights over social rules and hiring legal technicians as our referees. Our team spirit — our social spirit — is frequently nonexistent. The Canadian social game is also bogging down because we are cheering for all plays instead of the best plays. In declaring everything equal, we are ceasing to explore what is better and best, personally and socially. The attention given to the individual's rights and potential has been extremely important in this century, but it has become increasingly detached from what is socially beneficial, resulting in excessive *individualism*.

Together, individualism and relativism make social life difficult indeed, in the long run perhaps impossible. Individualism focuses on the individual to the detriment of the group. Relativism, taken to an extreme, erases agreement on the norms that are essential to social life.

Unbridled individualism and relativism are obviously not new problems. But conditions do not have to be new in order to be destructive. Moreover, conditions that don't go away may well be more threatening to societies at some points in history rather than at others. In our time, excessive individualism and relativism may well be two of the most serious threats to social life in Canada. With the movement of many of the world's nations toward greater freedom and individualism and toward pluralism and relativism, there is good reason to believe that the threat to social life will become increasingly global as well.

In its zeal to promote coexistence, Canada may find itself a world leader in promoting the breakdown of group life and the abandonment of the pursuit of the best. Individually, we have been emancipated; socially, we are in disarray. Despite a generally high level of affluence, Canadians these days seem frustrated, restless, and nervous. Author Pierre Berton recently said, "I haven't seen the country as mean-spirited since the Depression." In April 1990, Montreal *La Presse* columnist Lysianne Gagnon wrote, "Obviously the mood of the country is terrible." In the same month, *Winnipeg Free Press* editor John Dafoe described the nation as "fractious," saying that the most disturbing thing is "a certain lack of community. People seem to be very wrapped up in their own problems."[8] *Maclean's* editor Kevin Doyle summed things up this way: "At a time when the world seems to be on the brink of a new era of hope and change and freedom, symbolized by the events in Eastern Europe and the Soviet Union, Canadians [seem] to be blocked in a time warp, isolated and anxious about the future."[9]

Such is the madness characterizing the country today. It has an important history.

2

How We Got into All This

CONTRARY TO POPULAR BELIEF, all was far from well on the individual-group front in the past. True, the ties were there. Renowned political sociologist Seymour Lipset has recently released a major study comparing values and institutions in Canada and the United States. Lipset stresses that Canada historically has been characterized by an emphasis on community rather than the individual.[1] Canadians who lived between 1867 and the end of the 1950s were anything but islands unto themselves. During the first hundred years they were firmly interlocked with nation and community, family and church, school and work. Further, the bonds, whether of marriage, school, employment, or church life, were durable. Divorce did not come easily; education was mandatory; jobs were necessary; church involvement was expected.

Costly Connections

The quantity and durability of social ties during Canada's first hundred years have led many observers to idealize the past as a golden age of social life. For some people, such ties were very good and contributed to personal well-being. But a large number of Canadians paid a considerable individual price for social participation. Some quick examples:

In the early decades, the personal payoffs for citizenship were modest. National, provincial, and local governments were still in the midst of being formed for almost the first fifty years after

Confederation. Much-needed legislation aimed at ensuring and enhancing quality of life was consequently in the making for most of the country's first century.

Many people think community life was ideal in the pre-1960s. In rural and urban settings, many people had good social lives. Yet early communities also were characterized by strong cultural-religious group ties; many took on an English-Anglican or French-Roman Catholic or German-Lutheran flavor. Life was close-knit for those who shared in the dominant groupings, but not for those who didn't.

Between the 1860s and 1960s, the family was a centrally important social link for Canadians. Everyone was expected to marry; over 90 percent did. Married couples were expected to have children; over 90 percent did. Sexuality was tied to marriage. Premarital sex was severely stigmatized; extramarital sex was out of the question; homosexuality was denounced as perversion and declared a criminal act. People were expected to stay married, and most did. But "staying together" often masked difficulties, particularly those of wives and children. Husbands and fathers had wide-ranging authority over both. Wives frequently were subordinate helpmates, and many children were disciplined harshly. The readiness with which families ceased to stay together when they began to have the option not to suggests that, for a good many, things were probably far from satisfactory all along.

Involvement in organized religion was something of a national norm. In the first census, in 1871, almost all Canadians identified with a religious group. Membership and weekly attendance remained high through the 1950s. The Church made significant contributions to Canadians. It provided many with a refuge in a new land, instilled important social values, and worked to improve social conditions. Yet at times concern for the well-being of individuals was matched by the self-interests of the religious group. Many churches were frequently authoritarian and repressive.

Another important link between the individual and society was the school. The BNA Act of 1867 made education a provincial responsibility; it also set the stage for an array of educational disparities for years to come. Free and mandatory education came into being in Ontario in 1871 through the efforts of Egerton Ryerson, and the rest of Canada gradually followed. A major motive appears to have been the perceived need to control children who had been ousted from the workplace as the farm gave way to the city. Students in pre-1960 Canada were primarily young people who didn't go beyond high school. In 1867, there were seventeen universities and fifteen hundred students; by 1940 there were twenty-eight universities and forty thousand students. In the first hundred years, school provided basic literacy skills and a modest introduction to literature, history, and the physical sciences. Critiques of the educational system frequently lamented the failure to teach the three Rs rather than the failure to stimulate the fourth R — reflection.

Another important link to the social realm was work. Canadians were expected to work and work hard. For most men, women, and children who lived in the country's first hundred years, that meant work on farms and in small family businesses. The distinction between work and home hardly existed. With the coming of industrialization and urbanization, men no longer typically worked at home; children ceased to be an economic asset and were in need of care; and women — after years of being in an economic alliance with men — found themselves largely shut out from jobs. The workplace appears to have been a positive and gratifying environment for relatively few people. Assembly lines made work simple but tedious. There were few laws governing conditions and wages, and people faced accidents and health problems, as well as serious exploitation. Before the emergence of the often bitterly opposed unions, many Canadian workers were losing badly.

Obviously many post-Confederation Canadians experienced considerable gratification from group life. I am in no way trying to paint the pre-1960 situation as totally "black." However, the emphasis on group life and group loyalty was excessive to the point of often being detrimental to personal well-being. A large number of Canadians had their individuality extinguished. For many, the quality of life that was possible — socially and individually — simply wasn't there.

Two groups of Canadians paid a particularly high price for group involvement during Canada's first hundred years — women and cultural minorities.

WOMEN

Between the 1860s and the 1960s, Canadian women participated generously in social life. For their efforts they were rewarded by being treated first as noncitizens and later as second-class citizens.

Before 1872, married women were not allowed to retain property they had owned prior to marriage; nor could they control their own finances and property once they were married. They couldn't vote in any province before 1916 and didn't receive the federal vote until 1918 — fifty-one years into Confederation. In 1919, they were accorded the privilege of sitting in the House of Commons. It took until 1929 and a ruling by the English Privy Council to clarify the fact that women in Canada were indeed "persons" and therefore eligible, as full citizens, to hold any public office or position. Even so, Quebec withheld the provincial vote from women for another eleven years, until 1940.

WHEN WOMEN GOT THE VOTE IN CANADA

1916	Manitoba, Saskatchewan, Alberta
1917	Ontario, British Columbia
1918	FEDERAL ELECTIONS, Nova Scotia
1919	New Brunswick
1922	Prince Edward Island
1940	Quebec

AND ELSEWHERE. . .

1893	New Zealand
1917	U.S.S.R.
1920	U.S.A.
1928	Great Britain
1944	France
1945	Japan

SOURCE: Other countries adapted from Wilson, 1988:547

In 1917, Louise McKinney won a seat in the Alberta legislature, making her the first woman anywhere in the British Commonwealth to hold such an office. Four years later, Ontario's Agnes Macphail became the first woman elected to the House of Commons. It wasn't until 1935 that a second woman — sixty-nine-year-old Martha Black from Yukon — would sit in Parliament.

In 1930, Cairine Wilson became the first woman to be appointed to the Senate; in 1957, Ellen Fairclough was the first woman appointed to the federal cabinet. In late 1989 — 122 years after Confederation — a woman, Audrey McLaughlin, was finally elected as the head of a major national party.

In addition to being shut out of the political domain, Canadian women also were not treated equally in the educational realm. There was vigorous debate in the late nineteenth century on the advisability of educating female children.[2] From the start, men and women were educated for different reasons. Up through the 1950s, education for women was geared primarily to preparing them for marriage and family life. For men, job preparation was the objective. Schools taught that men work and women stay at home. Consequently, education did little to alter the aspirations and vocational flexibility of women — or the attitudes of men toward women.

Occupationally, women typically were expected to marry and stay home. Employment was for women who were single or disadvantaged. In 1921, 18 percent of women participated in the labor force. By 1951, the figure had only increased to 24 percent.

The available occupations for such "pre-marital" and "unavoidable" employment were restricted primarily to domestic and "nurturing" professions, particularly nursing and teaching. New "female" professions were gradually added to the list, including library work, social work, and physiotherapy. But the most burgeoning area through the end of the 1950s was clerical work, producing jobs that invariably placed women in inferior positions to men. By the end of the 1950s, women were still locked in "female" occupations, predominantly clerical. Those women who were in professions tended to be dieticians and librarians rather than doctors and lawyers.

Canadian women before 1960 were caught in a catch-22. Because their "appropriate" place was the home, few pursued higher education; of those who did, most gravitated to the limited number of "women's" fields. By 1960 only about one in four university students were women, with most enrolled in nursing, home economics, and education.

FEMALE ENROLLMENT IN UNIVERSITY BY FIELD OF SPECIALIZATION: 1891–1961

% of Undergraduate Enrollment

	Arts & Science	Agri-culture	Bus.	Ed.	Home Ec.	Law	Medi-cine	Nurs-ing	TOTAL
1891	22	—	—	—	—	—	3	—	12
1920	32	1	3	62	100	3	5	100	16
1930	33	1	14	64	100	3	4	100	24
1945	27	4	9	48	100	4	7	100	21
1961	29	4	7	48	100	5	10	99	26

SOURCE: Derived from Prentice, et al., 427.

Women who became part of the labor force experienced considerable discrimination. They were typically hired last, fired first, and paid less. For example, during World War I, as men left their jobs to join the armed forces, women — mostly unmarried — were brought into the labor force to make up for shortages. Yet they received only about 50 to 80 percent of the wages paid to men and were expected to relinquish their jobs at the war's end. During the depression of the 1930s, employers laid off women more readily than men, even in fields where they were dominant, such as the garment industry.

Asked again to make up for labor shortages during World War II, single and married women responded, with some mothers in Ontario and Quebec given help with child care. But again, when the war ended women were expected — and, in the case of federal government employees, required — to relinquish their jobs to returning servicemen.[3] The day nurseries were closed and the women went back to being wives and mothers. The public agreed:

a 1944 Gallup poll found that 75 percent of men and 68 percent of women believed that men should be given preference in postwar employment.[4] By 1961, the earnings of women employed full-time, year-round, were only about 60 percent of those of men in the same categories. Even full-time clerical workers earned just 75 percent of what men did.

Denial of full societal participation for women was hardly limited to the education and economic spheres. During the first hundred years after Confederation, women frequently were not allowed to participate in an array of other organizations. Some clubs, for example, hung out the "No Women Allowed" sign. Other organizations, such as political parties and religious groups, often had women perform "female" tasks — cooking, baking, and the like.

Nor does history have good things to say about the Church's prophetic voice. In Quebec, the Roman Catholic Church helped to restrain women. McGill University law professor Julius Grey notes that through the 1960s the Quebec Civil Code "consecrated a notion of 'paternal authority,' which made the husband the head of the family and gave him considerable powers over his wife and children."[5] Professor Alison Prentice and her associates, in their history of Canadian women, say, "In Canada as elsewhere, the Roman Catholic Church stood fast in its opposition to many of women's aspirations."[6]

Protestant groups also were generally guilty of sanctifying the status quo. Although women were often highly committed to faith and attended services more than men, they nevertheless were commonly relegated to "female" jobs. Very few were allowed to assume denominational and congregational leadership — as presidents, moderators, elders, board members, deacons, Sunday school superintendents, and the like. Most denominations were slow to ordain women as ministers.

The Prairie Bible Institute in Three Hills, Alberta, is known far and wide for its theological and social conservativism. Its founder and president, L. E. Maxwell, wrote these words of admission in 1984, at the age of eighty-nine: "In spite of the liberating power of the Gospel, strong prejudice against women's public ministry has persisted in certain segments of the church through its history. Some of God's choicest servants — missionaries, teachers, and evangelists — have been sorely hindered, severely criticized, and needlessly stymied. Their intolerable fault? They were *women*."[7]

Given the lack of concern on the part of male-dominated institutions, Canadian women had to organize in order to improve their status. Sometimes this meant working within institutions; often it meant working outside them. An example of the former was the women's missionary society. In 1869, a Baptist foreign-mission board rejected the application of Hannah Norm, from Nova Scotia, to go to Burma as a missionary. Norm turned to the women of the church for help, and they proceeded to establish the first of a number of female fund-raising societies that eventually made it possible for Norm to serve in Burma for forty-two years.[8] In the 1870s and 1880s, similar societies grew rapidly in all the major Protestant denominations. The early societies, suggest Prentice and her colleagues, "were the first large-scale women's organizations in which women were able to act independently and to develop confidence in their own abilities."[9]

Some of the early groups working outside existing institutions included the Woman's Christian Temperance Union and the National Council of Women. The WCTU was formed in 1874 to work for prohibition and to assist victims of alcohol abuse. It closely guarded its independence from male intrusion; men were allowed to be honorary members, but they could not vote.[10] The National Council of Women was established in 1893 by Lady Aberdeen, the wife of the governor-general. Its goal was to overcome the regional, social, and cultural divisions of women by coordinating the activities of provincial and local women's groups. It was middle class and conservative, but it was also reformist, and it sought to address pressing social problems such as suffrage, temperance, prostitution, profiteering, and equity of pay for women.

Throughout the century, other women's groups struggled to enhance the equality and dignity of women in Canada. Among them were the Canadian Suffrage Association, the Canadian Federation of Business and Professional Women's Clubs, the Women's Institutes, the Women's International League for Peace and Freedom, the Voice of Women, and the Canadian Federation of University Women.

Despite these efforts, severe inequities continued into the 1960s. Doris Anderson, a prominent figure in the Canadian Women's movement, has summed up the situation this way: "Women in the 1960s remained underrepresented in political institutions, faced the quota system in some universities, and were generally subject to a range of discriminatory policies and legislation in both the public and private sectors."[11]

In the face of the mounting strength of the women's movement and the pressure of a six-month campaign mounted by a coalition of thirty-two women's groups led by Laura Sabia, the federal government responded. On February 16, 1967, Prime Minister Lester Pearson announced the establishment of the Royal Commission on the Status of Women in Canada, with Ottawa journalist and broadcaster Florence Bird appointed as chairperson.

CULTURAL GROUPS

During Canada's first hundred years, many new arrivals to the country gave up much for their social participation. However, they were short-changed when it came to social benefits. Before we examine some of their difficulties, we need to look briefly at Canada's age-old cultural-group problem.

The French and British From the beginning, Canada's central cultural-group dilemma has been how to create one nation comprised of descendants from Britain and France. The historical background is well known. The host Native population was asked to share the land with uninvited newcomers who initially arrived primarily from the two European powers. In time, they were joined by an increasing number of people from other parts of the world.

Rather than gravitating to common areas where they interacted and integrated, the French and British tended to stick to different geographical and cultural turfs. Accordingly, observers referred to them as "the two solitudes." They shared no common vision and no consciousness of kind — two traits that are basic, indeed indispensable, to the existence of group life. Further, neither the French nor the British had illusions of coming to the new world to found a great nation. Very early, the French settlers were marooned when their parents had to give the land over to the British. The settlers from Britain soon found that their parents — although they owned everything in sight — were relatively indifferent to their existence.

Two strident founding peoples? Hardly. The French and British were more like orphans from two different families, stranded in a foreign land. Beyond their respective levels of alienation, they had little in common. Historians tell us that the reality of the two solitudes has represented Canada's central nation-building problem. For almost 350 years — from just after 1600 until the 1960s — we wrestled with the question of how the two dominant groups could comprise one country.

Following a period of pronounced social and economic backwardness from 1936 until 1960 under the Union Nationale and Maurice Duplessis, a new generation of Quebec leaders emerged. They were determined to bring the province into the modern age. Among them was a young lawyer by the name of Pierre Elliott Trudeau. "If . . . we continually identify Catholicism with conservatism and patriotism with immobility," he wrote in 1956, "we will lose by default that which is at play between all cultures; and the notion of French Canadian, with that of Catholicism which is grafted to it, will finish by becoming something very small indeed. An entire generation is hesitating at the brink of commitment."[12]

Aware that it had to demonstrate to Quebec that Canada could accommodate the renewed province, in 1963 the federal government established the Royal Commission on Bilingualism and Biculturalism.

Other Groups The Royal Commission found it necessary to address the cultural contributions of other ethnic groups and to report on how their contributions might be preserved. Many such groups had paid an exorbitant price to participate in Canadian life.

In the late nineteenth and twentieth centuries, a belief in evolving human progress and White superiority was pervasive throughout the Western world. English-speaking Canadians were among those who believed that Anglo-Saxon peoples and British principles of government represented the forefront of biological evolution. They felt that Canada's greatness depended upon a solid Anglo-Saxon foundation.[13] Howard Palmer of the University of Calgary says that Anglophones therefore assessed new groups largely on the degree to which their members conformed to the British cultural and physical ideal. The most desirable immigrants were British and American, followed by Western and northern Europeans, then other Europeans. Near the bottom of the pecking order were the pacifist religious sects — the Hutterites, Mennonites, and Doukhobors. Last were Blacks and Asians.[14]

Employment was difficult to obtain and easy to lose. Immigrants often had to settle for the most menial and dangerous jobs. In British Columbia, it was thought that Asians took jobs from Whites and were willing to work for less money. Unions, says Palmer, tended to exclude them, and "as a matter of policy, employers paid Asian workers less than others." Because of that province's legal and social practices, Chinese, Japanese, and South Asians were not allowed to vote, practice law or pharmacy, be elected to public office, serve on juries, or be employed in public works, education, or the civil service. Quebec, Nova Scotia, and Saskatchewan passed legislation prohibiting White women from working in restaurants, laundries, or any other business owned by the Chinese or Japanese.[15] Such laws had an outrageous antecedent — a 1876 tax on the pigtail worn by Chinese males![16]

In 1907, Japanese immigration was limited to four hundred males per year, and immigration from India was banned outright. Blacks were informally denied entry in 1910. Although seventeen thousand Chinese males were brought to Canada in the 1880s to help build the Canadian Pacific Railroad, the welcome was short-lived. First Chinese immigration was curbed with a head tax; then came the severely restrictive Chinese Immigration Act of 1923. Only forty-four Chinese people were admitted to Canada between 1923 and 1947.[17]

In both world wars, the armed forces were reluctant to accept Canadian citizens who were Black, Chinese, Japanese, or South Asian — although some people from each group did serve. Other groups also experienced problems. In World War I, Germans and immigrants from the Austro-Hungarian Empire were the targets of intense prejudice and persecution. They were called enemy aliens. Many were dismissed from their jobs; some were placed under police surveillance or in internment camps. In some instances, their language schools and churches were closed, their newspapers censored and suppressed, their businesses attacked.[18]

Governments of the day receive few marks for providing enlightened and courageous leadership in the face of racism. Sociologist Weinfeld of McGill notes that "government historically was the direct or indirect agency of minority misfortunes. Discrimination was either perpetrated or tolerated by the government well into the latter half of the twentieth century."[19] During World War I, the federal government hardly protected immigrants. On the contrary, it disenfranchised conscientious objectors and people who had become Canadian citizens after March 1902 if they

IMMIGRATION TO CANADA: 1867-1988

Yearly Average for Selected Periods
in Rounded Thousands

Period	Yearly Average
1867-1900	48,000
1901-1914	207,000
1915-1918	52,000
1919-1930	123,000
1931-1939	15,000
1940-1945	12,000
1946-1950	86,000
1951-1955	158,000
1956-1960	157,000
1961-1965	100,000
1966-1970	182,000
1971-1975	167,000
1976-1980	121,000
1981-1985	102,000
1986-1988	137,000

SOURCE: Computed from *The Canadian World Almanac*, 1989:94.

had been "born in an enemy country" or if they "habitually spoke an enemy language." From 1919 to 1953 in British Columbia, Doukhobors were denied the right to vote; they couldn't vote in federal elections from 1934 until 1955.[20]

During the Great Depression, Anglo-Saxon workers demanded, and often received, priority in obtaining and keeping jobs. Most non-Anglo-Saxons were forced to give up their jobs and accept government relief. Europeans and Asians were frequently victims of discrimination in the way relief was administered. The federal Immigration Act provided for deportation of non-Canadian citizens on relief; in 1931, seven thousand people were deported as "undesirables." In 1933, various categories of immigration were deleted, and even British subjects were discouraged from coming to Canada.[21]

With the coming of World War II, Germans, Italians, and pacifists encountered hostility. In 1942, Alberta passed a law banning all land sales to Hutterites for the duration of the war; from 1947 to 1972, the Alberta government put restrictions on the location and amount of land Hutterites could own.[22]

The handling of the Japanese is well known. On February 24, 1942, a federal government order resulted in some twenty-two thousand Japanese being evacuated from the Pacific coast area and relocated to the Interior of British Columbia and to other provinces. The government sold their property so the people couldn't return to the coast at the end of the war. Further, near the war's end, the government encouraged the Japanese to seek voluntary deportation to Japan.[23] In 1947, intense pressure from civil rights groups led to the dropping of plans to deport some ten thousand Japanese people.

As for the Jews, Canadian race relations expert Howard Palmer sums up a national tragedy: "Canada closed its doors to Jewish immigrants at the time when they desperately needed refuge from Nazi persecution in Europe."[24]

During World War II, Chinese and Ukrainians won new respectability through their support for the war effort. The involvement of all groups in wartime industry undermined social barriers.[25] Perhaps most significant, suggests Palmer, revulsion against Hitler and Nazism seemed to result in a reaction against public expressions of anti-Semitism and in a reaction against the concept of a superior race.[26]

On the heels of the war and in response to lobbying, Asians were at last given the vote — the Chinese and East Indians in 1947, the Japanese in 1949. Treaty Indians would have to wait until 1960. Some legal racism remained. In Nova Scotia, for example, Blacks were prohibited from attending White schools until 1954.

As late as the Immigration Act of 1953, immigrants could still be denied entry for many reasons, including nationality, ethnicity, and "peculiar customs, habits, modes of life, or methods of holding property."[27] A 1952 Gallup poll found that 55 percent of the population felt that "Canada does not need immigrants"; by 1959, the figure increased to 64 percent. In 1961, 52 percent of the nation agreed that "Canada should continue to restrict the admission of non-Whites."[28] The mood toward immigrants, wrote Queen's University historian Arthur Lower in 1958, was different for the French and English. "The French attitude has been simple: 'Let us keep the kind of society we have, unchanged, and unthreatened by the newcomer. We had to share our house once before with an intruder. We do not wish to do so again.' " Lower said that the English Canadian judged immigrants by their merits — providing that they had white skin.[29]

Similar to the case of women, Canada's major institutions — notably, the school and the Church — also failed to provide leadership roles in countering discrimination and bringing about equality. Canada's religious groups, for example, offered neither loud nor prophetic voices in the face of racial and cultural group injustice. Groups tended to be culturally insular, demonstrating limited interest in reaching out to people of different cultural backgrounds from their own. Some were outwardly hostile toward newcomers.

As immigrants continue to arrive on Canadian soil in the 1950s and 1960s, it was clear that a change in outlook was badly overdue.

Native Canadians In the course of trying to find a way to divide the spoils between the English and the French, as well as to learn how to accommodate newcomers, Canada somehow seemed to

MAKEUP OF THE CANADIAN POPULATION: 1871-1961 (In %s)

	1871	1901	1931	1961
British	60	57	52	44
French	31	31	28	30
Other European	7	9	18	23
Asian	<1	<1	1	1
Native	1	2	1	1
Other	1	1	<1	1

SOURCE: Dominion Bureau of Statistics.

lose sight — or perhaps simply felt no need to acknowledge — an obvious reality. The land that stretched from sea to sea was not vacant when the French and English laid their claims on behalf of their respective monarchs. The Native population had watched from the banks as the first ships arrived. The English and French seemed to feel that they had a divine right to the land occupied by what they called uncivilized savages. At their worst, they simply slaughtered the Natives who got in their way. In Newfoundland around 1800, three or four hundred Beothuk Indians are believed to have been herded onto a point of land near their favorite sealing site and shot down like deer.[30] The Beothuks' penchant for resisting the invaders seems to have caused the Europeans to treat them like wild animals who had to be destroyed.[31]

While a measure of peaceful coexistence was made possible by the extensive fur trade, that symbiotic arrangement began to break down with the arrival of larger and larger numbers of Europeans in the early part of the nineteenth century. The need for more land for settlers who wanted a piece of the expanding agricultural pie resulted in the negotiating of treaties with the Natives. Professor Anthony Hall, an expert on treaties, comments, "By and large Indian groups readily accepted the terms offered them by government representatives. . . . A good deal of trust existed between native people north of the Great Lakes and British military authorities."[32] Generally speaking, the treaties gave Natives a single payment of money or merchandise, along with the promise of annual payments in perpetuity.

Many observers have pointed out that the Indians and Whites had very different ideas of what the treaties meant. Leroy Little Bear, a lawyer and professor at the University of Lethbridge, writes that for the Native, "Land is communally owned." It rests not with individuals but with the tribe. "The land belongs not only to people presently living but also to past generations and future generations. . . . In addition, the land belongs not only to human beings but also to other living things, including the plants and animals, and sometimes even the rocks."[33] Historian E. P. Patterson of the University of Waterloo maintains that the evidence from Native testimony shows that Indians took the agreements to be indicative of sharing, friendship, and mutual respect. Obviously this was not the way the other signers interpreted the treaties; for representatives of the Crown and later of the Canadian government, the treaties "were regarded as legal purchases of land, with attending obligations such as the provision of annual payments, farm supplies, medical aid, and so forth."[34]

Some treaties and legislation established land reserves for Natives. The often revised Indian Act of 1876 gave status Indians — those who came under the treaties or were so designated in some other way — the right to live on reserve lands and receive certain government benefits. "These reserves were to be training grounds for assimilating the native peoples into the general society," Patterson writes.[35] The reserves were often a safe distance from urban settlements, removing Natives from undesirable influences, while also segregating them until such time as they became "appropriately civilized." Residential schools, frequently operated by Christian groups with government funding, played a central role in this process of "resocialization." The reserves came to number almost twenty-three hundred, and status Indians were fragmented into some six hundred bands. About two-thirds of the reserves and one-third of the bands were in British Columbia. Each reserve was about four square miles in area and housed bands ranging in size from a handful of members to several thousand.[36]

The federal government thus took on what has come to be regarded as a "trustee role," legally obligating itself to act in the best interests of Natives when acting on their behalf.[37] The Natives in turn became wards of the government, and frequently were treated like children incapable of emerging as constructive and productive adults without considerable intervention. Many Natives subsequently lost the initiative and confidence indispensable to self-expression. The idea that Natives would not be able to act responsibly without help became self-fulfilling.[38]

Isolated and marginal to mainstream Canadian life, Native peoples for much of the end of the nineteenth century and the first half of the twentieth were "out of sight and out of mind." One observer, Victor Valentine, aptly describes them as having been like "a cluster of satellites."[39] Their lack of purpose, severe poverty, poor health, inadequate education, and a wide range of additional severe personal and social problems — notably crime, violence, alcoholism, and suicide — tragically escaped national notice.

The exception to their missing presence, of course, was the interaction they had in the nearby small towns, or — when some attempted to make the big transition — in the larger cities. Such contacts seemed to foster negative stereotypes of Natives as being drunk, lazy, unintelligent, and "easy." "Like most non-white immigrants," notes Howard Palmer, "the Indians could not vote, were relegated to the bottom rungs of the economic order, were socially stigmatized, and encounted a good deal of prejudice."[40]

As a direct result of the firmly established reserve system, writes sociologist Carol Agòcs, Natives showed the demoralization and passivity seen in colonized peoples in other parts of the world. "Until the sixties there were few ways in which Indian residents of reserves could influence the paternalistic and quasi-colonial government bureaucracies."[41] But as the 1950s came to an end, a number of Native spokesmen, notably Harold Cardinal, began to clear their voices.[42] The slumbering hosts were about to emerge from their social asylum.

The Myth of "The Good Old Days"

Looking back at the inequities shown groups such as women and cultural minorities, the obvious question is, "Where were our minds?" Where were the people who were committed to the standards of fairness and equality and decency? Where were the voices speaking out and condemning such atrocities against women and minorities?

Some social critics will say that the voices were missing because many people — notably Anglo-Saxon men — were benefiting from the plight of the disadvantaged. Undoubtedly such an observation has much validity. But the unfair social arrangements appear to have been widely condoned by people who aspired to much better things — educators, religious leaders, politicians, journalists, social workers, and many others.

THE PRE-INFORMATION SOCIETY

It is fairly clear why the voices were missing. Canadians were part of a culture that largely had been imported from Western Europe. That culture accepted the "truths" of male dominance and British and White supremacy. As a result, the two institutions that probably had the best opportunity to intervene and call for a correction of injustices — education and religion — had both been infiltrated at the leadership levels. In turn, members of government, business, and the media who went through school and church doors came out little more inclined to challenge the unjust status quo.

Perhaps the tendencies toward the "groupism" and authoritarianism of the pre-1960s could have been offset by other sources of influence. But the fact of the matter is that people living in Canada between 1867 and 1960 were highly isolated. The dissemination of information — including alternative views of social reality — was slow and limited. Our grandparents and great-grandparents rarely traveled outside Canada. As well, reading, beyond the mandated educational experience, was limited by problems of illiteracy, disinclination, and inaccessibility. Even when people could read and wanted to read, they frequently didn't have access to libraries.

Although the mass media represented a potential source of information and stimulation, most newspapers in Canada then were rural weeklies that contained news of local interest; they didn't have a national or international focus. One historian comments that in 1931, rural papers "were, by and large, advertising sheets with only a smidgen of news and comment."[43]

There were some dailies by the time of Confederation, and the magazine that became *Maclean's* was launched in 1905. Radio arrived in 1919, with a forerunner of the CBC network set up in 1932. (Television did not make its appearance until 1952.) It is questionable, however, to what extent newspapers, magazines, and radio attempted to challenge the status quo. Certainly they had the potential to influence public perception, attitudes, and behavior. But they were typically staffed by people who were products of Canadian, American, and European cultures. To expect them to have risen above culture — especially when their publications and programs were financially dependent upon that culture — is probably to be expecting too much.

The print and electronic media would play a major role in transmitting information and stimulating thought from the 1960s onward. But as Canada said goodbye to the 1950s, their time had not yet come.

QUALITY OF LIFE

Life in the Canadian pre-1960s was far from perfect. For many people, simply staying alive was not easy. Thousands of Canadian babies died at birth. In 1831, about one in five children did not survive to age one; by 1981, the figure would drop to one in one hundred.[44] Thousands of Canadians died prematurely from diseases such as bronchitis, tuberculosis, and pneumonia. In 1926, when accurate national statistics became available, about 24 percent of deaths were the result of infectious diseases, compared with 7 percent in 1984.[45] Both my grandfathers died in the 1930s — one at thirty-two of mushroom poisoning, the other at forty-two of appendicitis. Such were the times. There was a desperate need for hospitals, medical personnel, and more knowledge.

Low incomes and poverty frequently were serious problems, made more difficult by the lack of legislation guaranteeing social help. Adequate housing was out of the reach of many, with legislation required that would establish housing standards and provide protection for renters. Adequate food and clothing were not a given for significant numbers of Canadians.

Canada's first century was a time when the support of the group was desperately needed. Fortunately, governments began to respond, especially after the Great Depression. But even with increasing government intervention, the country's well-being was severely rocked by the three cataclysmic events that dominated Canadian life during the first half of this century — World War I (1914-18), the Great Depression (the 1930s), and World War II (1939-45). The wars took their toll — some 60,000 and 42,000 lives, respectively. All three events put excruciating economic pressure on many people. And together they placed an inestimable amount of emotional strain on Canadians.

GOVERNMENT PROGRAMS IMPLEMENTED

- 1914-18: workers compensation (Ontario, Nova Scotia, British Columbia, Alberta, New Brunswick)
- 1927: old age pensions: means test (federal-provincial)
- 1939-44: student aid (federal-provincial)
- 1940: unemployment insurance (federal)
- 1944: family allowances (federal)
- 1951: old age pensions: no means test (federal)
- 1957-61: hospital care (federal-provincial)

Families, friends, and religious and cultural groups helped many people cope. Perhaps it is this group support in the face of adversity that some older Canadians have in mind when they think of life as having been somehow better in the past. Relationships sometimes may have been better; physical conditions, however, definitely were not.

Technological advances were considerable between the 1860s and the 1960s. Still, for much of that time, work outside the home was arduous and difficult. Farming, manufacturing, railway construction, and the like were neither easy nor efficient. The same was true of work in the home. In 1941, 30 percent of the country was without electricity, and 40 percent had no running water. Only half had flush toilets.

Long hours of labor often left little time for leisure. Even here, the options were limited. Socializing was a possibility; for some,

HOUSEHOLD AMENITIES IN 1941

In %s

	Electricity	Running Water	Telephone	Refrigerator	Flush Toilet
CANADA	69	61	40	51	52
Farm areas	20	12	29	22	8
Rural non-farm	60	41	28	36	33
15,000-30,000	99	96	54	67	85
30,000 and over	99	99	57	79	89

SOURCE: Adapted from Prentice et al. 1988:245.

reading. But the motion picture did not arrive until the 1920s, and radio and television, as noted, did not make their debuts until 1919 and 1952, respectively.

But then again, when one has to give so much of one's resources to the struggle simply to stay alive, it is difficult to "live well." When our ever-present realities include the possibility of our own death or the death of someone we love, when we are not able to find a job or don't know how long we can keep the one we have, such concerns dramatically color the rest of life. A world war, a depression, and then another world war, followed by the ongoing threat of still another war and another depression, profoundly influenced the everyday outlooks of many pre-1960 Canadians. It was not a time when the living was either easy or particularly good.

When the little granddaughter, borrowing the words of the singer on the radio, approaches the gray-haired man in the recliner and says, "Grandpa, tell me 'bout the good ol' days," he can be forgiven for pausing, thinking for a few moments, and then, with a smile, spinning total fiction. The truth would be less believable than the fairytale.

Times needed to change.

3

THE SEEDS OF TRANSFORMATION

AS CANADA EVOLVED from an agrarian society to a modern industrial nation, the three dominant emphases common to such development were increasingly being felt — individualism, pluralism, and relativism. Though all three themes are prevalent in highly developed societies, our nation did a particularly good job of enshrining them. Canada, accordingly, has been somewhat extraordinary in both the benefits it has reaped and the costs it has borne.

The Sources of Freedom

THE AMERICAN FACTOR

By the end of the 1950s, Canadian society was being significantly influenced by some important developments. To the south, the American civil rights movement was making unprecedented strides. Institutionalized racism was being dismantled. Another important movement, primarily involving college students, was beginning to gain strength: the emergence of the youth counterculture would shake up the American status quo at virtually every level in the 1960s. Also south of the border, the women's liberation movement was making significant headway and would escalate with the publication in 1963 of Betty Friedan's *The Feminine Mystique.*[1] Greater freedom and greater equality were major American themes in the late 1950s and 1960s.

Through the influence of media on both sides of the border, Canadians of the period were becoming more sensitized to the goal of a just society. Young people would sit around Canadian camp fires, strumming guitars and singing imported songs of peace, such as "Blowin' in the Wind," or freedom, such as "We Shall Overcome." Their earnestness was usually matched by their ignorance; they liked the songs but most had little sense of what the lyrics were all about. I know. I was one of them. Still, the influence of the emphasis on emancipation stateside was felt by large numbers of Canadians. Weary from war and anxiety about a looming battle with Russia – all the more an ongoing issue because of Vietnam – the message of justice and peace hit a responsive chord.

These were times that were good to the individual. The theme that cut through these movements in America was that of freedom. Blacks needed to be free to participate fully in all of life. Young people needed to be free to turn their backs on materialism and war. Women needed to be free to live out life with no preset barriers.

The day probably had no more eloquent a spokesman than Martin Luther King, Jr. Who can forget his "I Have a Dream" speech before the Lincoln Memorial in Washington on August 28, 1963. "I am happy to join with you today in what will go down in history as the greatest demonstration for freedom in the history of our nation," he began. He told the massive crowd that 1963 was not the end but the beginning of the movement for freedom, that they needed to continue the struggle with dignity and discipline, meeting "physical force with soul force." There was no place for polarization; the presence of many "white brothers" that day was a reminder that "injustice must be carried forth by a biracial army." He spoke of his dream of equality "on the red hills of Georgia," in the state of Mississippi, and down in Alabama, of a day when his four children would "live in a nation where they will not be judged by the color of their skin but by the content of their character." And then there was that remarkable conclusion:

> This will be the day when all of God's children will be able to sing with new meaning, "My country 'tis of thee, sweet land of liberty". . . Let freedom ring, let freedom ring. And when we allow freedom to ring, when we let it ring from every village and hamlet, from every state and city, we will be able to speed up that day, when all of God's children . . . will be able to join hands and sing in the words of the old Negro spiritual, "Free at last, free at last; thank God Almighty, we are free at last."[2]

THE HUMAN FACTOR

It wasn't as if the individual suddenly was born in the 1960s. A certain amount of historical stereotyping sometimes leave us with the impression that people in earlier times were indistinguishable from groups. Our images of primitives sitting around fires, medieval Europeans unreflectively submitting to religious dogma, and Canadian settlers being perfectly cohesive groups are strange distortions of reality.

The inclination of individuals to act and think however they want has been so pronounced that it has always posed one of the great dilemmas for social life. Throughout history, individuals have been hard-pressed to give a little for the good of the group. Individuals have little inclination to abandon their own whims in order to adhere to the laws and conventions of the group. The data are abundant: we need only look at young children to get the poignant picture. Only with indoctrination and coercion is social life possible.

Throughout history, we have had high-profile individualists. Among them have been inventors and artists, philosophers and writers, eccentrics and killers. Societies have not always done a good job of telling the difference. We have been known to exalt the destructive and execute the productive. Mindless conformity has received much greater applause than creative nonconformity. Many great individuals died long before they were appreciated. Nevertheless, history is dotted with an endless array of individuals who have stepped out and taken chances. They have been variously regarded as our heroes and villains, the former praised as having "left their mark on history,' the latter seen as having made history more difficult.

At certain times, the individual has been particularly exalted. For example, in the Graeco-Roman period and in the European Enlightenment of the seventeenth and eighteenth centuries, intellectuals and artists gave expression to the enormous capabilities and potential of the individual. As well, individuals who have been willing to take on the group have played an indispensable role in bringing about change. It is hard to envision that the course of history would have been the same without religious figures such as Moses, Buddha, Jesus, and Muhammad; or stripped of such political figures as Caesar, Jefferson, Lenin, and Hitler.

The individual was there all along. In the post-1950s, people increasingly maintained that individuals had the right to the freedom to be everything that they are capable of being. There was a growing belief that everyone should be able to live out life without being limited and debilitated by inequality and injustice.

THE ECONOMIC FACTOR

Part of the sense of urgency was due to the significant social changes that had been taking place in American and Canadian life. The speed was different, with the U.S. leading by a number of years. But the pattern was the same. In Canada, the new century brought with it an economic transformation. An economy heavily based on agriculture was displaced by an economy based on manufacturing. This movement from an agrarian to an industrial society contributed to a number of important social alterations.

Two patterns were particularly significant. First, the workplace moved out of the home. Second, the workplace moved away from the farm. These two trends had a radical influence on life in Canada. The movement of the workplace from the home meant a major reshuffling of roles. Family life, previously fairly homogeneous, became increasingly specialized. Husbands moved into the workforce; women looked after the homefront; children gave more primacy to school. The change in locale of the workplace meant that people left the farms for the cities; immigrants similarly bypassed rural Canada in favor of the buregeoning urban centers.

URBAN-RURAL POPULATION DISTRIBUTION 1871-1986

	URBAN	RURAL
1871	20	80
1891	32	68
1911	45	55
1931	53	47
1951	63	37
1971	76	24
1986	77	23

SOURCE: *Statistics Canada.*

City life was not country life. In the city, the emphasis was on the individual. For starters, jobs were specialized to an extent inconceivable on the farm, with such specialization accelerating only in response to advancing technology and expanding industries and services. Institutions were similarly expected to play highly specific roles. Growth within such realms as leisure, education, and social services meant that no one institution could any longer dominate the entire range of social life — such as the Church had attempted to do in Quebec before 1960.

In rural Canada, life had revolved around the church and the school. In the cities, people found themselves with choices such as they had never seen before. Jobs and schools, shopping outlets and entertainment, political parties and religious groups now were available in optional form — representing something of a consumer's paradise. But city living was also characterized by resource limits. Canadians obviously had only so much money and time; through the 1970s they would continue to say that their top two personal concerns centered on insufficient quantities of both.

TIME AND MONEY CONCERNS

"How often do these common problems bother you?"
% Indicating *"A Great Deal"* or *"Quite a Bit"*

	MONEY	TIME
NATIONALLY	52	66
British Columbia	44	65
Prairies	52	69
Ontario	52	63
Quebec	58	67
Atlantic	49	66
Male	47	64
Female	58	67
18-29	41	63
30-39	61	73
40-49	54	71
50-59	37	65
60+	37	45

SOURCE: *Project Can80.*

The combination of unprecedented choice on the one hand and resource limits on the other accentuated the individualistic tendencies of Canadans. We became fussier and more demanding — in short, we became highly selective consumers. We ignored those companies and organizations that failed to offer us what we wanted, and we formed consumer groups to collectively confront suppliers whose products failed to meet our ever-rising expectations.

As consumer met supplier, the pace quickened. Suppliers in all spheres felt the heightened competition for limited dollars and time and consequently were forced to work ever harder to maintain or increase their share of their markets — be those markets food and clothing, entertainment, religion, politics, or whatever. No one received an exemption. Products had to be tailored to individual taste; stores had to specialize. Department stores suddenly were in trouble; new outlets and franchises that proved successful were increasingly those that did very little very well.[3] Many organizations ably handled the transition. Through vastly accelerated advertising, for example, companies did much more than merely meet consumer demand. They also dramatically expanded that demand, convincing Canadians that we needed far more than we wanted.

Industrialization was first felt in southern Ontario and Montreal, later in the West and the rest of Quebec, last in the Atlantic region. By the late 1950s, we were well on our way to becoming a consumer society. What was pronounced in the cities was soon disseminated to the small towns and rural areas. Moreover, what was in place was only the tip of the iceberg: television had barely had a chance to make an appearance.

When it came to needs, we had options galore; when it came to wants, we seemed open to an endless number of propositions. In much of life, personal emancipation was taking the form of free wheeling and free dealing.

The Components of Freedom

INDIVIDUALISM

The new emphasis on freedom in the 1960s was turning the focus of gratification from the group to the individual. In the cities, as choices increased, so did the possibility of being able to have what we wanted — from clothes and television programs to occupations and relationships. Consumer supply intensified consumer demand. Canadians no longer had to put up with the things they didn't like — even in such previously unnegotiable areas as religion and marriage. This side of the law, there no longer was the necessity of being led by the dictates of others.

What was becoming increasingly valued was personal fulfillment — physical, social, intellectual, and spiritual. The emphasis on communalism of our first hundred years was being replaced by a new emphasis on individualism. Canadians were coming to think of well-being in highly personal rather than social terms. Of considerable importance, involvement in the core groups of their parents and grandparents was becoming optional. To an extent unknown before in our history, the spotlight was on the individual. Group life was becoming disassociated from personal well-being.

PLURALISM

In a culturally diverse society, individual freedom is possible only if people are allowed to coexist. In the pre-1960s, we showed a distinct reluctance to allow people of different backgrounds to participate fully in Canadian life. However, the influence of the American freedom movements and consumer gratification helped to change that disinclination.

In Canada's first century, it may have been appropriate to speak of culturally extinguishing the Natives or absorbing French Canada; newcomers were forced to assimilate, and women had to stay home and leave education, business, and politics to men. By the 1960s, the emphasis on individualism — officially, at least — was changing all that. Assimilation and segregation were seen as racism that needed to be stamped out.

Neither our pluralistic country nor our pluralistic planet could move toward the actualization of freedom without at least respecting the reality of diversity, and responding with tolerance and acceptance. In Canada, we would do more, going beyond mere cognizance of our cultural diversity and enshrining it in a policy of multiculturalism.

Individualism and pluralism become mutually reinforcing. Once a society like ours gives official affirmation to pluralism, the rights not only of groups but individuals become unquestionable. Further, when a policy of pluralism is officially endorsed, citizens must respect a variety of lifestyles and outlooks. An emphasis on "truth" and "right" is replaced by an emphasis on "viewpoint" and "what's right for you." Any stronger evaluations become a threat to social stability. This leads us to a third important consequence of freedom.

RELATIVISM

In a pluralistic society, truth can be dangerous. Our ancestors believed in truth. They wanted, for example, to know the true shape of the earth, the true meaning of life, the true reason for criminality. The search for truth often led them into difficulty. Their belief in discoverable truth encouraged them to search for the best in everything, but it also created some serious problems for group life and contributed to closed-mindedness and intolerance.

The growing movement toward personal freedom in a pluralistic Canada left little room for dogmatic truth claims. In relativism, individualism found its perfect rationale.

Relativism is probably as old as the first two dissenting humans. But in Canada in the 1950s, in a country weary of war and conflict, it had new attraction. It also had scientific support. The emerging social sciences of anthropology and sociology were gaining momentum in North American educational circles. As noted earlier, their cross-cultural research was uncovering a concept they called cultural relativism. People around the world, said social scientists, address common needs in diverse ways — but one expression is not more true or better than the other; they simply are different. To equate a culture's ways with the right ways is to be guilty of ethnocentrism.

The theme of relativism was pronounced in other circles. In 1966, Joseph Fletcher published a highly influential book entitled *Situation Ethics* that had a significant influence on the realm of religion. In the book, Fletcher argued that what is right or wrong is dependent not on a set of rules but rather on how people "operationalize" the concept of love in specific situations.[4] Bishop James Pike offered his support of Fletcher's idea, writing that lying, theft, and extramarital sex, among other things, are sometimes "right" if love is served.[5]

In the last half of this century, the idea that truth is relative has come to be widely accepted. Our world is one where relativsim reigns. American philosophy professor Allan Bloom, who taught for a time at the University of Toronto, writes that almost every student entering university believes that truth is relative. Students are astonished by a person who doesn't regard such a proposition as self-evident, says Bloom, "as though he were calling into question 2 + 2 = 4. These are things you don't think about."[6] Since the 1960s, few Canadians could be heard making statements about having "the true" this or "the right" that; similarly, fewer people were referring to the views of others as "false" or "wrong." Relativism had become too widespread for such attitudes to be exhibited — at least publicly. Bloom comments that, today, "The true believer is the real danger. The study of history and of culture teaches that all the world was mad in the past; men always thought they were right, and that led to wars, persecutions, slavery, xenophobia, racism, and chauvinism. The point is not to correct the mistakes and really be right; rather it is not to think you are right at all."[7]

Relativism was right for the Canadian individualistic and pluralistic times. It gave intellectual legitimacy to the personal pursuit of well-being in a multicultural setting.

The Leader-Architect

One important source of social change is the so-called human factor. Change, after all, is not the inevitable consequence of abstract global forces. Societies are affected in different ways by dominant world trends. Individualism and relativism, for example, could have had any number of consequences for Canadian life. Specific individuals are often critical catalysts.

"The two Luthers," four centuries apart, serve as poignant examples. The Protestant Reformation was not simply the result of invisible and invincible social and economic forces. The movement of rebellion against the Roman Catholic Church needed to coalesce; it did so in part because of the stand taken by one priest, Martin Luther. The U.S. civil rights movement needed powerful leaders who could symbolize racial injustice and articulate it to Americans. Martin Luther King fulfilled such a role.

The ingredients for a major social transformation were present in Canada. We had the desire for increased individual freedom and had legitimized such a pursuit through our emphasis on pluralism and relativism. What was needed was an architect who could pull those strands together.

4

The True North Finally Free

WITH THE COMING of the 60s, Canada finally began to emerge from its colonial shadow, with Pierre Elliott Trudeau playing no small role. On February 15, 1965, on the heels of a very long and bitter Commons debate, our new flag was hoisted to the top of the Peace Tower in Ottawa. Our national anthem, "O Canada!", was approved by Parliament in 1967 and officially adopted under the National Anthem Act of June 27, 1980. On April 17, 1982, Queen Elizabeth II proclaimed from Parliament Hill that Canada now had its own Constitution. In the words of one American commentator, "By the end of his time in office, Trudeau had managed to rid Canada of the last symbolic tatters of colonial status and thereby to bring it to full political maturity."[1]

More than twenty years ago, Trudeau wrote that in the face of Quebec's "attempting to reduce federal power to nothing . . . to defend federalism, I entered politics in 1965." He had a game plan. In 1990 he and a colleague recalled: "We went to Ottawa not to gain power for power's sake but to transform our society according to a set of liberal values. Make no mistake, we were an ideological government — ideological in the sense that we were motivated by an overarching framework of purpose. That framework was grounded in the supreme importance we attached to the dignity and rights of individual human beings."[2]

Canadian society has felt the cumulative impact of both the Trudeau government and the times.

Emancipated Groups

In the 1960s, Canada attempted to come to grips with two of its major areas of inequity: cultural minorities and women. The first hundred years of Confederation had left considerable room for improvement. The time had come to take remedial steps.

CULTURAL GROUPS

Queen's University historian Arthur Lower wrote at the end of the 1950s that although everyone hates compromise, "where you have a country of two primary cultures, two primary religions, and two pulls on fundamental allegiance — one to the past and one to the country — and now, another large, heterogeneous group which must be built into the original structure, only one attitude becomes possible, short of endemic civil war, the attitude of compromise."[3] With the coming of the 1960s, Canada attempted to establish such compromises between its divergent groups.

The resolving of the inequities of Canada's cultural groups involved first and foremost resolving the fundamental question of how Quebec and the rest of Canada could exist as a nation. In 1965, The Royal Commission on Bilingualism and Biculturalism released its preliminary report; six further volumes would be released over the next seven years.[4] The commission reported that Canada was in the throes of a major crisis that could only be resolved when Quebeckers were convinced that they could experience equality and mutual respect with the rest of the country, individually and collectively.[5] Francophones in Quebec and across the country were experiencing considerable linguistic, economic, and occupational inequities in both the public and private sectors.

Out of the commission's recommendations emerged the official policy statement: It was decreed that Canada had two founding peoples — the French and the British. Hereafter, the nation would have two official languages — French and English. Canadians would be free to live out life in either tongue. In 1969, the concept was enshrined. With the passing of the Official Languages Act, the first of Canada's two major intergroup building blocks — bilingualism — was dropped into place.

A second major intergroup issue that needed to be resolved was that of the place of other cultural groups. The 1953 Immigration Act had continued to blatantly discriminate against the entrance into Canada of non-White groups. Such unfair treatment concerned the government of John Diefenbaker, resulting in a lifting of racial barriers to immigration in 1962. In 1967, the Pearson government introduced a "points system" for selecting immigrants, emphasizing "education, training skills, and other special qualifications."[6] But changes in immigration policy did not solve the problem of how Canadians responded to newcomers.

The second important intergroup issue was addressed by the Royal Commission, something as an afterthought in Book Four of its six volumes. Having spent three volumes dealing with the French-English issue, the commission recommended that people of other cultural extractions should also have the opportunity to retain what is good from their national heritages. Cultural diversity, it was argued, would enrich Canada. We would become a nation of nations. In 1971, the second of the two critical Canadian building blocks — multiculturalism — was set in place beside bilingualism. In making the announcement, Prime Minister Trudeau summed things up this way: "A policy of multiculturalism within a bilingualism framework commends itself to the government as the most suitable means of assuring the cultural freedom of Canadians."[7]

Trudeau offered something of a classic statement on the nature and purpose of multiculturalism in an address to a Ukrainian group in 1972:

> [Canada's multicultural composition] and the moderation which it includes and encourages, makes Canada a very special place, and a stronger place as well. Each of the many fibres contributes its own qualities and Canada gains strength from the combination. We become less like others; we become less susceptible to cultural, social or political envelopment by others. We become less inclined — certainly less obliged — to think in terms of

> national grandeur; inclined not at all to assume a posture of aggressiveness, or ostentation, or might. Our image is of a land of people with many differences — but many contributions, many variations in view — but a single desire to live in harmony. . . . On a planet of finite size, the most desirable of all characteristics is the ability and desire to cohabit with persons of differing backgrounds, and to benefit from the opportunities which this offers.[8]

Consistent with such a spirit, a new Immigration Act was passed in 1975 that took effect two years later. The act established the objectives of Canada's policy, including the pursuing of demographic, economic, and social goals, family reunion, nondiscrimination, obligations to refugees, and cooperation between government and the private sector in facilitating the adaptation of immigrants to Canadian society.[9]

As far as resolving long-standing grievances of Native peoples, Trudeau's position was clear. Just as he was opposed to special constitutional status for Quebec, so he advocated the eventual removal of special status for Indians by, among other initiatives, drawing treaties to a close.[10] Nonetheless, the Constitution of 1982 explicitly protected aboriginal and treaty rights, including any rights "that may be acquired by the aboriginal peoples of Canada by way of land claims settlement."[11]

Canada's policy of bilingualism attempted to ensure the preservation of the historically dominant English and French cultures. The policy of multiculturalism encouraged the preservation of other cultures and languages, yet stopped short of advocating additional official languages. The two policies were aimed at ensuring the collective rights of cultural groups. They make coexistence — indeed, Canada — possible.

In the light of such developments, McGill professor Morton Weinfeld, who was so critical of the way the Canadian government had handled discrimination in the pre-1960s, could write in 1988: "The Canadian state has moved from active oppression and past indifference to championing the rights of minority groups. The state and its institutions are formally committed to ensuring for Canadian minority groups both equal economic opportunity and continued cultural survival."[12]

CULTURAL GROUP ORIGINS OF CANADIANS: 1986

In %s

British		34
French		24
British and French		4
British/French and Other		13
Other than British/French		25
Other European	16	
Asian	4	
Native	3	
Other	2	

SOURCE: Derived from *Canadian Social Trends*, Summer 1989:1.

The publicity given to the "English only" movement in 1990 – in which close to fifty Ontario cities, including Sault Ste. Marie and Thunder Bay, declared themselves unilingual – obscured what has been a slow but increasing inclination for the country as a whole to accept the federal bilingualism policy. As of late 1989, 58 percent of Canadians endorsed the two-official-languages policy, compared with 55 percent in 1980 and 49 percent in 1975. In every region, there has been a slight increase since the 1970s in the proportion of Canadians who favor bilingualism – a noteworthy trend, given that the policy became law only in 1969.[13] In 1987, a comprehensive national survey of fifteen- to twenty-four-year-olds found that 69 percent of the emerging generation support bilingualism.[14]

Such findings show that bilingualism gradually has been gaining acceptance across the country. The process has been slow, with reception particularly cool in western Canada. Differences by age and education, however, suggest that the level of acceptance could continue to increase with time — unless, with issues such as Meech Lake, the positive trend is sabotaged.

Research also shows that there has been an increase in the acceptance of multiculturalism since the mid-1970s. As of late 1989, 68 percent of Canadians endorsed multiculturalism.[15] The 1987 national youth survey found the support level for multiculturalism among the country's fifteen- to twenty-four-year-olds to be 74 percent.[16]

Since the 1970s, survey results show that there has been a softening of negative attitudes toward Canada's cultural minorities.[17] The proportion of Canadians who say that they feel comfortable with East Indians, Natives, Jews, Blacks, and Orientals has increased.

FEELING AT EASE WITH MINORITIES

	% Indicating "*At Ease*"				
	JEWS	ORIENTALS	NATIVES	BLACKS	EAST INDIANS
1985	91	91	90	88	83
1980	93	91	86	89	77
1975	91	86	87	84	*

* Item not included.

SOURCE: *Project Canada* surveys.

Attitudes toward marriage between members of various ethnic or racial groups provide an index of the extent to which Canadians are accepting of people of diverse backgrounds. Since the 1960s, there has been a considerable decrease in opposition to racial and religious intermarriage. For example, the proportion of Canadians opposing Whites marrying Blacks has dropped from 53 percent in 1968 to a current level of about 25 percent.[18] During the same two decades, opposition to Protestant-Catholic marriages declined from 28 percent to around 10 percent. Younger people are least opposed to intermarriage, suggesting acceptance will continue to increase in the future.

Clearly, discrimination continues to exist in Canada. The country is still a long way away from full cultural and racial harmony. Yet the news is far from all bad. In the two decades since bilingualism and multiculturalism were officially enshrined, in the midst of frequent charges of rising racism and intergroup conflict, there are signs of steady improvement.

WOMEN

In late 1970, three years after its creation, The Royal Commission on the Status of Women in Canada tabled its findings in the House of Commons.[19] The 488-page report contained 167 recommendations and assumed that "equality of opportunity for Canadian men and women was possible, desirable, and ethically necessary."[20] Issues addressed included equal pay for work of equal value, family law, educational opportunities, access to managerial positions, birth control, maternity leave, and day care. Four principles were outlined: women should be free to choose whether or not to take employment outside their homes; the care of children is a responsibility to be shared by the mother, the father, and society; society has a responsibility for women because of pregnancy and childbirth, and special treatment related to maternity will always be necessary; and, in certain areas, women will for an interim period require special treatment to overcome the adverse effects of discriminatory practices.

By the 1980s, writes Professor Cerise Morris, "most of the [report's] 167 recommendations . . . had been partially implemented and many had been fully implemented." She adds that several controversial recommendations, however, "had not been acted upon by the federal government."[21]

Changes are apparent everywhere. The movement of women into the labor force has been described by a Statistics Canada demographer as "perhaps one of the most important social revolutions of the last quarter-century in Canada."[22] The percentage of women working outside the home rose from 29 percent in 1961 to 53 percent in 1988; women comprised 44 percent of the workforce in 1988 (compared with only 28 percent in 1961), including just over one in two married women.

Educationally, whereas only 26 percent of undergraduates were women in 1961, that figure climbed to 37 percent by 1971 and to 51 percent by 1988. Equally significant, women were finally making numerical inroads into areas such as law, medicine, and business. More than four in ten undergraduates in those fields were women in 1981, compared with one in ten in 1961. As of 1985, women received 42 percent of all master's degrees and 26 percent of all doctorates.[23]

There also have been noteworthy changes in attitudes since the 1950s. Gallup poll data from the past thirty years dealing with the home, paid employment, and the women's movement was reviewed in 1984 by sociologist Monica Boyd. She concluded, "Although vestiges of traditional attitudes persist, the analysis shows that Canadians are becoming more egalitarian in their attitudes and opinions about women and women's issues."[24]

Seymour Lipset comments that women's groups in Canada have known greater success than their American counterparts in achieving political objectives. He notes that Ontario specifically has gone much further than any American state in enacting legislation requiring equal pay for jobs of comparable skill in the public and private sectors. Canadian women outnumber U.S. women in their participation in higher education and in the labor force.[25]

It has taken a long time for a male-dominated Canada to provide full citizenship to women. Advances are evident in education and the workplace and, to a lesser extent, in politics and religion. Consequently, Canadian ambassador Yves Fortier, in his February 1990 report to the United Nations Committee on the Elimination of Discrimination Against Women, could say that strides are being made toward equality. There is evidence of progress—the Charter of Rights, amendments to the Canadian Pension Plan, and the establishment of women's directorates across the country.[26]

However, it is also clear that the utopia of gender equality is hardly at hand. The National Action Committee on the Status of Women, an umbrella organization that represents some five hundred groups, denounced Fortier's report. "I think it's misleading," said Alice de Wolff, the NAC's executive coordinator. She added, "Canadian women's lives are getting harder." The NAC issued a parallel report arguing that legislation is failing to

WOMEN IN PROFESSIONAL PLACES:* 1986

	% of Total
MALE-DOMINATED PROFESSIONS**	
Pharmacists	50
Optometrists	32
Educational administrators	31
University professors	28
Chemists	27
Lawyers	22
Physicians and surgeons	21
Dentists	14
Judges and magistrates	12
Architects	11
Clergy	11
Nuclear engineers	10
Electrical engineers	5
OTHER PROFESSIONS	
Dietitians and nutritionists	96
Elementary-kindergarten teachers	81
Librarians and archivists	81
Postsecondary school teachers	74
Social workers	68
Psychologists	60
Educational-Vocational Counsellors	56
Secondary school teachers	46

* Occupations where 45% or more of people had at least a bachelor's degree in 1981.

** Occupation in which 65% or more of people employed in it in 1971 were men.

SOURCE: Adapted from *Canadian Social Trends*, Spring 1989:15.

ensure that discrimination against women will end, and that unemployment, underemployment, and poverty remain very serious issues for women.[27]

There's no question that problems persist. Poverty continues disproportionately to afflict young single mothers and elderly women. When women enter the workplace, they often are not treated fairly: Statistics Canada data for 1987 show that although the pay gap is closing, women working full-time still are making only two-thirds of what men make. The difference persists at all educational levels.[28] Depersonalizing stereotypes continue to thrive: a glance at rock videos and beer commercials, for example, reminds us that the dichotomy between the rugged male and the sex-symbol female is far from a thing of the past.

Further, women continue to be the victims of a disproportionate amount of violence. In many parts of Canada, anxiety and fear are part of their daily lives. A March 1990 poll found that 50 percent of women feel that there are areas within a kilometer of their home where they would be afraid to walk alone at night. Only 16 percent of men expressed the same fear.[29] Anxiety and fear all too frequently are experienced not only outside the home but also inside the home. In countless situations, women are not treated with the same respect, professionalism, and sexual detachment shown men.

The problems facing Canadian women have not been resolved. But the emphasis on individual worth and individual rights has done much to raise awareness of many key issues, as well as bring forth a sizable preliminary response.

Emancipated Individuals

Complementing the two major group rights policies was the inclusion of the Canadian Charter of Rights and Freedoms in our 1982 Constitution. In addition to reaffirming collective rights, the Charter guarantees the freedom of individuals — of conscience, religion, thought, belief, opinion, expression, peaceful assembly, association, movement, and liberty. The Charter declares that all Canadians are equal, unequivocally giving legal protection to the rights of every individual. It also explicitly permits laws,

SOME PROGRESS . . . SOME DISTANCE TO GO

% Agreeing

	MEN	WOMEN
"Do you think men ever help with the housework?"		
1958	26	23
1981	49	37
"Do you think married women should take a job outside the home if they have young children?"		
1960	4	6
1982	36	41
"Do you think married women should take a job outside the home if they have no young children?"		
1960	58	72
1982	85	88
"Do you think women who do the same work as men should receive the same pay?"		
1954	49	63
1970	84	89
1985*	96	96

SOURCES: Computed from Gallup data in Boyd, 1984; **Project Can85.*

programs, and activities aimed at "the amelioration of conditions of disadvantaged individuals or groups."[30]

The Charter's potential for personal autonomy was verbalized recently by former Prime Minister Trudeau. Testifying before the Senate Submissions Group on the Meech Lake Accord in late 1989, Trudeau explained that the Charter "was meant to create a body of values and beliefs that not only united all Canadians in feeling that they were one nation but also set them above the governments of the provinces and the federal government itself." As a result, he said, "people have rights which no legislative body can abridge, therefore establishing the sovereignty of the Canadian people over all institutions of government."[31]

Looking at things from the U.S. side of the border, sociologist Seymour Lipset sees the Charter and the ensuing judicial intervention to protect individual rights and civil liberties as "important, even revolutionary." He writes: "[The Charter] probably goes further toward taking the country in an American direction than any other enacted structural change, including the Canada-U.S. free-trade agreement. The Charter's stress on due process and individual rights, although less stringent than that of the U.S. Bill of Rights, should increase individualism and litigiousness north of the border."[32]

For their part, Canadians are not yet sure of the personal implications of the Charter. A May 1987 Gallup poll found that while 40 percent think that their rights and freedoms are better protected now, another 40 percent feel things are pretty much the same.[33] Beyond public perception, the enactment of the Charter at minimum appears to reflect the growing sense of the importance not only of cultural groups in Canada, but also of the individual — with or without a group tie.

NEW OUTLOOKS

The strong emphasis on the rights of groups and individuals has given Canadians new glasses with which to view old realities. Researchers tell us that levels, for example, of racism, sexism, child abuse, sexual harassment, and even homicide have not increased significantly in Canada since the 1960s. The proportion of Canadians who are homosexual has remained about the same. What has increased in each case is not *incidence* but *visibility*.

Of course, racism and sexism were there all along. But we didn't define such behavior as particularly abnormal. Through the 1950s, many Canadians didn't wince about saying they bought groceries from the "Chinaman"; they passed on jokes about beautiful but mindless women who liked to talk and shop. Some people exhibited homosexual tendencies, but we tended to neutralize their behavior through humor and caustic labels, such as calling them "fairies" and "fruits." In the 1950s, unsolicited physical touching was common in Canadian life — including employment, school, and religious settings — to the point where, for many people, it was at worst seen as annoying. People who indulged in sexual innuendo were called "forward"; a sexual invitation was called a "proposition." Abuse of children by parents, siblings, and others was not uncommon. But one didn't tell teachers and the police about the misbehavior of a father or mother or sister or brother or guardian or whomever. Murders took place, but usually didn't involve strangers.

SEEING IS BELIEVING

"Have you, yourself, ever been discriminated against because of age, sex, religion, racial origin, or some other identifiable characteristic?"

	% Indicating "*Yes*"
NATIONAL	24
18-29	29
30-49	27
50 & over	16
University	31
High School	24
Less High School	12
Female	27
Male	20
English Origin	29
Other Origin	25
French Origin	13

SOURCE: *Gallup Canada, Inc.*, November 26, 1987.

Times were not the same. Asked in 1990 why the police weren't notified about child abuse by Roman Catholic brothers at an Ontario training school in 1960, the former deputy minister said it was because such reporting wasn't the practice of the government at that time. The normal procedure was to fire people accused of engaging in abuse. Only in extremely serious cases were the police called in. "We're talking about what happened thirty years ago," said the seventy-year-old former official. "Things were handled differently in those days."[34]

Given our desire to have a more humane and just Canada, we are redefining old practices in new ways. There have been at least two major consequences. First, Canadians are changing their behavior. The change is motivated by both a desire to relate in a more humanitarian way to others, as well as by the need to protect themselves against highly damaging accusations. Second, in the light of the new norms, people are "seeing" more inappropriate behavior than ever before. Significantly, those Canadians who report the highest levels of personal discrimination "due to" their age, gender, religion, or race tend to be those who are best equipped to "spot" such inequities — people who are young, better educated, female, and of English origin.

NEW FREEDOM

On the individual level, to an extent never known before, we have been emancipated. We have been given the green light to focus on ourselves, to give attention to our personal development — mentally, physically, socially, spiritually. We are acquiring more and more education, reading books and taking courses aimed at personal growth; we are concerned about health, fitness, and diet; we are giving unprecedented attention to polishing our social skills; we are treating spiritual quest as a personal journey. Sociologist Lipset notes that a new tone of individualism and confidence is found in Canadian literature. He cites an 1982 observation made by literary critic Ronald Sutherland:

> [A] new hero, as it were, suddenly exploded from the pages of Canadian fiction. In many respects he is an exponent of traditional American rather than Canadian values — self-reliance, individualism, independence, self-confidence. . . . Clear examples of the new hero are found in novels from both French and English Canada, indicating that Canadians of each major language group

are simultaneously and at long last creating a new image of themselves.[35]

Previous barriers to individual expression and growth have been breaking down like a series of Berlin Walls. Race and ethnicity, gender and physical attributes, marital status and personal relationships are among the many walls that are at various stages of demolition.

Age is a good example. Increasingly, people are viewing age as a poor basis for commonality in relationships. Frequently it is being ignored by participants. The reason is that, although people are more free than ever "to grow," they are doing so at very different rates. Young people, for example, are developing informed, sophisticated minds; people in their forties and fifties are developing young bodies; spiritual commonality often transcends age boundaries; social skills are often precariously related to year of birth.

Dating and marriage have come to know an expanded range of age possibilities. Older women are more frequently becoming involved with younger men, complementing the age-old and ongoing pattern of older men and younger women. People are marrying and remarrying at virtually any age. The age at which people will have children is going up. In 1970, 12 percent of Canadian women in their thirties who gave birth were first-time mothers; in 1986, the figure had jumped to 26 percent.[36] The age at which people assume a partner's children is even more a matter of guesswork.

The business world has lost little time catching on. The J. Walter Thompson ad agency of New York, for example, with worldwide revenues of close to $4 billion U.S. annually, reports that it no longer defines parents in terms of their own age but rather by the age of their children. Chief executive officer James Patterson says, "We have found that studies based on age such as 50 plus, the graying of America, or lifestyle studies, such as yuppies, are obsolete as we enter the 1990s. If we think of people in terms of their life stage rather than their age or even socioeconomic position, we will have a more accurate window into their needs and desires."[37]

As never before, the individual is "in." The fountain of wisdom and the fountain of youth have both appeared in the form of personal growth: young people are becoming older; older people are becoming younger.

NEW RELATIONSHIPS

The accelerated emphases on the individual and the personal nature of what is right also have had a profound impact on personal relationships in Canada. In the 1950s, the well-known Presbyterian minister and U.S. senate chaplain Peter Marshall, of *A Man Called Peter* fame, described marriage as "the coming together of two tributaries to form one great river."[38] The view of relationships and marriage as the fusion of two lives was common before the 1960s. Widely used terms told the unsubtle story: marriages were called "unions," the participants "partners." Individuality and personal freedom were largely lost. For many, perhaps most, marriage was something they served, rather than something that served them. Canadians were inclined to ask, "What am I supposed to be like now that I am married?" rather than, "What do I want to be like now that I am married?"

People readily acknowledged that marriage was something that fulfilled and enriched them and helped them to overcome some of the limitations they experienced as single people — loneliness, sadness, boredom, insecurity, inferiority, fear. Ideally, marriage was thought to help two weak people to become strong, and two strong people to become stronger. The cure-all for the problem of being single was thought to be a wife or a husband. At its best, fusion meant infusion. Marriage helped many people cope with life.

But frequently there were significant personal costs. The ideal of two fused lives left little room for individuality. Particularly for women, marriage often suffocated expression, ambition, and personal development. Education, careers, and personal interests and activities were put on the back burner — or sometimes never reached the stove — because family demands and allegiances came first. Supportive clichés spoke volumes: "Behind every successful man there is a woman," and "Every man needs a good woman." Married people were applauded for making "sacrifices" for each other and their children; charges of selfishness and lack of loyalty were sometimes made if a spouse wanted to pursue a personal rather than a family interest, or if a couple chose not to have children.

In part because "the tributaries" often failed to flow into one great river, in part because of the acceleration of individualism, a very different view of relationships began to gain prominence as Canada said goodbye to the alleged "happy days" of the 1950s. A position that sociologist Robert Bellah and his associates[39] have called "the therapeutic model" of relationships began to be widely advocated and widely accepted as scientifically appropriate and personally emancipating for countless people, particularly women. The therapeutic model assumes that, in order to have healthy social ties, people first need to work on themselves. Paradoxically, once they have themselves "together" and don't need anyone, they then are in a position to have a healthy relationship with someone. Put another way, personal deprivation is viewed as a relational liability. It needs to be overcome before one can relate successfully to others.

Good relationships, then, involve healthy people relating to healthy people for mutual enrichment. In the language of some proponents of the model, "winners attract winners." Healthy, "winning" individuals are essentially self-sufficient; they are not drawn into relationships by need. The pop singer Meatloaf, in a hit a decade ago, announced, "I want you, I need you; but there ain't no way I'm ever going to love you."[40] People who endorse the "autonomy model" of relationships slightly revise the lyrics, in effect saying, "I want you, I love you — but there ain't no way I'm ever going to need you." Psychiatrist and author Scott Peck, in his enormously successful *The Road Less Traveled*, sums up this emphasis: "Two people love each other only when they are quite capable of living without each other but *choose* to live with each other. . . . Again and again we tell our couples that a good marriage can exist only between two strong and independent people."[41]

The emphasis on autonomy rather than fusion in relationships has been heralded as a major breakthrough. Individuals enter relationships not out of weakness but strength and are enhanced by such nondependent ties. People can demand more of relationships than ever before. In marriage, for example, people "will not tolerate a cold, conflict-ridden, or unfulfilling family life," writes sociologist Metta Spencer. "Their expectations are high, precisely because real possibilities for family warmth exist."[42]

Post-1960 Canada has been a time of great emancipation for groups and individuals. Inequities involving cultural minorities and women have been significantly addressed. Individual rights and freedoms have been constitutionally guaranteed. The quality of interpersonal life shows signs of improving. These are no minor social alterations. However, they represent only part of the Canadian transformation.

Emancipated Institutions

Encouraged by pluralism, freedom has become a dominant theme within all of Canada's major institutions. Emphasis on the individual and choice can be seen everywhere.

THE FAMILY MOSAIC

The family of Canada's first 100 years has been radically transformed to meet the needs of individualistically minded Canadians. Once the country's primary social link for almost everybody — complete with children and clearly defined roles and responsibilities — it now is a colorful mosaic of forms and functions. Family expert Pat Armstrong, a sociologist at York University, begins an article on the family in *The Canadian Encyclopedia* with these words: "There is no such thing as the 'Canadian family'."[43] According to Statistics Canada, the term "census family"

> refers to a *husband-wife family* (i.e., a husband and a wife, with or without never married children, living in the same dwelling), or a *one-parent family* (i.e., a lone parent of any marital status, with one or more never married children in the same dwelling). Persons living in a common-law type of arrangement are considered husband and wife.[44]

Since the 1960s, structural and functional choices have accelerated. The remaining functions of the family are said by some experts to have been reduced to four — reproduction, economic sustenance, socialization, and affection. Others say only the last two remain; still others maintain that even those two functions are increasingly questionable, given realities such as daycare and divorce.[45]

Options abound. Canadians are increasingly free to marry, cohabit, or not marry; continue a marriage or terminate it; have children in marriage, outside marriage, or not have them at all; engage in marital sex, nonmarital sex, or be celibate; be heterosexual, homosexual, or both.

If we opt for a relationship of some kind, there also are myriad additional choices that arise concerning such areas as the division of labor within the home, who will work outside the home, who will take what responsibilities for raising children, and so on.

Children in turn find themselves in an increasing number of role possibilities. They may be the children of one parent or two; they may have parents who are married, previously married, or never married. Both parents, one parent, or no parent may be employed; both parents, one parent, or no parent may be taking the lead in child-raising.

Sexually, the relationships may be significant; they also may not. Whether or not nonmarried couples engage in sexual relations has come to be seen as a private issue in Canada, a matter of personal preference. As sex has come to be viewed increasingly as an individual rather than a marital issue, the key criterion for many has changed from commitment to feelings. People engage in sexual relations "if they feel like it." The major issue is not an intent to marry or commitment to a serious relationship. Cautionary measures need to be taken to avoid unwanted pregnancy and disease, notably AIDS. But if two people want to have sex, so the thinking goes, then why not?

Some fast family facts[46]:

- The liberalizing of divorce laws has resulted in a rising divorce rate. Between 1921 and 1968 the rate rose from .06 to .55 per 1,000 population; by 1969 it had jumped to 1.24, by 1985 to 2.44.

In 1969 the median length of marriage before divorce was fifteen years; by 1986 it had dropped to about ten years. We still are behind the Americans; there, 44 percent of marriages end in divorce, compared with 28 percent here.

HIGH RELATIONSHIP EXPECTATIONS: 15- TO 24-YEAR-OLDS

In %s

	Will eventually marry or make a relationship commitment	Will stay with same person for life		
		Very Likely	Fairly Likely	Not Very Likely
Nationally	92	69	29	2
Males	91	66	32	2
Females	93	71	27	2
15-19	93	66	31	3
20-24	92	71	27	2
B.C.	94	65	35	1
Prairies	97	73	25	2
Ontario	94	72	25	3
Quebec	86	61	35	2
Atlantic	93	71	27	2

SOURCE: *Project Teen Canada 88.*

- The number of lone-parent families increased from 347,000 in 1961 to 854,000 in 1986, with 82 percent headed by women. Children living in such settings doubled during the same period from half a million to 1.2 million.
- Divorce and single-parent snapshots should not obscure the moving picture. New relationships are formed; remarriage is common — 76 percent of divorced men and 44 percent of divorced

women eventually remarry; a divorced person is involved in 30 percent of all current marriages, compared with just 12 percent as recently as 1967. Lone-parent episodes for women, when seen as ending in remarriage or children leaving home, last an average of 5.5 years.

• Canadians are delaying getting married at all. In 1961, 70 percent of males twenty to twenty-four had not yet married; as of 1986, the level has jumped to 79 percent; for females in the same age group, the increase has been even greater — from 40 percent to 60 percent.

• Between 1961 and 1986, the number of births dropped from 3.8 births per woman to 1.7. Total family size during the same period fell from 3.9 persons to 3.1. In 1961, 80 percent of women fifteen to twenty-nine were mothers; by 1981, the figure stood at 59 percent.

• From the time of Confederation, homosexuality had been punishable by up to 14 years in prison. In 1969, the law was amended, exempting consenting adults. Although 70 percent of Canadians do not approve of homosexual relations and about the same proportion say they are inclined to feel uncomfortable around homosexuals, 76 percent nonetheless assert that "homosexuals are entitled to the same rights as other Canadians."[47]

• About 90 percent of fifteen- to twenty-four-year-olds and 80 percent of adults eighteen and over approve of nonmarital sex when people love each other. Behaviorally, some 45 percent of unmarried fifteen- to nineteen-year-olds and 80 percent of twenty- to twenty-four-year-olds indicate that they currently are sexually active.[48]

For all the sexual freedom, some basic rules do remain fairly solidly in place. One forbids extramarital sex; at last count, only 4 percent of Canadians said such activity is "not wrong at all."[49] Another rule — enforced by law — is that the sexual partners cannot be related. And one marital configuration is championed by virtually no one: polygamy. Monogamy remains almost "an absolute" in Canada, standing as one widely accepted "truth" in a culture where truth is rare.

There is also an accelerated concern for the well-being of family members. Particular attention has been drawn to the abuse of wives and children. It is not that such abuses are new problems in Canada or elsewhere. However, there has been a growing sense that these long-standing problems of abuse will no longer be tolerated, that membership in the family is not to be bought at the price of the physical and emotional harm of anyone. Across the country, women's organizations and other groups have raised the profile of abuse of wives and children. Governments have begun to respond to such concerns.

THE EDUCATION MOSAIC

Things have come a long way since the days when the primary goals of education were control and the acquisition of basic skills, the dominant means discipline and memorization. A culture that has placed increasing importance on the autonomy of the individual could not be expected to leave education untouched.

To begin with, access to education has come to be seen as an individual right. For example, surveys have found that approximately 90 percent of Canadians feel that a person who cannot afford it nevertheless has a right to a university education.[50] Further, Canada's industrial and post-industrial expansion has been seen as dependent on education. Consequently, education reforms have taken place because they have been seen as both socially just and economically necessary.[51]

The result has been a dramatic increase in the attention given to education at all levels since the 1960s.[52] At of the end of the 1950s, only 15 percent of Canadians had high school diplomas and a mere 5 percent had university degrees. By 1990, high school grads stood at about 80 percent, those with degrees at almost 15 percent, those with some post-secondary education jumped during the period from about 20 percent to 35 percent. Institutions and enrollments have boomed. In 1955, Canada had some forty-five universities; in the next twenty years, approximately twenty more were added. Enrollment during that 1955-to-1975 period jumped from under 150,000 to over 350,000. Currently, about half a million people attend universities full-time, some 300,000 part-time. Community college programs also accelerated in the sixties. By 1990, they numbered almost two hundred, compared with about thirty in 1960 with full-time enrollment standing at almost 325,000 students.

In the words of sociologists Sid Gilbert and Ian Gomme, the system in the post-1950s has "changed from elite education to mass education. It is no longer only a select and fortunate few who advance to post-secondary certification." Canada now stands second only to the United States in the percentage of the labor force with college diplomas or university degrees.[53]

Beyond education becoming an individual right, it also has come to have a strong individualist focus. In giving direction to education in the post-1950s, the Royal Commission on National Development in the Arts, Letters and Sciences, headed by Vincent Massey, in 1951 defined education's individualistic mood. "Education," it said, is "the progressive development of the individual in all his faculties, physical and intellectual, aesthetic and moral." The result of such disciplined growth, according to the commission, is an educated person who has fully realized his or her human possibilities.[54]

Since the 1950s, the individual has been at the center of education in Canada. In view of the fact that the school had its origins in the need to harness and refine unwieldly and uncultured children, the attendance-education exchange was not particularly balanced in pre-1960 Canada. Curricula were typically rigid and discipline was strict. The early grades were organized to simulate a home atmosphere, complete with female teachers whose nurturing skills were viewed as an asset in molding young people into productive citizens.

In part reflecting the liberal conception of education put forward by the American philosopher John Dewey — emphasizing the development of the individual, the promotion of social equality, and preparation for adult work roles — things have changed. An effort has been made to make education less authoritarian and more flexible. Considerable experimentation has taken place to develop programs and physical environments that are sensitive to the individual needs of students, including the gifted and handicapped.

Queen's sociologist Robert Pike comments that, in comparison with some countries such as Japan, "individualism is more pivotal for educational philosophy and practice" in Canada. The practical applications of individualism, he says, are evident in such postwar reforms as promotion by subject rather than grade, the maximizing of student choice in high school courses, and the assessment of graduating high school students individually by their teachers rather than through uniform provincial exams.[55] Individualism can also be seen in education goals, Pike maintains. While there is still official acknowledgment that students should develop social responsibility, "such a goal is often subordinate to other goals that emphasize the importance of achieving self-worth and self-reliance."

The idea of a "liberal" education has also carried with it a strong emphasis on the presentation of all points of view. Reflecting the national emphasis on multiculturalism, a great deal of attention has been given to respecting the rights of cultural and religious minorities. Teaching is expected to be non-doctrinaire; prayer is viewed as having no place in the classroom; holidays — including Christmas, Remembrance Day, Thanksgiving, and Easter — should not be colored by any one religion.

For example, in January 1990, the Ontario Court of Appeal ruled that public school religious courses that aim to indoctrinate students in any one faith violate the Charter of Rights and Freedoms. Caution in other areas is suggested in this excerpt from an Ontario school board administrator's letter to high school principals regarding guidelines for Remembrance Day:

> Remembrance Day gives us the opportunity to appreciate the qualities of endurance and courage and devotion to the principles of freedom within our community. We must express a sensitivity to the fact that for many students the word "remembrance" has a very familiar meaning. Staff should be aware that some students may not want to share their memories.
>
> Symbols of remembrance may be very different depending on the culture where a student comes from (for example, crosses may not be meaningful to Iranian, Israeli or Sri Lankan students and others who do not have a Christian

> background). In our multi-cultural society, it is advisable to use only appropriate symbols such as flags, poppies and wreaths, rather than symbols pertaining to any particular faith.[56]

At the university and college level, the individualistic theme takes on a somewhat different meaning. Professors insist on their right to freedom of expression, in print and in the classroom. The University of Lethbridge, where I teach, includes in its statement of philosophy: "The University asserts its right and responsibility for free expression and communication of ideas. It is self-evident that a university cannot function without complete autonomy in this domain."[57]

Still, professors, like school teachers, are expected to be detached and objective. They are not to be biased or take moral positions, but rather to present the pertinent facts and interpretations. Outside the physical sciences, the key arbitrator of truth is the individual, who decides what will be right for him or her. Here the school and university become the key sources of relativism.

Education stands out as an institution that not only has been strongly influenced by individualism and relativism but also has done much to legitimize the two themes. Indeed, the mark of a well-educated Canadian is that he or she places supreme importance on the individual while recognizing that truth is relative. To decry individual fulfillment or to claim to have found the truth would be a dead giveaway that one has not graced the halls of higher learning.

THE WORKPLACE MOSAIC

We already have seen that the economic transformation of Canada has been a major source of accelerated individualism. But individualism also has had a powerful effect on the workplace as we have moved from an economy based on agriculture to one based on heavy industry to one based on information and service industries. The cultural emphasis on relativism also has had a profound impact on values and outlook in this important sphere.

For the vast majority of Canadians, of course, work on farms and in small family businesses belongs to history. As of 1986, there were fewer than 300,000 farms in Canada, compared with 733,000 in 1941.[58] Industrialization has brought with it economic centralization, urbanization, and job specialization. A major correlate has been the increasing movement of women into the workforce.

Most of us work in settings where our individual work assignments have become more and more specialized — and interdependent. Beyond literal assembly lines, what is of paramount importance in Canadian organizations ranging from large bureaucracies to small companies is the coordination of varied work roles so that the goals of the organization can be accomplished.

An interesting paradox that has resulted from the prevalence of interdependent, specialized roles is that both employers and employees have gained an extremely high level of freedom in the form of independence. While employers need to have roles carried out, they seldom are dependent upon any given employee; to be so is to invite organizational disaster should that employee be lost. Good people are still coveted — but the human options have to be plural. Canadian employers consequently view the vast majority of their employees as specialized parts in organizational machines. They are dispensable; they have to be. What is of central importance is that the organizational role be played; it doesn't matter *who* plays it. Role performance and role coordination are the central ingredients of goal attainment.

Toronto lawyer Brian Grosman offers a corporate example in his book, *Corporate Loyalty: A Trust Betrayed*. He writes that a valued employee is a loyal employee who "works hard, protects corporate assets and does not move from one company to another." But, says Grosman, "in a world of downsizing, restructuring, massive mergers, friendly and hostile takeovers, sales and acquisitions, a major assault upon the concept of loyalty is in progress." Competition means leaner and meaner operations, firings, early retirements, and so on. Loyalty toward employees has become precarious.[59]

But employees are also highly autonomous. The average Canadian employee is an individual who has the qualifications — or

POST-INDUSTRIALIZATION IN THE POST-1960s

% of Employers in Work Sectors

	1960	1970	1980	1988
Manufacturing	24.7	22.7	19.7	17.2
Services*	24.5	25.7	28.9	33.2
Trade**	16.5	16.8	17.2	17.7
Agriculture	11.5	6.3	4.5	3.6
Utilities	8.6	8.8	8.5	7.4
Government	n/a	6.2	6.9	6.7
Construction	7.0	6.0	5.8	5.9
Finance	3.8	4.8	5.7	5.9
Mining	1.6	1.6	1.8	1.5
Forestry	1.6	0.9	0.7	0.3
Fishing and Trapping	0.3	0.3	0.3	0.6

* Service is provided but no goods are produced.

** Refers to sale and distribution of merchandise.

SOURCE: Derived from *The Canadian World Almanac*, 1989:367.

at least the potential — to play an organizational role. In most instances, his or her relationship to the organization is primarily financial. We agree to perform a specialized role in return for remuneration. Our organizational commitment varies; we may care about the organization, be indifferent, or even be negative about how it fares. The primary link to the workplace for most Candians is not dedication but dollars. This is not the family business or farm. If the organization that employs them is having difficulty meeting its goals — turning a profit or fulfilling its mandate — individuals are free to take their skills elsewhere, and they frequently do. They no longer "sink or swim" with the ups and downs of the small family operation.

While we invariably dislike being informed that we are "replaceable," the truth of the matter is that we ourselves convert the proverb into a fulfilled prophecy by freely moving from one job to another. Why? Usually because we see such moves as being "in our best interests." Grosman writes that people involved in investment banking "jump from firm to firm to accumulate as much wealth as they can in the shortest possible time," like "baseball free agents, not . . . belonging to anything larger than themselves."[60]

What Grosman is saying about people in investments seems equally appropriate to the vast majority of Canadians in the workforce. Individuals are not seen as adequately motivated if they do not keep a keen ongoing eye on the labor market, always on the lookout for an opportunity to make an "upward move." An April 1990 Gallup poll found that, although 70 percent of Canadians think their job "is safe," 45 percent think it is likely that they will change employers within the next five years. The Gallup organization suggests that the findings reflect a situation in which "allegiances to a particular employer are diminishing." Whereas it has been maintained that Canadian workers in the past frequently "began and finished their careers with one employer, today's worker is decidedly less faithful and rooted."[61]

For employees, the emergence of role-centered organizations means that livelihood is based not on the performance of the company but on personal role performance. Such a limited investment is perceived by most to have significant advantages. Many early critics of the division of labor, notably Karl Marx, were very wary of the alienating effects specialized work would have on individuals who were divorced from the product and the process of their labors. Wrote Marx, "Work is external to the worker . . . and consequently he does not fulfill himself in his work. . . . [He] feels himself at home only during his leisure time, whereas at work he is homeless. . . . A man who lives by the favor of another considers himself a dependent being.[62]

These days, it seems clear that, particularly in large bureaucracies, most employees have limited awareness of the "product" of the organization, or of its profit margin. Relatively few, however, appear to care. Most people appear to be content to carry out their highly specialized tasks; they don't want to endure the pressure and anxiety that come from having their own businesses or even from having to take chances on the job. The 1987 national survey of fifteen- to twenty-four-year-olds, for example, found that the job attribute valued the least was having the opportunity to "make most of the decisions."

VIEWS OF "A GOOD JOB": CANADIAN YOUTH

"When you think of 'a good job,' how important is work. . ."
% Indicating "*Very Important*"

	TOTAL	MALE	FEMALE
That is interesting	81	78	83
That gives me a feeling of accomplishment	75	69	80
Where other people are friendly and helpful	71	66	75
Where there is a chance for advancement	70	71	68
Where there is little chance of being laid off	62	63	61
That pays well	56	58	53
Where you make most of the decisions yourself	32	35	28

SOURCE: *Project Teen Canada 88.*

Individualism and relativism have given specific labor market meaning to the term "free market economy." The two cultural themes have contributed to unprecedented freedom for large numbers of employers and workers.

THE MEDIA MOSAIC

Nowhere are the themes of the individual and choice more apparent than in the media. The varied media forms in Canada — both of national and U.S. origin — respond to the cultural presence of the two themes, as well as aggressively promote them.

While "mass," the media are also intensely personal. Charles Templeton recalls how, in his early days of television, an NBC producer reminded him that when he looked into the camera, he wasn't speaking to millions of people, just one.[63] The successful newscaster, writer, reporter, disc jockey, talk-show host, and entertainer is a person who succeeds in relating to a wide audience of individuals — so much so that when they meet their public face to face, celebrities discover that the masses relate to them on a first-name basis, as if they were longtime friends. In a sense, they are.

The fact that media forms are frequently consumed in social situations does not negate the fact that songs, articles, movies, front-page stories, TV shows, magazine features, and sports scores are all read, seen, heard, and felt by individuals. Media forms address all of our emotions. They make us laugh and make us sad, make us cheer and make us mad, engender courage and engender fear, remind us what's real as well as feed our fantasies, stimulate our minds as well as give them a rest.

As individuals in need of supplements to our limited personal experiences and first-hand knowledge, we have come to rely heavily on the media to find out what's happening in the world. In the 1990s, the media are like reliable, informed friends to us. As we sip our coffee in the morning, we are told what happened while we slept, given a short update at noon, the latest word as of suppertime, and a final briefing just before we go to bed. The media inform us of major events, ongoing developments, rumors, social problems, research findings. They also function as a resource, helping us to raise our child, improve our marriage, upgrade the house. In short, the media offer us unlimited information.

The media's capacity to scan the entire globe at a single bound makes their influence awesome. Our television sets have become our windows on the world. From the comfort of our family rooms we watch a massacre in China, the proclamation of freedom in Poland, riots in South Africa, a siege in El Salvador, an earthquake in Iran. We assume that when an important event happens anywhere in the world, the media will deliver it to us live and in color. In order to be informed, we turn to the media. And when the media speak, we listen. However well exposed we may be to the world, we are at best experiential specialists. Media supplementation of knowledge and information is inevitable — and necessary.

As for relativism, in the course of carrying out its array of functions, ranging from informing to entertaining, the media officially maintain a position of objectivity and fairness. Operating in a pluralistic milieu, their implicit message is that, in matters

WHAT CANADIANS WATCH ON TELEVISION

Type of Program by Origin (In %s)

	TOTAL	CANADIAN	U.S.
Drama	33	4	29
News	20	17	3
Comedy	13	<1	13
Variety	12	6	6
Sports	6	5	1
Other	16	4	12
TOTALS	100	36	64

SOURCE: Derived from *Canadian Social Trends*, Autumn, 1989:14.

of lifestyle and beliefs and attitudes, no views are better or worse than others. "Everything's relative."

In large part, such "open-mindedness" is dictated by market considerations. It is not wise to alienate audiences, readers, and advertisers. When Jimmy the Greek made what was regarded as a racist slur against Blacks on a pregame show on CBS a few years ago, he was promptly bounced by the network. It was not only inappropriate; it was bad for business. Relativity is the media's watchword. One can be controversial, but not to the point of alienating the audience. It kills the ratings.

Rather than doing unnecessary things to limit markets, the media have been engaging in an incredible amount of diversification in recent years. The explosion of different forms of media in the United States and Canada is a reflection of the media's effort to match diverse choices with individual tastes. Television and radio networks and stations are in touch with social reality. While other institutions and organizations wonder "what's going on out there," the electronic media are surveying the public to death, guided by ratings more than probably any other entity in our society — even the politicians. They do not have to be taught that the customers are into selective consumption. The trick is how to get people literally to buy one's media offering.

If market research shows the product people want doesn't exist, the solution is simple: create it.

Canadians do not lack for a wide variety of media options. The print media are readily available in the form of newspapers, books, and magazines. The electronic media seem everywhere with the partial list including radio and television, motion pictures and videos, records and tapes. But when it comes to consumption — and probably influence — television appears to be a runaway leader. Canadian writer Michelle Landsberg goes so far as to say that "television is not part of our culture; it is our culture."[64]

Television has reached its present level of dominance in less than four decades. It has come a long way since its belated and shaky 1952 start in Montreal, Vancouver, and Toronto, where the first image beamed to southern Ontario was the CBC logo — upside down and backwards.[65] By 1985, as many Canadian households had television sets as had telephones (98 percent).[66] Today, the average home has at least one color set; 50 percent have at least two. One in two households also has a VCR, dramatically up from 6 percent in 1983. Cable runs into 70 percent of homes.[67] Statistics Canada reports that TV viewing accounts for an average of about one in five of people's waking hours." In 1987, Canadians watched an average of 3.4 hours per day. The average for women was 3.8, for men 3.2.[68]

This is not to say that other media do not have a place. Radios are listened to, but in most cases they provide background music and information while people are doing other things. The same is true of recorded music. The average Canadian spends less than thirty minutes a day reading newspapers, books, and magazines. Somewhat more than three in ten read the paper every day; about two in ten give some time to reading a book; one in ten will browse through a magazine on a given day but, as with radio listening, while doing something else.[69]

Two quick illustrations of retrenchment. Library borrowing had been on the rise into the past decade, but has slowed somewhat since 1982. Significantly, the borrowing of talking books, videos, and recordings has been increasing more rapidly than the borrowing of books.[70] Movie-going has plummeted since the early 1950s, when the average Canadian saw some seventeen shows a year. But people haven't stopped going—the national average is about three a year — it's just that a new norm has been established as a result of television and the VCR. Having to adjust to fussy customers, the theater owners cut the number of outlets from 1,950 in 1955, to 1,200 in 1970, and to 788 in 1985. But the number of screens increased, to 1,450 by 1985, via an expansion of multiscreen operations.[71]

ACCESSING OF MEDIA:
15- to 24-YEAR-OLDS

% Indicating Engage in "*Daily*"

	NATIONALLY	15-19	20-24
Listen to music	94	95	93
Watch television	79	80	78
Listen to FM radio	66	62	70
Read the newspaper	47	42	52
Listen to AM radio	47	49	44
Read books	29	31	28
Read magazines	20	23	18
Watch rock videos	20	28	11

SOURCE: *Project Teen Canada 88.*

John Carey, the esteemed Oxford historian, has written, "The advent of mass communications represents the greatest change in human consciousness that has taken place in recorded history." Within a few decades, says Carey, we have seen a change from a situation in which most people around the globe had little knowledge or curiosity about how others were faring, to one in which ordinary people have and must have "accurate reports about the doings of complete strangers." Carey says that this development "represents a revolution in mental activity which is incalculable in its effects."[72]

The effect that the media have on Canadians is phenomenal. They are the modern-day creators of the world. They decide which nations are heroes and which are villains. They define superstars and also-rans. They create reality and instill models for individual living. Education specialists Robert Patterson and Nick Kach write, "While the influence of the traditional socializing agencies has been waning, the power of the mass media has been increasing significantly. . . . Television, especially, has become the purveyor of values, beliefs and knowledge. Mass media broadens perspectives, leading to greater openness, pluralism, and relativism."[73]

Historically, the media generally and the news media specifically have known a high level of freedom of expression in Canada. The early newspapers of the 1800s were mostly weeklies that had clear political sponsorship. Still, some were the targets of hostility and violence. The proprietor of a St. John's paper incensed some local Irish Catholics, who cut off his ears to teach him a lesson; publishers William Lyon Mackenzie and Joseph Howe were charged and acquitted of libel.[74]

Historian Paul Rutherford says that out of such encounters the notion of the freedom of the press began to take root in Canada, supported by public opinion and justified by liberal assumptions. In 1832, Mackenzie wrote: "Remember, that wherever the Press is not free the people are poor abject degraded slaves, that the Press is the life, the safeguard, the very heart's blood of a free country."[75] Rutherford adds, "The notion of the freedom of the press has been inextricably linked to the notion of popular sovereignty."[76] With minor opposition, the idea that the Canadian press is free and independent persists. The assumption has been explicitly enshrined in the Canadian Charter of Rights and Freedoms.

An important footnote: along with education, the media have most explicitly promoted the importance of the individual and the relativity of truth. In Canada, to speak of the impact of the media on Canadian life is not to speak only of the Canadian media. The influence of American media on our culture and perceptions has been profound.

We have been eager consumers of American books; their bestsellers become our bestsellers. Our shelves are stocked with American magazines and newspapers. On television, we are inundated with U.S. channels and programs. Back in 1952, when Canadian television stations were launched, there were already close to 150,000 TV sets in Canada — all with antennas pointed toward the United States, where stations had appeared in 1947.[77] In 1987, Canadians gave 60 percent of their viewing time to U.S. programs.[78]

The American influence is not about to decrease. Cable television, nonexistent in 1970, now includes perhaps ten or more U.S. channels in a cable package. That package is being brought to more than seven in ten Canadian homes in big cities and hamlets alike. The impact on Canadian minds is in the process of escalating greatly. Of particular significance, the tremendous American emphasis on both individualism and relativism is being transmitted as never before to Canadians.

THE POLITICAL MOSAIC

Individualism and relativism have also invaded politics. Age-old *provincial primacy* continues to be evident in the provinces' dealings with the national government. The style has its roots, of course, in the fact that our founding fathers opted for a federal system, subdividing powers between Parliament and the provinces. Needless to say, the power balance and relations have varied over time.

Consequently we have a national government comprised of the provinces, yet, in theory, transcending them. When Parliament meets, the power distribution reflects the population differences of the ten member provinces.

The tremendous disparity in provincial populations creates a disparity of power. Equity has always been a big issue in Canada. Prince Edward Island, with less than 150,000 people and four Members of Parliament, clearly does not have the clout Ontario has, with its one hundred MPs. The west and the Atlantic regions have been defensive over the years, given the superior power of Ontario and Quebec.

The voluntary nature of the provinces' tie with Canada has been particularly apparent in times of strong discontent, when Quebec and the west, for example, have threatened to separate from the federation — something virtually unheard of south of the border.

Provincial individualism is hardly new. The emphasis on the coexistence of autonomous, interdependent parts is as old as Canada. But the growing cultural emphasis on individualism has intensified and given legitimacy to provinces pitting themselves against the federal collectivity. Individualism has made it inappropriate for the central government to be heavy-handed manner in its dealings with the provinces.

Individualism is showing signs of having a pronounced influence on the political styles of Canadians. In general, people are exhibiting a declining interest in political parties. Many people at the 1988 NDP leadership convention, for example, observed that the membership — once the youngest among the country's three major parties — was noticeably gray.

Further, it takes the publicity of a Meech Lake for Canadians to discover their politicians. A Gallup poll taken in the spring of 1990 revealed that 95 percent of Canadians could identify Brian Mulroney as Canada's prime minister and 87 percent knew that George Bush was the U.S. president. But the long-standing quip about "Joe Who?" was living on: after having been the country's Minister of External Affairs for five years, Joe Clark was known as such by just 57 percent of Canadians. Three months after she was elected as head of the NDP, Audrey McLaughlin was known to only 37 percent of the populace.[79]

Political parties are suffering from a crisis of credibility. Canadians have less respect for and confidence in political parties than in public schools, churches, large corporations, and labor unions.

When it comes to their voting styles, many Canadians give further evidence of their limited interest in — or loyalty to — political parties. On the heels of the November 1988 federal election, a *Maclean's* poll found that a quarter of voters said that they had changed their minds at least once during the fifty-one-day campaign as to what party would get their vote. One in five voters chose a party during the last two weeks; one in seven waited until election day. Allan Gregg, head of Decima, the company that conducted the survey, commented, "The level of volatility was stunning. It suggests that an increasing number of Canadians are prepared to extend or withdraw their support based on their own assessment of merit. . . . The old notion of standing behind

DECREASING RESPECT FOR POLITICAL PARTIES

"How much respect and confidence do you have in . . ."
% Indicating "*High*" or "*Very High*"

	1989	1979
Public schools	62	54
Supreme Court	59	57
Organized religion	55	60
Newspapers	36	37
Large corporations	33	34
House of Commons	30	38
Labor unions	28	23
Political parties	18	30

SOURCE: *Gallup Canada, Inc.*, February 9, 1989.

a party through thick and thin is disappearing." Political scientist George Perlin, of Queen's University, notes that Canadians often name the party they voted for most recently when they are asked which party they identify with. He adds, "It does not necessarily mean there is any enduring loyalty."[80]

The poll found that almost 50 percent said that the leading factor influencing their vote was issues; 18 percent said the leading factor was the candidate; another 18 percent cited party leaders. Only 15 percent said that they were guided primarily by party loyalty.[81] People have learned that political results are achieved not through solo efforts but through collective action. But in banding together in coalitions, they have been collectively pursuing individual concerns.

What they have in common is a personal issue rather than ideology. Thus it is that diverse individuals join in speaking out on the environment, nuclear disarmament, abortion, violence, racism, poverty, and other issues. People in some groups may be linked by a specific variable, such as province, gender, ethnicity, religion, or age. Yet even here, commonality tends to be influenced by the issue involved. One only has to differ with the group to be deleted from the movement.

The implications for candidates are sobering. Those who want to win have to champion not parties but constituency issues. To be closely aligned with a party is at best dubious benefit, at worst downright dangerous. Many candidates are caught in the cross fire between federal and provincial branches of the party; often a constituency will be hostile toward either or both. Smart candidates downplay their party ties. Today, winning depends on convincing constituents that one is committed to their concerns and is the best person available to advance them.

The cultural emphasis on individualism has contributed to a growing interest in using the political process to realize personal concerns. Individualistically minded Canadians are insisting that government be for the people — we support those who support us.

THE RELIGION MOSAIC

Involvement in organized religion was once something of a national norm. In the late 1950s, some 85 percent of Roman Catholics and 40 percent of Protestants said that they attended services every week. The church appears to have played a significant role in the lives of most Canadians. In Quebec, the Roman Catholic Church dominated everyday life. Elsewhere, Protestant denominations joined the Roman Catholic Church in exercising considerable influence on Canadian life. Other religions were also important.

But Canadians today, living in a culture that has been giving increasing attention to individuals and their viewpoints, are taking quite a different approach to religion. They have become highly selective consumers.[82] Most Canadians want religion *à la carte*. They pick and choose beliefs, practices, programs, and professional services from increasingly diversified religious smorgasbords. Weekly service attendance currently has dipped to under 30 percent. Attendance is only one indication that the selective consumption style of Canadians offers no institutional exemptions.

Moreover, attendance problems are far from over. A late 1987 survey of the nation's 15- to 24-year-olds has found that many traditional beliefs and practices remain high. But when it comes to groups, attendance and enjoyment are both extremely low. Less than one in five Canadian young people attend services

SERVICE ATTENDANCE INCREASINGLY SELECTIVE

"Did you, yourself, happen to attend a church or synagogue in the last seven days?"

	1946	1956	1965	1975	1986	1990
Protestant	60	43	32	25	27	24
Roman Catholic	83	87	83	61	43	37
NATIONALLY	67	61	55	41	35	27

SOURCE: Gallup Canada, Inc.

weekly. Just 6 percent report that religious groups are a source of high enjoyment.

Nevertheless, 80 percent continue to "think they are something," identifying primarily with the Roman Catholic Church (45 percent) and Protestant groups (32 percent); only 3 percent have other religious group preferences. Further, a surprising 75 percent say they expect to turn to religious groups for birth-related ceremonies in the future, with some 80 percent saying the same about weddings. More than 85 percent say they anticipate one day turning to the churches for funerals.[83]

Additional research findings suggest that many of the 20 percent who say they are "nothing" will do so only temporarily. As they require rites of passage, they will "reaffiliate," primarily with the dominant Roman Catholic and Protestant groups of their parents.[84] In support of such an expectation, the survey found that — among the young people who currently say they have no religious preference — 47 percent will be looking to religious groups for baptisms and the like, 69 percent for weddings, and 77 percent for funerals![85]

In present-day Canada, the core for whom religion is significant — perhaps about 15 to 20 percent — have faith constantly undermined by a society for which religion is marginal. Yet, the majority for whom religion is peripheral continue to accept it in its specialized place. The result, says religious studies professor Terence Penelhum, is one where the committed experience "partial secularization" in the form of the "devitalization of faith," while in the case of the skeptic, "something as complex and deeply rooted as Christianity can hardly be abandoned in all details in a few generations."[86]

Contrary to rumor, Canadians young and old are not abandoning the churches. Religious identification for most is not particularly overt, but it certainly shows little sign of ceasing to be at least latent. But Canadians have become highly selective about what they want. They also give little indication of being interested in giving much in return. For the vast majority of Canadians the phrase is about as self-evident as grass being green: religion is a personal matter. The fact that the idea is taken for granted is symptomatic of the extent to which the cultural emphasis on individuality has invaded, dominated, and reshaped religion.

RELIGION: YOUTH AND ADULTS

		YOUTH	ADULTS
BELIEFS:	God	84	83
	Divinity of Jesus	81	78
	Life after death	65	65
PRAY:	at least sometimes	80	74
GROUP TIES:	Attend weekly	17	25
	High enjoyment	6	16
	Identify	80	89
ANTICIPATED RITES:	Birth	75	85
	Marriage	80	86
	Death	85	91

SOURCES: *Project Teen Canada 88* and *Project Can85*.

Generally speaking, the response to the demand for consumer religion has been unconscious and unintentional. Nonetheless, the harsh reality is that Canadian religious groups have tended to function as suppliers, serving up religion *à la carte* to specialty-minded customers. The desire for religious fragments on the part of Canadians has put tremendous pressure on religious organizations to diversify their offering or lose business to more specialized religious and secular groups. Most have been inclined to bow to the demand.[87]

Religious offerings have become more diversified than ever before. A person who descends on virtually any church of any group in any large city will find the menu to be large and varied. There is something for everybody — worship, Sunday school, choirs, Bible studies, women and men's groups, youth and seniors' groups, social activities, married and singles' groups, membership classes, personal growth classes, social justice groups, fitness sessions, early morning prayer, early morning aerobics — and these are just for starters.

They also will find the church "big enough" to include a wide range of dispositions and theological orientations; should they not, they need only drive a little farther. Within their own groups, people who identify with Roman Catholicism, Anglicanism, the United Church, or Conservative Protestantism have the choice of being evangelical or agnostic, charismatic or formal, detached or involved, socially concerned or pietistic.[88]

Decreasing importance is placed on religious truth. Pluralism has declared its quest inappropriate; relativism has declared it futile. Most Canadians know little about the traditions with which they identify; only about half, for example, can identify "Peter" as the person who "denied Jesus three times"; just 20 percent of Toronto Diocese Anglicans can name the author of their historically hallowed Book of Common Prayer.[89] If few people are knowledgeable about their traditions, even fewer seem to care. One major religious group's truth claims seem to be about as acceptable and accurate as another's. Only the claims of cults and sects are regarded as suspect.

For their part, Canada's religious groups tend to make few claims about truth, especially outside their own physical and social confines. To make such claims is to flirt with the possibility of being labeled dogmatic and intellectually shallow. The rules are clear: people are allowed to express opinions, as long as they don't step on the toes of other individuals and groups. They can offer ideas, as long as they refrain from asserting that they have the truth. In the case of Christian groups, for example, our culture permits Jesus to be one way, but it gasps at any suggestion that he is the *only* way. One has to be careful, the message fairly tentative. Vagueness is a virtue.

Individualism and relativism have proven religiously emancipating for many people. In 1975, more than half the people asked said that a key reason for decreased involvement was that "religion had been forced on me as a child."[90] These days it is possible to differentiate between commitment and coercion. Faith has the opportunity to be the product of urgency rather than imitation.[91]

The two themes have also contributed to a Canadian religious environment that is quite different from the pre-1960s. Pluralism has decreed that groups extend to each other the basic courtesy of tolerance. Conflict between groups, while not extinct, has no place in the public arena. Competition is watched with a wary eye. Coexistence receives the Canadian stamp of approval.

An Amber Maple Leaf

We have come a long way. Today, more than 90 percent of Canadians describe themselves as "very happy" or "pretty happy"; this compares with about 85 percent for the so-called "happy days" of about 1960. Further, 93 percent say they receive considerable enjoyment from their friends; 94 percent describe their marriages as "very happy" or "pretty happy"; 74 percent say their present financial situation leaves them satisfied (the 1963 figure was 68%); 71 percent say they get considerable enjoyment from the area where they live; and 79 percent of those employed full-time report high levels of gratification from work; for part-timers the figure stands slightly higher, at 84 percent.[92]

The satisfaction that Canadians express with life in their provinces and the country is summed up well in what they report about where they would like to live. Given the hypothetical chance of living in any province, most would stay put. If they were to move, the favorite destination is beautiful British Columbia. If they could live in any country, only 8 percent would head for the United States, 12 percent would be en route to other parts of the world. The rest say they would stay in Canada.[93] "Whatever uncertainties surround the economy and the environment, Canadians appear optimistic that, individually if not always collectively, they will prosper in the future," wrote *Maclean's* in 1990.[94]

Canadians report higher levels of satisfaction with life than do people elsewhere. We also think we are faring better. In comparing ourselves with Americans, for example, nine in ten of us indicate that we have much better health care, and six in ten think we enjoy greater world respect. Almost seven in ten maintain that, overall, we have a superior quality of life.[95]

Pluralism, individualism, and relativism seem to have been very beneficial to Canada. Many of the imbalances of the country's first hundred years are being corrected. Individual behavior and expression have been increasingly emancipated in all spheres of life. The two major losers in earlier times — women and cultural groups — are faring better. Our quality of life has undoubtedly improved: we are staying alive longer, and in most cases are living very well. In 1986, the standardized per capita income of Canadians was $15,900 U.S., second in the entire world only to the Americans, who earned about $17,400; the rate of increase in the Canadian economy between 1985 and 1989 was second only to Japan's.[96]

But there's more to the story.

5

Success in Excess

No one is questioning that there was a need for changes. Throughout Canada's first century, emphasis on the group was costly. The losses for individuals and for society were significant. Personal and social well-being were far from ideal.

The new emphases on individualism and the relativity of truth in the 1960s were therefore refreshing. The ensuing emancipation of individuals and institutions in Canada was a necessary and profound historical development. Today, Canadians are free to live out life as they see fit. Our institutions, with no exceptions, have embraced individualism and relativism.

Canada's status as a world leader in promoting freedom through emphasizing individualism, pluralism, and relativism has been accompanied by major rewards. Few nations know a higher standard of living, a more peaceful existence, a greater level of freedom. But just when it seems that we can finally sit back, relax, and put our pluralistic society on display as a model for the world, some unexpected warning lights are beginning to flash.

Excessive Individualism

THE PRICE OF BONDLESSNESS

Social theorists and practitioners have always had to deal with this basic problem: how much individuality can a society have and still be a society? Sigmund Freud, in his classic work *The Future of an Illusion*, wrote that civilizations are possible only when the desires of the individual can be reconciled with the needs of the group. The inclination of individuals to go their own ways, if not harnassed by something like religion, needs to be controlled in some other way, such as personal volition. Otherwise, social life is not possible.[1] Social philosophers including Hobbes, Locke, and Rousseau maintained that unbounded selfishness and chaos are checked when people are willing to cooperate with each other — when they enter into a "social contract." Sociologist Emile Durkheim saw less developed societies as being held together by moral consensus, by shared sentiments, beliefs, and values that reflected "a collective conscience." In modern societies characterized by individuality and specialization, Durkheim maintained, solidarity persists not through consensus but through our interdependence.[2]

In Canada, the problem has been summed up well by Pierre Trudeau. In 1968 he wrote, "The oldest problem of political philosophy . . . is to justify authority without destroying the independence of human beings in the process. How can an individual be reconciled with society? The need for privacy with the need to live in groups? Love for freedom with need for order?"[3]

The problem has not gone away, in Canada or anywhere else. On the surface, for a country like ours to opt for a pluralistic model and declare itself to be a nation of nations sounds workable. And as the idea of the cultural mosaic spills over into other areas, such as relationships and family life, education and the media, the idea of being able to choose freely from many options sounds inviting.

Trudeau maintained that Canada was tied together by two convictions: the uselessness of national uniformity, and the value of tolerating the differences that would otherwise divide us.[4] In accepting difference, we find our oneness. Like a mosaic art-piece mounted on a wall, our different parts can add up to a unified whole. In an area like family life, the application of such a principle means that we find our togetherness in accepting each other's right to be different.

However, the mere presence of diverse parts does not for a moment ensure an integrated piece of art — let alone an integrated and prosperous society. In Canada, the time has come to address a centrally important question, both as a country and as individuals relating to each other in various spheres of life: if what we have in common is our diversity, do we really have anything in common at all? University of Toronto political scientist Gad Horowitz once wrote that multiculturalism in reality is "the masochistic celebration of Canadian nothingness."[5]

Is Horowitz right? Does pluralism, by legitimizing everything, in the end create nothing? In stressing the rights of individuals and the ultimate rightness of nothing, does pluralism become a threat to collective life? In a recent, insightful critique of life in the United States, Berkeley sociologist Robert Bellah and his associates assert that, south of the border, excessive individualism is threatening group life — love and marriage, community involvement, national identification. "What has failed at every level — from the society of nations to the national society to the local community to the family — is integration. . . . we have put our own good, as individuals, as groups, as a nation, ahead of the common good."[6]

Ironically, their critique may well be more applicable to Canada than to the United States. Bellah's colleague Seymour Lipset, in his landmark comparative study of the United States and Canada, maintains that individualism — along with antistatism, populism, and egalitarianism — is at the heart of "the American creed."[7] Canada, on the other hand, has tended to be far less individualistic, remaining "more respectful of authority, more willing to use the state, and more supportive of a group basis of rights. . . . The country has an extensive welfare state and considerable government ownership; its trade union movement is much larger proportionately than the American; and the constitutional rights to ethnocultural survival given to French Canadians have been extended greatly, as have those of other ethnic groups not of Anglo-Saxon background."

Lipset's emphasis on U.S. individualism and Canadian collectivism has been widely shared by academics. However, the argument fails to take into account a centrally important historical and current reality: American individualism has coexisted with an intense commitment to group life. The two characteristics have been anything but mutually exclusive. Princeton sociologist Robert Wuthnow puts it this way: "As a nation, our culture combines themes of rugged self-reliance with themes of altruism and benevolence. In our personal lives, we mix together our concerns for ourselves and our concerns for others."[8] In his analysis, Lipset cites a Canadian scholar, Sacvan Bercovitch, who speaks of an "ideological consensus" typical of the United States. Bercovitch recalls the first time he came into contact with "the American Consensus," in the late 1960s. Crossing the Canadian border, he found himself in a country which despite its arbitrary frontiers, despite its bewildering mix of race and creed, could believe in something called the True America. . . . Here was the Jewish anarchist Paul Goodman berating the Midwest for abandoning the promise; here, the descendant of American slaves, Martin Luther King, denouncing injustice as a violation of the American way; here, an endless debate about national destiny. . . ." His Canadian background had not prepared him for such a "spectacle. [There were] a hundred sects and factions, each apparently different from the others, yet all celebrating the same mission."[9]

This intense commitment to ideological consensus has helped to bind Americans together. Americans are committed to nation and family, community and region, high school and college. In American ideology, individualism has always had a pronounced group context. The family, school, university, church, community, and region are ropes that tie individuals fairly tightly to social locations.

But there is no need to limit oneself to rhetoric in making such an observation. Some impressive, readily available data sets exist that tell the story, among them attachment to high schools and colleges. Anyone who has looked at cars bearing U.S. license plates knows that it is a common practice for Americans to stick high school and college decals on car windows. Many of those same drivers return to their high school settings for football and basketball games — a practice foreign to most Canadians. Statewide tournaments are keenly followed by large numbers of loyalists. At the college level, the attachment to schools and alma maters is nothing short of phenomenal. On a typical Saturday in any autumn of your choice, university stadiums all over the States are packed with football fans — fifty to a hundred thousand of them. They are students, state residents, and alumni who travel miles to see "their team" play. Yet, those who show up for the live performances represent only part of the ardent followings: American universities and colleges also realize remarkable revenues from network and cable television. Beyond the conference contracts, Notre Dame, the beloved syncretistic symbol of Catholicism, athletics, and scholarship, has a personal television contract with CBS for the televising of all of its home games, coast to coast.

In most parts of Canada, there is virtually no such attachment to high schools. University football games are usually played in near-empty stadiums. Most students, graduates, and residents couldn't care less about "the big upcoming game" of the University of Toronto Blues, the University of Manitoba Bisons, or the University of Alberta Golden Bears.

Mere sports, you say? Hardly. Those attendance figures provide very good measures of distinctly different inclinations stateside and this side when it comes to identification with one's school and college, one's community, and personal biography.

A second example. This past Sunday, nearly half of Americans attended a religious service, compared with about a quarter of Canadians. Most Canadians continue to identify with one religious group or another and will come out of the woodwork for rites of passage and on other special occasions. But there is little sense of religious group commitment. Americans continue to outdistance Canadians in participating in religious group activities.

Americans have historically stressed "rugged individualism." But the American creed has also stressed "we, the people" — the theme of collectivity. In sharp contrast, Canada has had no such "creed that binds." Group life has not been grounded in ideology. As Lipset reminds us, "There is no ideology of Canadianism."[10]

A tip-off is that Americans have heroes; Canadians ignore the historical record and, as Thomas Berger notes, almost exclusively adopt "the heroes and heroines of other nations."[11]

A TREND AWAY FROM JOINING

"Are you a formal member of any of these groups?"
% *"Yes"*

	1975	1985
Church or synagogue	58	35
Sports club	27	24
Labor union	26	24
Service club	23	15
Hobby-related group	22	15
Fraternity or sorority	16	6
Political group	10	9
Nationality group	7	6
Farm organization	7	2
Any other group	10	8

SOURCE: *Project Canada Series.*

THE UNASSEMBLED MOSAIC

In Canada, we have discarded the melting pot for the mosaic. In place of a dazzling charter myth, we have a working agreement between divergent groups. And when it comes to loyalty to collectivities, well, one is hard-pressed to provide evidence that suggests that Canadians are very excited about *any* collectivity. We increasingly view the traditional family structure as optional; we scarcely think of supporting the old high school or university; we stay away from the churches; we typically are less than enthused about community involvement; many of couldn't care less about the region from which we came. Forget about decrying excesses of American patriotism. The harsh reality is that Canadians are not very loyal to very much of anything.

What has held our country together is not commitment to shared ideology but rather a tenuous willingness to coexist. While individualism in the United States is buffered by a group-endorsing ideology, in Canada there is no such ideological protection. To use a crude sports analogy, individualism in the States is like a football player taking a handoff and facing a number of defenders; in Canada the individualist ball carrier finds himself in the clear. Consequently, the accelerated emphasis on individualism in the Western world is a far greater threat to social solidarity in Canada than it is in the United States.

The Canadian emphasis on pluralism translates into freedom for individuals. But pluralism does not go on to indicate how individuals are brought back into community. Pluralism breaks the whole into protected parts, but it doesn't put the parts back together again.

Let's put it this way: if different parts only have to coexist side by side as inanimate components of art on a wall, all is well. But if each of those different parts needs to come alive as interdependent components of a living organism, that's quite a different story. In Canada, diffuse individual contributions do not necessarily add up to anything.

In assessing Canada, sociologist Kevin Christiano of the University of Notre Dame makes the point that if groups of people are to persist, they must somehow be told what makes them a group. They must be given an identity. But, says Christiano, "the language of individualism . . . is ill-suited to the task of bestowing identity, for to accomplish it one must speak of history and destiny in ways that circumvent, if not obliterate, the individual." Though an emphasis on the individual may bring with it democracy and equality, it also "removes persons from the guidance of the group and the comfort of tradition and further forces upon them a new identity as autonomous citizens."[12]

There is good reason to believe that our strong Canadian emphasis on individual rights and personal gratification is making group life very difficult in Canada; in the long run it may make it impossible. Canadians find themselves torn between wanting good ties with other people while responding to a culture that tells them to put themselves and their own well-being first. Young people are placing high value on personal rather than social matters. Older Canadians are doing the same. Professor Joseph Levy of York University writes that large numbers of "Grays" have adopted a "Look out for Number One" philosophy and are "purchasing the biggest and most expensive cars, taking exotic holidays, and leaving society, their family and friends to fend for themselves."[13]

Such an imbalance in favor of the individual is putting a serious strain on relationships of all kinds. Friendships, marriages, family life, work ties, and local, national, and global citizenship are among the potential casualties. Folk and academic wisdom notwithstanding, when it comes to individualism, we may well be leaving Americans in the dust.

INDIVIDUALISTIC ASPIRATIONS
Canadian Youth, 15-24

"As you look to the future, how important are the following to you?"

% Indicating *"Very Important"*

	NAT	BC	PR	ONT	QUE	ATL
A good marriage and family life	82	84	88	84	74	81
Strong friendships	75	73	79	78	71	70
Success in my line of work	74	77	75	76	72	74
Getting a good education	70	67	73	70	71	66
Correcting social and economic inequities	16	12	16	17	17	18
Being a leader in my community	6	2	6	6	7	6

SOURCE: *Project Teen Canada 88.*

Excessive Relativism

Canadians deserve to be nominated as "champions of choice." We pride ourselves on giving people choices. Even if the available options are not what we would choose, we regard it as a virtue to defend the right of others to choose whatever they want. It's the Canadian way. Increasingly, we have come to regard truth as a matter of personal preference. Such an idea has become so pervasive that Canadians who don't know the meaning of *relativism* commonly use the phrase, "It's all relative." The tip-off that the concept is an idea divorced from comprehension is the fact that the phrase often comes out, "It's all *relevant*!" Relativism has becomes a Canadian cliché.

CONFUSING CHOICE WITH BEST

Emphasis on the personal quest for truth has been an important corrective to the authoritarian imparting of ideas that tended to characterize the pre-1960s. The emphasis on memorization in schools and the tendencies of religious groups to indoctrinate, for example, were not only personally stifling. In inhibiting personal growth and creativity, such styles also seriously retarded social development. Intellectual liberation has been a breath of fresh air for everyone.

However, with the assistance of pluralism, the importance of ceasing to be dogmatic about possessing truth has become confused with the importance of pursuing truth. The fact that both two-parent families and single-parent families are permissible does not mean that both contribute equally to personal and social well-being. Maybe they do. But the mere fact that choices exist does not mean that they have the same individual and societal payoffs. All religions have the right to exist in Canada. But this is not to say that the sheer existence of religious claims means that all claims are equally accurate, or that the consequences of practicing Anglicanism, Pentecostalism, Hinduism, and Satanism all have the same emotional outcomes.

Pluralism legitimizes the expression of viewpoints. But, if anything, it makes the evaluation of viewpoints not less important but all the more important. Precisely because we encourage choices, we need to champion the critical concept of discernment. People need to learn *how* to choose.

Such thinking is hardly heretical. Physical and social scientists assume that some explanations are better than others. The better ones are those that help observers understand the world. They do a better job of describing, explaining, and predicting what is happening. We are free to hypothesize anything; but that is not to say that every hypothesis has equal merit. These are evaluated, then supported or discarded. For example, despite diverse opinion, the earth *is* round, not flat. Most objects *do* fall — rather than rise — on their own. Some factors *do* influence heart attacks and cancer. Our facial features *do* have genetic sources. Education *does* have an influence on prejudice. Age is *not* randomly associated with church attendance.

As for personal well-being, we all know that all things do not have equal returns. The path to physical health, for example, is not simply guesswork. We may differ between cultures and within cultures when it comes to what we regard as a good meal. But the fact is that some foods will kill us and others will be nutritious. Similarly, we may differ from culture to culture when it comes to what we do to stay fit. But for all of us, being unfit has similar physiological consequences, regardless of what culture we call home.

People have varied ways of addressing physical, emotional, intellectual, and spiritual needs. Yet this is hardly to say that all the results are equally efficacious. The fact that people hold a variety of ethical views is not to say that all lead to the same interpersonal results; the fact that people subscribe to a number of personal development programs is not to say that they all have the same impact on individual well-being. Options say nothing about consequences.

OPEN-MINDED MINDLESSNESS

Such concerns about excessive relativism in the American context were expressed in 1987 by philosopher Allan Bloom in his book, *The Closing of the American Mind*. Bloom maintains that university students typically believe that truth is relative and that openness is therefore a moral virtue. Relativism, he writes, "has extinguished the real motive of education, the search for a good life."[14] In Bloom's words, "The unrestrained and thoughtless pursuit of openness . . . has rendered openness meaningless. . . . History and the study of cultures do not teach or prove that values or cultures are relative. . . . The fact that there have been different opinions about good and bad in different times and places in no way proves that [no claim] is true or [that no claim is] superior to others."[15] Bloom calls for a willingness to think and pursue knowledge and truth, drawing on history and the array of available cultures.

By way of illustration: Canadian youth was asked to respond to the statement, "A preschool child is likely to suffer if the mother works"; 51 percent agreed, 49 percent disagreed. Bloom raises this issue, and points out that, in dealing with the question of whether children experience loss when both parents are employed, we typically respond that the potential loss is made up by parents equally sharing the child-rearing. But Bloom protests that we commonly stop with such an egalitarian resolution, and fail to think the choice through — namely, does .5 + .5 *really* equal 1 when that "1" is one of the adults choosing to stay home and take on child raising in a focused, full-time way? The answer is probably no — which doesn't mean parents shouldn't be employed, but rather that their choices carry different consequences.[16]

Following Bloom, in Canada, everything is possible. But that is not to say that everything is equally good, personally or socially. As Canadians, we are coming precariously close to worshiping choice as an end in itself. Rather than carefully examining the benefits and costs of available options and then sticking our necks out and suggesting what in fact might be "best," we instead take the easy way out. We decree — with the authorization of pluralism — that an educated, enlightened, sophisticated Canadian is a person who tolerates almost everything and seldom takes a position on anything. If a person dares to advocate a position in an ethical, moral, or religious realm — on premarital sex, marriage structure, homosexuality, or, religion, for example — such a person typically is viewed as narrow-minded. The late Toronto Anglican archbishop Lewis Garnsworthy went so far as to say, "To speak up on anything in Canada is to run the risk of being labeled a bigot."[17]

Even such a seemingly central trait as honesty runs into trouble. While some 90 percent of Canadian adults and young people say that they place a high value on honesty, they show a reluctance to label any behavior *dishonest*. They are socialized to think that to do is to sound judgmental.

For example, during the Dubin inquiry into the Ben Johnson scandal, The Sports Network asked viewers each morning whether coach Charlie Francis was justified in what he did, whether coaches and athletes giving and using performance-enhancing drugs should be banned for life, and whether Johnson's 1987 world record set in Rome should be allowed to stand. The results were in favor of Francis, against the life ban, and for letting Johnson's record stand. *Toronto Star* sportswriter Ken McKee commented, "If those callers are indicative of Canadian thinking, we have a much larger problem than the lying and deceit of a group of elite athletes, their coach and others over the last eight to ten years."[18] An April 1990 Gallup poll provided some data on how indicative the sports channel's results were. Some 20 percent of Canadians felt that no action should be taken against athletes using banned drugs, while 55 percent felt a two-year suspension was appropriate. Just 25 percent favored a life suspension.[19]

In short, relativism has contributed to a situation in which many Canadians are not differentiating between being judgmental and showing sound judgment, between exhibiting discrimination and being discriminating. Living in a society that instills the idea that an individual is free to have values but is not free to impose those values on others, we find ourselves endorsing choice *per se*. In dispensing with discernment, we cease to pursue the best of possible options. What we are left with is unreflective, mindless relativism. We may no longer be as authoritarian as we were in the past. But we also are not any more inclined to be critically reflective and creative.

We have been rewarded with citizens who clamor to assert their diverse choices in viewpoint and behavior. We are left with little sense of what is right, good, or true. Mindless relativism has destroyed those kind of nerve endings.

VISIONLESS COEXISTENCE

Excessive individualism and excessive relativism can create significant problems in any society. What makes them so dangerous to social life in Canada is the fact that they descend like powerful missiles on a society that already is fragile because of its explicit commitment to sheer coexistence. The possibilities for social devastation are unlimited.

Since the founding of the country, Canadian leaders aspired first and foremost to simply "get along." Professor William Stahl points out that Confederation enabled people of "every stripe and faction [to] claim the new nationality as their own, without having to give up anything of what they were." He adds, "Other than a few bands and firecrackers, Confederation was not attended by much emotional outpouring."[20] While the Americans emphasized "life, liberty, and the pursuit of happiness," our founding fathers emphasized "peace, order, and good government."[21] The Americans dreamed of pursuing happiness and well-being; Canadians simply wanted to coexist.

Of considerable significance, the post-1950s Canadian national leadership applauded such an ideal. Pierre Trudeau saw the founding charter as striking in "its absence of principles, ideals, or other frills," and appropriate for a heterogeneous, "disjointed half-continent."[22] His version of federalism, writes Christiano, does not involve imposing a national consensus, but instead "deliberately reduces [it] to the greatest common denominator between the various groups composing the nation." Trudeau's federalism attempts to find a rational compromise between the divergent groups history has thrown together. Members are asked only to abide by the terms of the social contract.[23]

Central to Trudeau's thought is the idea that a truly democratic government cannot be "nationalist," but rather must pursue the good of all its citizens, without prejudice to ethnic origin. It stands for and encourages good citizenship, never nationalism. For Trudeau, nationalism is "the faith that takes the place of reason for those who are unable to find a basis for their convictions in history, or economics, or the constitution, or sociology."[24] History shows that nationalism destroys peace between nations and order within them. "A people's consensus based on reason will supply the cohesive force that societies require," Trudeau has argued. As for Canada, his words are stirring yet chilling: "I am suggesting that cold, unemotional rationality can still save the ship."[25]

In a careful critique of Trudeau's thinking, Christiano suggests that Trudeau's political philosophy equipped him well to be the chief executive of a fractious modern state. But, says Christiano, "that same philosophy's unwavering adherence to individualism may have precluded a lasting solution" to Canada's problems.

Why? Because, he says, it admitted neither of the existence nor the appropriateness of any set of symbols that would integrate emotionally the entire nation.[26]

> Unfortunately for Trudeau, nations are not reasoned into being. They issue forth not as the products of dialogue, deliberation, and discussion, but out of the facts of history. Around these facts are arrayed songs of noble and daring deeds, stories of virtue under trial, and claims to uniqueness among the peoples of the earth. Together these items form the symbolic substance of nationhood. This substance may be altered or augmented with difficulty, but it is denigrated or denied only at the risk of peril to the nation itself.[27]

What is left in Canada is a value system that contains nothing that marks it as exclusively Canadian. No history or heroes give it legitimacy. The ideals of tolerance and understanding "are fatally universalistic. Anyone may embrace them, and thankfully some nations do, and seriously so. But there is no reasoning offered for why *Canadians* are compelled to accept this choice, only the assertion of the unassailable truth that it is the courteous thing to do."[28]

In his 1969 Dominion Day address, Prime Minister Trudeau told the nation, "It is the tolerance towards one another which forms such a basic part of the character of Canadians. Toleration and moderation," he said, are the standards against which "we can judge our stature as a country and as a people."[29] Two decades later, his newest book would bear a title that would capsule the same theme: *Towards a Just Society*. In the introduction, Trudeau's words of 1970 are recalled: "The aim of life in society is the greatest happiness of everyone, and this happiness is attained only by being just towards each and every person."[30] Justice, equality, tolerance, coexistence—the themes of the Trudeau years — the ongoing themes of present-day Canada. But the time has come to move on.

When a country like Canada enshrines pluralism through policies such as multiculturalism and bilingualism and the guaranteeing of individual rights, the outcome is coexistence —

no more, no less. It's a good start in building a society out of diverse peoples. But there's a danger. If there is no subsequent vision, no national goals, no explicit sense of coexisting for some purpose, pluralism becomes an uninspiring end in itself. Rather than coexistence being the foundation that enables a diverse nation to collectively pursue the best kind of existence possible, coexistence degenerates into a national preoccupation. Pluralism ceases to have a cause. The result: mosaic madness.

Some twenty years ago, Trudeau expressed the problem with typical eloquence: "The best ideologies, having arisen at specific times to combat given abuses, become the worst if they survive the needs which gave them birth."[31] In Canada, our emphasis on pluralism has become purposeless. We are expending much of our energy on ensuring that social and individual equality is being realized. Equality is a critically important start in pursuing optimum living; but in Canada, it has blurred the finish line.

And so it is that we have groups warring against groups and individuals, individuals warring against groups and other individuals. Mosaic madness is everywhere. In the caustic summation of Saskatchewan MP Simon deJong, the Constitution has become a legal straitjacket; many issues important to Canada are not being resolved by politicians but by "a panel of old men" on Supreme Court benches.[32] Ron Ghitter, who chaired Alberta's 1983-84 Committee on Tolerance and Understanding and has championed equality, recently told an Edmonton multicultural association, "I suggest that rather than building bridges between the various segments in our community, [multicultural] programs tend to ghettoize and divide." Ghitter continued, "Is it not time to ask the question: what can be done to bring our communities together, rather than dividing them?"[33]

Coexistence is an inadequate national dream. It's not enough; it has never been enough. In times past, leaders would occasionally attempt to rally "mythless" Canadians around the idea that they occupy common geographical turf. National goals and dominant values, noted John Porter in *The Vertical Mosaic*, seemed to be expressed in geographic terms, such as "from sea to sea."[34] As recently as March 1990, Prime Minister Brian Mulroney, in a televised address on Meech Lake, was described by a Canadian

Press reporter as spending "as much time rhapsodizing about deep snow-covered forests, prairies that stretched to the horizon and mountains that seemed to touch the sky as he did trying to explain the deal and define distinct society to a public that does not understand it."[35] Appeals to geography and landscape have never stirred the Canadian masses.[36]

Similarly, coexistence as an end in itself fails to inspire anyone. It is visionless. If we want to live well, then the achievement of peaceful coexistence is only a preliminary personal and social goal. Coexistence gets us a junior high school diploma. Only when we go further and work together to create the best possible society do we get our advanced degrees.

Canada has come a long way. We have put behind us much of the "groupism" and authoritarianism of the pre-1960s. We have experienced considerable social and mental emancipation. The problem is that we have come too far. We have replaced oppressive connection with visionless coexistence. We have substituted the mindless acceptance of truth with the mindless acceptance of relativism. The casualty list is not a short one.

6

The Interpersonal Casualty List

When it comes to interpersonal relations, Canadian life should be better than ever. Our language and cultural policies, along with the Charter of Rights, has seemingly set the stage for very good social ties. However, our strong emphasis on the well-being of the individual, as well as our relativizing of interpersonal standards, is resulting in far less than what is possible.

Impoverished Interaction

Anyone who has spent time in various parts of Canada knows something that is familiar to world travelers: cultures carry with them very different styles of interaction. An encounter with strangers in a Toronto or Montreal subway car typically involves different interaction from what occurs on a city bus in Winnipeg or Victoria. People in a shopping mall in Ottawa or Vancouver tend not to treat each other in the same way as people in smaller malls in Charlottetown, Moose Jaw, or Red Deer. Canadians who take initiative in talking to strangers are likely to be seen as coming from the Atlantic provinces or western Canada, from smaller cities and towns or rural areas — or perhaps from the United States, which leads to a crucial point.

Although styles of interaction vary, nonetheless some general national characteristics are unmistakable. Complement my travel experiences with your own, and see how well some of the following "interaction impressions" fit . . .

To ride the trains across Britain is to discover quickly that the people sitting across from you in the southern part of England are remarkably apt at demonstrating "British reserve" — they don't speak unless spoken to, at which point they are pleasant and courteous. They bear little resemblance to the friendly folk who live in Yorkshire, the outgoing and humor-loving Scots, or the warm and quick-witted Irish. The reserve of the English in London pales, however, in comparison with the Swedes on the streets of Stockholm, Russians in the shops of Leningrad, or the widespread social oblivion of the Finns in Helsinki. In all four cities, social interaction is virtually nonexistent, except for fairly terse encounters in clearly defined situations, such as when one is a customer in a restaurant or shop. People who don't know one another simply ignore one another. On crowded streets, eye contact is out; physical bumping and cutting off are in.

The French on Paris streets tend to glance at people passing by more noticeably than the Swiss in Zurich or the Portuguese in Lisbon. Even the Anglophone Canadian who commonly faces language barriers feels surprisingly more at ease with strangers in these countries than in parts of England. Australians and New Zealanders seem to be somewhat more outgoing than the southern English, while Fijians have a low-key but sociable manner.

Those people who break the tranquility of hotel lobbies in Stockholm or Oxford or Calgary are frequently Americans — as often as not outgoing and noisy. Their volume and hard-hitting style bring them as many enemies as their money brings them friends. Still, whether a Canadian is in New York or Los Angeles, Chicago or Atlanta, Austin or Pullman, what is highly consistent is the American style of looking and conversing. Many of the uninitiated from other countries have been taken aback by such a style, variously welcoming it as "friendly" and "helpful" or denouncing it as "presumptuous" and "superficial."

I have yet to see firsthand how people interact in Asia and South America. But I — like you — have seen enough to know that nations and regions and communities have an array of styles. I have also seen and experienced enough styles to know that some elements of those styles uplift the human spirit better than others. There are explicit acts and gestures that convey warmth versus callousness, caring versus indifference, respect versus disdain. Some types of interaction make us fly; other types ground us.

As freedom sweeps across the globe, people nationwide and worldwide find themselves with a vast range of interaction possibilities. What is disconcerting is that, by every indication, excessive individualism and excessive relativism lead to interaction that is on a bare, subsistence level.

The increasing legitimizing of cultural and individual diversity in Canada requires that we ask a fundamentally important question: What kind of interaction do we want to have? It's not enough simply to say that we will put all groups in the national playground and let everyone relate to each other however they want. Not to advocate some quality of interaction is to get nothing more than diverse interaction. Here the idealism of Pierre Trudeau and others is showing, and showing badly. The expectation seems to be that if we encourage tolerance, somehow "the least common denominator" that results will be optimum living. In 1972 the former prime minister wrote:

> There is no such thing as a model or ideal Canadian. What could be more absurd than the concept of an "all-Canadian" boy or girl? A society which emphasizes uniformity is one which creates intolerance and hate. . . . What the world should be seeking and what we in Canada must continue to cherish are not concepts of uniformity but human values: compassion, love and understanding. Our standards in all activities should be one of excellence, but our routes to its achievement may be as numerous as there are Canadians who pursue it.[1]

The pursuit of compassion in the face of individualism and the pursuit of excellence in the face of relativism are precisely the goals that are critical to personal and social well-being. Unfortunately, human history does not support the assertion that these pursuits naturally rise to the top. They need to be consciously and constantly cultivated. Most certainly, they will not be the natural outcome of an emphasis on sheer coexistence.

WHAT KIND OF VALUES DO WE WANT?

Select Values of Canadian Youth
by Country of Birth and Race

% Viewing as "*Very Important*"

	CANADA: NON-NATIVE (1,865)	CANADA: NATIVE* (100)	IMMIGRANT WHITE (81)	IMMIGRANT NON-WHITE (59)
GOALS				
Friendship	83	82	86	83
Being loved	78	67	74	65
Success	76	77	65	86
Freedom	75	79	78	81
A good education	63	72	63	83
Concern for others	64	57	64	56
Family life	62	65	63	58
Acceptance by God	28	39	25	53
MEANS				
Honesty	84	78	82	77
Cleanliness	74	77	65	72
Reliability	74	59	68	61
Politeness	68	66	57	60
Hard work	62	63	60	61
Intelligence	59	57	57	74
Generosity	55	50	52	47
Imagination	42	30	49	30

* Separate non-probability sample, drawn from reserves across Canada.

SOURCE: *Project Teen Canada 88.*

Selective Compassion

Some people might argue that Canadians do, in fact, care about each other. Our pluralistic policy and our Charter of Rights indicate that we aspire to be tolerant and respectful. Our throne speeches include statements about being a caring Canada, and our social programs are admired by many countries. Our caring for one another can be seen in the support we give the fund-raising drives of many groups. But things are not always what they appear to be.

For starters, even in the presence of good intentions, our active concern for the well-being of other Canadians is tempered by limits. Pressures of time and money have resulted in our matching selective consumption with selective compassion. We can't support every cause or care about every person. And we don't. Most of us focus our compassion and caring on our relatives, our friends, and perhaps one or two pet charities or favorite causes. The old quip "God Bless me and my wife, my brother John and his wife — us four, no more. Amen" is proving to be a more accurate depiction of many outlooks than first thought. York professor Levy is even more scathing. He cites one expert who observes, "We want so much to 'make it' for ourselves that we [are] hesitant about making a commitment to anyone or anything, including our own flesh and blood."[2]

For example, most of us watched with emotion as Eastern bloc countries, one after another, declared freedom in 1989. A *Maclean's* poll late that year found that 75 percent of Canadians felt that the changes taking place in Eastern Europe are making war less likely. However, only about 30 percent said that Canada should offer large-scale financial assistance to encourage reform and stability — especially if it meant higher taxes. Writer Bob Levin summed things up this way: "In general, most Canadians clearly took a rosy view of the change sweeping Eastern Europe — as long as they did not have to help pay for it." Incidentally, the government nonetheless pledged $72 million to help Hungary and Poland, and sent medical supplies worth about $500,000 to Romania early in 1990 to help children in institutions.[3]

Asked to comment on such findings, Bruce O'Hara, a British Columbia sociologist, suggested that "it's not that people do not have concerns about Third World poverty and so on. But they are overloaded with immediate concerns." Two-career couples, for example, face heavy combined work schedules, with the result that "the increased work load per family has left less time for idealistic pursuits. A lot of the fullness of life," says O'Hara, "has been gutted."[4]

NEVER SEEM TO HAVE ENOUGH TIME

Hours/Minutes Spent Per Workday: 1986

	TOTAL POPULATION	EMPLOYED MEN	EMPLOYED WOMEN	OTHER WOMEN
SLEEPING	8:25	7:53	8:06	8:37
WORKING FOR PAY	3:35	7:04	5:49	:22
FAMILY CARE	3:03	1:47	3:13	6:02
MEDIA	2:55	2:35	1:56	3:04
TV/Rented Movies	2:20	2:08	1:31	2:29
Reading	:27	:22	:19	:26
Other	:08	:05	:06	:09
OTHER LEISURE	2:32	2:09	2:12	2:57
EATING	1:25	1:21	1:15	1:39
PERSONAL CARE	1:11	1:00	1:16	1:09
VARIED OTHER	0:54	0:11	0:13	0:10
TOTAL	24:00	24:00	24:00	24:00

SOURCE: Computed from *Canadian Social Trends*, Winter/1989:24.

Part of the problem, of course, is sheer numbers. Years ago, German sociologist George Simmel wrote a fascinating essay entitled "The Metropolis and Mental Life."[5] He argued that in urban settings, where there are large populations of diverse people, individuals cannot possibly relate deeply to everyone. For their own protection, they limit themselves emotionally and psychologically. They develop what he calls a "blasé attitude." It's not that they're down on people; it's just that they have to limit themselves in order to cope with the events involving the large number of people among whom they live.

The blasé attitude can be seen in the person who picks up the newspaper, notes the headline in a corner of page one that "Four

Perish in Fire," murmurs "That's terrible," and flips to the sports pages to see who won the game last night. It can be seen in people backing over each other as they get into an elevator — or walking into each other on a sidewalk — as if the other person were invisible.

There's nothing personal about it — that's the whole point. It's not that people are trying to be offensive; it's just that they develop an obliviousness. To use social-work parlance, people who fail to limit their energies in these ways develop "compassion fatigue." People who take on too heavy a load of other people's problems, leaving little time or energy for themselves, become disillusioned and depressed. Care-giving professionals — doctors, social workers, and therapists — are said to be particularly vulnerable.[6]

Officially, we care; compassion in Canada is officially "in." Fund-raising drives for worthy causes receive the endorsement of everyone from the NHL star to the business community to the civic group to the local disc jockey. People like Terry Fox, Steve Fonyo, and Rick Hansen have become nationally and internationally applauded celebrities. Virtually everyone feels that people who cannot afford medical care nevertheless have a right to such care. Some nine in ten Canadians maintain that people have a right to incomes adequate to live on. What's more, seven in ten of us think that Canadians are generous.[7]

But in reality we aren't particularly big-hearted. Between 1969 and 1985, the percentage of our incomes that we gave to charities slipped from 1.1 percent to 0.8 percent. During the same period, the percentage of profits that corporations gave dropped from 0.7 percent to 0.4 percent.[8] A 1988 report released by the Canadian Centre for Philanthropy found that, although we think we are more generous than Americans, we aren't. In 1985, individual Americans gave three times more to charity than Canadians did. American companies gave 4.4 times as much as Canadian firms, a substantial increase over 1970, when they gave 1.5 times as much. The report did not find Canada's affluent to be particularly generous. In terms of giving as a percentage of income, farmers led the country in 1985, followed by pensioners and self-employed professionals. The most generous region was the poorest — Atlantic Canada.[9]

THE DELEGATION OF CARING

Precisely because we "officially care" but limit how much we extend ourselves to people personally, caring has been evolving into a professional activity. For example, somewhere between the rhetoric of expressing concern for Canadians and doing something for Canadians, many of us point out, "It's the job of the government. The government needs to look after the people out there who have problems." Frequently, when someone comes to the door wanting to collect for a charity, we find ourselves mumbling, "Where's the government? Given the taxes they're taking our of our paychecks every month, why on earth should *we* have to support all these charities?"

Closely related to the idea that caring for those in need is the job of the government is the idea that caring is something carried out by specialists. It is no accident that we hire people to work in what we call the "caring professions" — doctors, nurses, social workers, counselors, clergy, and the like. The expectation is that people who go into those professions will care about people. Usually they oblige at least officially. For example, a recent paid public relations item released by a provincial nurses association read, "Nursing is not just a job. It starts with a sincere desire to help and care. It's not surprising that everyone knows a kind compassionate nurse."[10] Princeton sociologist Robert Wuthnow sums up the transition to "care for pay." The story of the Good Samaritan provides a model for the compassionate person, he writes. "He rides along with other things on his mind, suddenly sees someone in need, is moved emotionally, and interrupts his journey (probably missing an important business deal) in order to care for the injured stranger." Wuthnow points out that today's Good Samaritan is a paid professional:

> He's taken CPR and the Red Cross course in first aid; in fact, he's going to Jericho on a routine rescue squad mission; this road, after all, is frequented with bandits who beat people up and leave them on the side of the road; when he spots someone, he knows just what to do; certainly he doesn't prolong his commitment; he takes the stranger to the hospital and goes on his way. And the priest and Levite? Well, they didn't need to be bothered because they knew the rescue squad was on its way.[11]

In a highly specialized Canada, we all officially care. But in practice, we contract it out to the government and the specialists. Such delegation may be unconscious, but it has a very important social result. If you and I are not employed specialists in the caring industry, then caring usually is not part of our job descriptions. Whereas indifference to people may be fatal to the career aspirations of a nurse, it is not seen as jeopardizing the future of an aspiring accountant. And so it is that thousands of Canadians engage in "noncaring professions." They feel no need or obligation to take an interest in helping their customers, clients, students, and others to solve the problems that they are encountering.

For example, people involved in taking our money are not especially known for their caring styles. I have a friend who ran into some financial problems a few years ago. She told me she proposed the renegotiation of a loan with a loans officer. Hearing her personal problems, the loans person exclaimed, "What do you think we are, a social assistance department?" Another acquaintance was audited and told that the tax people wanted a sizeable amount of money — on the spot. She made the mistake of suggesting, "Could I possibly give you one cheque now and postdate a second?" The thoroughly annoyed auditor responded, "What do you think we are, a finance company?" Put succinctly, these kinds of occupations — along with thousands of others — are not defined as helping professions. The loans officer and the auditor are not expected to be particularly compassionate or even pleasant — nor is the police officer or the lawyer or the school principal. For many of us on the receiving end, it would be nice if they were, but they don't have to be. Significantly, when they are, we act pleasantly surprised.

SYMBIOTIC TIES

Our indifference to many Canadians is not solely the result of resource limits, large populations, and specialization. The inclination to care also has been severely dulled by excessive individualism.

A surprising proportion of people — approximately one in two Canadians — openly admit that concern for others is not something they value highly. Only about the same proportion say they place a high value on generosity. The widespread cultural emphasis on individual gratification assumes that involvement will bring a personal payoff. If we're going to relate to people or engage in group life -- a marriage, a friendship, education, employment, church life and the like — we need to get a return on our investment. Otherwise, the response is well known: "Who cares?"

Even those who are involved in social issues such as abortion, war, the environment, and child abuse may not be acting compassionately. It is clear that for many participants, social crusades represent the collective expression of their individual concerns. For example, women participating in the feminist movement frequently have limited compassion not only for men, but also for women who are not sympathetic to their concerns. In the abortion debate, people who are pro-life and pro-choice both claim to be motivated by compassion for life, yet they commonly show questionable compassion for each other.

Further, our interest in the well-being of Canadians is typically highly conditional. Surveys asking Canadians about the right of people to adequate incomes, medical care, and education, while endorsed, frequently receive qualifiers such as, "providing they're willing to work," "as long as they are contributing to the country," and so on. The idea seems to be, "Yes, we'll look after them, but there are some conditions."

COMPASSION, BUT . . .

	% Agreeing
People on welfare should have to work	84
The government is spending too much on welfare	40
Families should receive a minimum annual income	40
People on welfare could get along without it if they tried	35

SOURCE: *Gallup Canada, Inc.*, December 1, 1988.

Given our societal emphasis on individual gratification, it is hardly surprising to find that such conditional caring is widespread. Much of life is based on exchange. "What's in it for me?" is a fairly good rule of thumb that guides interaction. Conditional caring is everywhere to be seen. Groups appealing to individuals and corporations to give to their particular organizations give major emphasis to the fact that donations are tax-deductible. Companies stress that they are friendly and conscientious; some even make the outright claim, "We care." Such virtues are seen as good for business. In such a milieu of exchange, we opt for the people, services, and organizations that add something to our lives.

The problem with all of this is that there are times when we're interacting with people who really need unconditional caring of the "no strings attached" variety. While all Canadians want to live and live well, many are having difficulty; some are hurting badly. Unconditional caring is in considerable demand.

Unfortunately, the norm of exchange places a premium on unsolicited concern. It is not an exaggeration to say that, these days, Canadians need a license to care. To attempt to care "just because some people need it" is to invite trouble. The potential recipient of our caring, like us, has been influenced by the exchange model that pervades our society. They, too, are readily aware that caring has rules. It is supposed to be selective, follow friendship and family lines, bear some kind of a return and — if none of the above — be carried out by a professional care giver. If such rules are not followed, suspicion is aroused.

We need only examine some of the clichés associated with the idea of unconditional caring. One of the most well-worn is "Don't take candy from a stranger." Sounds solid, a good piece of advice. No question, it's an important guideline if the possibility exists that a stranger will use candy to exploit or harm a child. However, while it may be a good rule of thumb with respect to potential violence, it is a poor rule of thumb when it comes to caring. It also means that well-meaning strangers will never be allowed to give candy to children.

People who aspire to care for other Canadians just because they need it run the risk of being perceived as having a hidden agenda.

Such is the extent to which the norm of exchange has come to dominate our culture. Experience, advice, and the media have all made their case: if strangers are overly helpful, they "must be up to something." Tragically, for some recipients who are unaccustomed to receiving something for nothing, in lieu of the giver having a tainted motive, one is created. The giver is variously said to be guilty or strange, perverse, and even masochistic.

Should a Canadian who aspires to give unconditionally get past the barrier of the recipient, there still is the serious problem of the social audience. Likewise located in an exchange-oriented culture, they express their collective doubts. For example, sexual harassment and child abuse are significant problems that have required an ameliorative response. However, the spin-off of such major attention is a national paranoia surrounding the interaction of men with women and adults with children. A male who speaks to a female stranger places himself in a potentially dangerous situation. An adult — especially a male — thinks twice before he runs to help a young girl who has just fallen off a bike in a park.

I have gotten on an elevator and had a woman blatantly wait for me to push the button first, so that she will know I am not going to try to follow her. One understands, but it seems somehow tragic. From the standpoint of an adult, there is something that is rather debilitating about making a playful comment to a child in a restaurant, and having a mother respond with mistrust. Again, one understands, but it seems that everyone somehow is losing.

A society that does not allow us to give candy to a child we do not know, or engage in a conversation with a stranger, is a society in which it is virtually impossible for us to extend ourselves in any way to people we do not know. Precisely at a time when large numbers of Canadians need people who will care about them unconditionally, the culture has made such caring all but impossible. Our cautiousness has done much to destroy the potential for compassion.

The net effect of selectivity, delegation, and individualism is not going unnoticed. A late 1988 national survey found that one in three Canadians feel that most people are demonstrating less care for one another than they did ten years ago.[12] These findings are just for openers.

SOPHISTICATED EXCUSES

Our way of relating to strangers is typically justified by relativism. We are told that we can only expect certain kinds of behavior in large cities, versus smaller communities. People in Toronto possess the blasé attitude to a much greater extent than do people in Barrie or North Bay. That's why Torontonians frequently cut each other off as they walk down those crowded sidewalks, or back into one another in those stuffed elevators — as often as not minus an "excuse me." In the presence of strangers, people in large cities tend to avoid eye contact and are unlikely to initiate conversations. That's big-city life — or so the argument goes. Manners and courtesies and caring are said to be relative to community size. Interpersonal behavior is not any worse or better in the city or the town, just different.

Interaction with members of cultural minorities, such as Sikhs or Asians, is often fairly abrupt and formal. If a member of the majority or another minority group complains that they aren't very friendly, the predictable response is that Sikhs and Asians are not accustomed to being outwardly friendly — in contrast, for example, to Scots and Americans. "It's all relative," we are reminded. "Don't impose your cultural standards on them."

The problem with all of this is that, as Canadians, we find ourselves unable to advocate any vision of "good" interaction. Our commitment to a pluralistic view of society leads us to say that one form of interaction is just as valid as another. The human consequences of different kinds of interaction seem to be regarded as insignificant.

In taking such a position, our "mindless relativism" is showing and showing badly. Obviously we are free to act in any number of ways when we deal with each other. And obviously the range of possibilities has cultural sources.

But that is not to say that all forms of interaction have the same impact when it comes to well-being. To argue that politeness and rudeness, kindness and callousness, abruptness and patience all have the same personal and social effects is sheer nonsense. Clearly we feel different when we encounter courtesy, friendliness, and helpfulness, from what we feel when we experience insensitivity, coldness, and apathy.

A friend who teaches at Washington State University recently commented to me, "New York is something very different, even to Americans. New York is an island of incivility." A foundation known as "New York Pride" is trying to change things. It has launched an advertising campaign to "crack down on bad manners" in a metropolis described by one writer as comprised of "surly cabbies, sharp-elbowed bus riders and kamikaze bike messengers." Spokesman Herbert Rickman, a lawyer who was former mayor Edward Koch's special assistant, described the foundation as "a citizen army" whose objective is "to make New York livable once again. When people participating in exit surveys are asked why they don't want to come back, one of the reasons is the rudeness and the mean spiritedness," says Rickman. Television ads admonish viewers, "Come on, New York, ease up. Let's keep this the world's greatest city." The foundation also plans to plant thirty thousand trees during the year, start a weekly radio talk show, and conduct anti-litter and anti-graffiti campaigns in every neighborhood of the city.[13]

A utopian goal? Probably. A worthwhile goal? Undoubtedly. If "good" and "negative" interaction are decreed to be totally relative, then we are setting ourselves up to experience a quality of life that is vastly inferior to what is theoretically possible. Rather than taking the position that any form of interaction is just as acceptable as another, we need to explore what kinds contribute the most to personal and social well-being. Then we need to advocate them. At this point in our history, we are a long way from such a place.

Impoverished Relationships

A Canadian society that enthusiastically embraces the freedom of the individual could not have expected less than dramatic changes in male-female ties. The dilemma of reconciling the individual and the group is no more apparent anywhere than in the area of intimate relationships. To put it mildly, we're not faring particularly well.

STARTING WITH SELF

The emphasis on personal autonomy in relationships has been highly acclaimed. It has been professionally endorsed and widely adopted. People enter relationships out of "want" versus "need." Freed from having one's life determined and suppressed by others, individuals are at last able to experience the fullness of who they are. Self-love, self-expression, self-development, and self-actualization are among the themes commonly stressed. Quite obviously "self" is given central play. One personal growth seminar leader put it this way: "Love is a beautiful thing involving one person: *you*."[14]

The autonomy model is emphasized by many therapists and counselors. Workshops and programs aimed at enhancing relationships through refocusing on oneself have exploded in the past three decades. The more popular in Canada tend to come from the United States; they include transactional analysis, Personal Best, and Context Training.

The autonomy model has some significant personal payoffs. A lot of Canadians have self-esteem problems. Surveys have found that approximately 50 percent of Canadians young and old admit to being bothered by feelings of inferiority.[15] Individuals who take the autonomy model seriously often come away with an enhanced self-image and an improved sense of what they can accomplish. They frequently claim to feel liberated, exhilarated, and motivated, freed, and empowered to pursue excellence in all areas of their lives.

ENDING WITH SELF

But there is a major problem with the autonomy model: it doesn't work. The giveaway as to why lies in the answer to the central relational question the model raises: "If I don't need you, then why should I want you?"

The answer? "You add something to my life." But here things get highly conditional. At the point that you don't bring me anything and, even worse, begin to subtract from my expression and development, the relationship is history. Such conditional relationships are disposable. We say, in effect, that we will be willing to love someone, providing he or she loves us the way we expect to be loved. The commitment is not to the relationship, but to our own personal well-being. Seen in such a light, marriage in Canada today frequently signals little more than the formal consummation of mutual self-interest. As a result, when we reach the point where we are not sufficiently gratified, we terminate the relationship and try again.

Today in Canada, individualism is contributing to an almost consumerlike approach to relationships. People have become like individual islands, self-governed and self-sufficient. When they feel it will be personally beneficial, they consent to being joined together by a highly portable bridge. But the bridge remains in place only so long as mutual well-being is enhanced. At the point that the arrangement ceases to be beneficial for one island, the deal is off and the bridge is dismantled and stored — temporarily.

Such an emphasis on mutual payoffs raises an obvious question. Does love not go beyond mere taking — physically, financially, emotionally — so that one person extends himself or herself to the other, because he or she wants to bring something to that person? Put another way, if we really love someone, do we ever dispense with conditions?

If, following the autonomy model, our starting place of concern is ourselves, it seems that the best we can hope for is a mutual "win." The problem is that there are times when the person we are involved with is not able to offer us a "win." They may require some emotional subsidizing. In the language of the theologian, they may be in need both of "grace" — receiving what they don't deserve — and "mercy" — not receiving what they do deserve. The "win-win" formula might call for an amendment to "lose-win".

In relationships, grace and mercy are sometimes desperately required. With its emphasis on self-gratification, the autonomy model is unlikely to come through with an adequate amount of either.

The old fusion model and the newer reciprocal model both have reflected dominant cultural emphases — in the first case on the group and in the second on the individual. Taken to their extremes, neither style leads to widespread personal or social well-being. The old fusion model of relationships may have resulted in longevity without freedom. But the new autonomy model results in freedom without longevity. Both add less than is possible to the quality of one's life and the lives of others.

The relational costs of the excessive emphasis on the individual and the relativity of what is best have been extremely high. Much of the liability lies with our major institutions.

7

The Institutional Casualty List

THE THEME OF FREEDOM has come to pervade all of Canada's major institutions. In turn, it has been championed by them. There have been many important benefits for everyone. Yet, the excessive institutional focus on the individual and choice is seriously limiting their contribution to personal and social well-being.

The Media

If isolated individuals want to express their opinions and their views of reality, the social consequences are initially fairly marginal. Lone Rangers and lone crusaders have to start small, gain some allies, and attempt to mount a social movement in order to be heard by society and taken seriously by legislators. Most individual voices never get beyond being cries in the wilderness. Freedom of expression consequently carries a limited social tab. When adopted by the media, however, the emphasis on individual expression has far-reaching effects.

THE POWER OF THE PRESS

Given the tremendous power of the media in the 1990s, the values of media personnel are of central importance. There is no such thing as value-free journalism. The mere selection of one event or issue over another reflects someone's values. Beyond selection, the position taken on the event or issue reflects values. The same is true for such seemingly innocuous offerings as entertainment and commercials. One can support, decry, or remain indifferent to some people, some issues, some models for living. The key determinant? One's values. Reflecting on the potential impact of the international expansion of American television, forecasters John Naisbitt and Patricia Aburdene comment, "Unlike cheeseburgers and jeans, the globalization of television is explosive and controversial because it conveys deeper values." It "crosses over the line of superficial exchange," they note, and "goes right to the ethos of a culture, addressing the fundamental spirit that informs its beliefs and practices."[1]

The media are the modern-day creators of the world. Historically, the gods have tended to carry no little responsibility. Reality construction is important and difficult business. For starters, it requires a vision of the kind of society that one would like to create. If the gods are careless, they may make life unnecessarily difficult — bringing forth the indignant wrath of inferior but vocal creatures who have little patience with heavenly bungling.

These days, it is not at all clear that the media's concern with expressing their freedom has been matched by their concern for responsibly constructing reality.

A recent and important example. On the heels of the death of the Meech Lake accord, the media hardly warranted a nomination for a Nobel peace prize. At a time when "perception was everything," the media had us looking for an abrupt separation — which didn't happen — and an economic disaster — which didn't happen. In lieu of news of that dramatic variey, our undaunted media focused on "the new outbreak of nationalism" in Quebec, citing as "evidence" attendance at that province's revived, but traditional, St. Jean Baptiste Day parade, along with select interviews with Quebec nationalists. And then, of course, there was the irresistible opportunity to fuse post-Meech Lake hysteria with the visit of the Queen. Negative reactions to her short stop in Hull were maximized as further evidence of Quebec's newfound disenchantment with Canada.

This was not a careful and objective reporting of news; it was a selective and, frankly, sadistic taunting of English Canadians. Quebec's apparent jubilation stirred our fears; the alleged rejection of the Queen stirred our anger. If we were a family, our life together would very quickly disintegrate.

SOME QUESTIONS FOR THE MEDIA

Beyond this specific instance, a number of problems are readily apparent — for example, in the reporting of news generally.

Catering to Customers It is significant that, from their beginnings in Canada, the media were hardly financially autonomous. Newspapers that, in the 1840s, depended on patrons depend in the 1990s on companies that will advertise and subscribers who will read those ads. The same is true of other forms of media. Even publicly owned services such as the CBC and publicly sponsored networks such as PBS want listeners and viewers.

Frequently, in reporting "news," the media go with what sells — violence, catastrophes, scandal, sexual abuse, drug use, diseases that kill — and therefore is profitable. Similarly, many filmmakers, with an eye to the box office, give people what they want instead of having some concern for what they may need. Particularly confusing for many people is the unclear line between news and entertainment. A television talk-show host like Geraldo is adamant that he is a journalist who, in his phrase, is "democratizing the news." Yet the difference between "Entertainment Tonight" and "A Current Affair" is not especially obvious. Even with newsmagazine shows such as "60 Minutes" and "W5," one is sometimes hard-pressed to know whether the material presented is "entertaining news" or "entertaining events presented as news."

The media have tended to give Canadians what they want. Unfortunately, the economic benefits of magnifying the sensational and the deviant have "created" a planet and a nation that, on paper, screen, and radio, are far more problem-plagued and violence-prone than "the real world." Canadians, frequently with the assistance of a U.S. portrayal of life south of the border, have come to believe that their society is extremely violent, that wife-beating is close to the norm, that drug use among young people is epidemic. Significantly, national surveys have found that we Canadians are inclined to see American social problems as *our* social problems. The debt has two main sources: the American media and our failure to remember that the objective problems in the two societies tend to be very different.[2]

Depiction leads to perception, perception to personal and social consequences. In the widely cited phrase of social psychologist W. I. Thomas, "If we define things as real, they are real in their consequences."[3] What brings results is not what *is* real but what we *think* is real. The media's role in instilling the perception of what is real in Canada is unrivaled. As a result, the model of life that the media have for Canadians and Canada is critical to personal and interpersonal well-being.

Its impact is felt in every age group. An instructor at a community college in Edmonton, Andrew Blake, has been trying to dispel "the myth" that older people are common targets for lurking criminals. "Some elderly are barricading themselves in their homes and refusing to go out because they are convinced the streets aren't safe. It's just not true," maintains Blake. He points out that only four in every thousand seniors will ever be robbed, considerably lower than for other people. Says Blake, "Their perception of being a victim of crime causes anxiety, and concern for safety detracts from their quality of life. We have to tell them their perception is invalid." It won't be easy. Following his presentation at a recent seniors' conference, one woman immediately asked if she should put bars on her windows.[4]

The media have created a society in which anxiety and distrust are high, in which good things that happen are more the exception than the rule. Such a construction of reality undoubtedly "sells," and the media subsequently turn a profit. Ironically the public pays a hefty bill.

Choosing What Will Be News In view of the implications for individuals and society, the selection of news must be carried out thoughtfully and responsibly. Often this is the case, particularly with major papers and stations. However, in a large number of cases, editorial decisions lie with a small group of people or with only one person. The top news stories for the day are subsequently decided by vote, by rank, and even by whim.

The danger here is that some editorial staff and individuals give evidence of having little more than "a wire service mentality." They pull material off the newswire and news-service tapes with limited rationale for why one item warrants play over another. News services, for their part, appear to have questionable safeguards against "bad research" and "bad surveys." Most important, given what "makes the news," large numbers of media personnel either do not understand or have little concern for the social and personal implications of printing or airing given items.

Creating News If there is nothing happening, the media frequently create news. A popular procedure in Canada is for newspapers and networks to commission public opinion polls. That's fine. What's not so fine is that members of the media rarely distinguish between *perception* and *behavior* in reporting the results of those polls.

For example, in February 1990, the *Toronto Star* ran a headline that read, "Intolerance on rise, 54% say." The poll, conducted by the reliable Angus Reid, in fact revealed that a minority of Canadians were exhibiting racist sentiments about such issues as turbans in a Legion hall, the treatment of Natives by the justice system, immigrants threatening Canadian society, and preference for White over non-White immigrants. Nevertheless, the writer focused on people's *perception* that intolerance is increasing, rather than on their *behavior*, and began the story, "Many Canadians pay lip service to the ideals of tolerance to ethnic minorities while harboring racist or discriminatory sentiments."[5] Here the fabrication of news comes full circle: the media create the perception that racism is increasing, and then — even when the findings indicate it is not — offer as news the fact that Canadians "think it is."

Probably one of the most naive notions of the average citizen is the idea that the media simply report the news. In reality, a news quota exists. What is important on any given day is limited to the amount of space on the front page or to the news spot of five minutes, two minutes, or thirty seconds. Items compete for space; news will be found in proportion to the time and space available. If nothing is happening, if it is "a slow news day," the media will not be lost for material. One only has to find a slant, an angle, even if the factual support is precarious. In 1986, I submitted a news item to the *Edmonton Journal* indicating that racism had been decreasing in Canada since at least the mid-1970s. One exception to the trend was the Prairies, where there was little or no change between 1980 and 1985. The paper ran as its headline, "Racism Highest on the Prairies."[6]

News is constantly "in the making," but not only in terms of the popular notion of high-flying, fast-breaking events. Writers and reporters are working overtime to create stories that will sell. In 1979, a writer from *Maclean's* contacted me, wanting to find some data that would support her thesis that religion is making a comeback in Canada. She pointed out that the assignment had come from a senior editor who was impressed with the apparent burgeoning interest in religion in Toronto, especially in some Pentecostal groups. For three hours we went over extensive national data that offered no support for her thesis. Nonetheless, sometime later the story appeared, the writer's argument supported by anecdotal stories in lieu of "hard" evidence.

Short Attention Spans Lewis Garnsworthy, the late Toronto Anglican Archbishop, in attempting to get a little more thick-skinned in the course of being assailed by the media, reminded me of the old saying that "the paper that carries tonight's headlines will carry out tomorrow's garbage." He was right. News has a short life span. Consumers don't want to hear the same news twice, unless it is a captivating story that can be expanded into a series. But after a story has been tapped from every angle possible, the media move on to other things. Their love affairs with stories are short-lived. On a given day they report with grimness an item that can upset and stir up people. But they quickly move on, often with little regard for the impact of the story on individuals and communities.

Significantly, coverage does not end when stories are "completed" — when the rapist gets caught, the priest is cleared, the feared business collapse doesn't take place. Rather, attention to an item ends when coverage no longer sells papers or interests listeners. In the midst of the AIDs epidemic, whatever happened to herpes? Has the threat of nuclear war simply disappeared? What ever became of the energy crisis? In 1989, events in China were monitored tenaciously by the media. To a large extent the students there were abruptly forgotten when the abortion issue began to hit an array of Canadian courts. The generalization is not an exaggeration: news is like the music industry's top 40; nothing stays on the charts for long.

Filling the Window Documenting the widespread nature of television viewing in Canada, Ted Wannel and Craig McKie of Statistics Canada wrote in 1986: "It is evident that television has captured the attention of Canadians as a source of information and entertainment. If there is a central question here it might well be: what will fill Canadians' television windows in the future?"[7] There has never been so great a need for media that can contribute to well-being, that will responsibly "fill the information windows." Yet, precisely at a time when the media-creator — like the gods of yore — needs to be careful and wise, there is good reason to believe that content is being driven largely by concerns relating primarily to "ratings, readers, and revenues." Such lofty goals are not the kinds of ingredients of which social well-being is made.

Beyond the news industry, programs, films, and videos, for example, hardly show a consistent tendency to be aimed at enhancing life. One wonders, for example, if members of the media, in providing models for living, have any vision of something worth striving for, or is profit the only name of the game? Do we want a world of Rambos or Cosbys or Mr. T's or Woody Allen, or what? Do people involved in the motion-picture industry understand or care about the social impact of an endless string of *Friday the 13th* horrors, versus pro-relational offerings such as *Parenthood* or *When Harry Met Sally*?

Because of the media's unprecedented power, Canadian life, to a greater extent than ever before, urgently needs its help. Unfortunately, at this point in time the media's emphasis on freedom and commitment to profits has made them far less than godlike sources of personal and social well-being.

Education

Educators are clearly in a position to have a profoundly positive influence on Canadian life. However, their cultivation of an appreciation for the individual and choice has been excessive to the point of counterproductivity. A number of areas can readily be cited.

INDIVIDUALISM WITHOUT INDIVIDUALITY

There is little doubt that Canadian young people are coming through our educational systems with individualism well-entrenched. Regardless of the type of education that they have experienced, fifteen- to twenty-four-year-olds differ little in their inclination to endorse individualistic versus social values.

Ironically, while young people place a high value on the individual and individual gratification, they do not place a high value on individuality. If anything, the evidence suggests that Canadian youth are consumers of "mass culture." They are not individualists who strive to be personally imaginative and reflective. On the contrary, few characteristics are valued by them less highly than imagination and creativity. It is noteworthy that the two traits are also not highly valued by Canadian adults.

The drive toward conformity as a means of individual gratification clearly has a variety of institutional sources. One of the most important appears to be the school. Young people at all stages of the educational system in Canada often have been receiving a double message. On the one hand, they have been encouraged to develop as individuals, to tap their potential and be all that they can be. On the other hand, the behavioral and thought expectations continue to be highly confining. A strong case can be made for the argument that, into the 1990s, "the good student" — whether at play school, high school, or grad school — continues to be one who follows the rules, memorizes the material, and makes no waves. Our societal reward is young people who emerge from school with high personal expectations, having mastered minutiae and embraced mass culture, while devaluing imagination, creativity, and risk-taking.

SELECT VALUES
15- TO 24-YEAR-OLDS

% Indiciating "*Very Important*"

	NAT	BC	PR	ONT	QUE	ATL
Success	76	72	73	76	78	78
Freedom	75	71	78	78	70	79
Concern for Others	64	67	66	76	42	68
Generosity	54	48	50	57	57	55
Imagination	42	38	42	45	44	36
Creativity	35	34	35	35	38	27

SOURCE: *Project Teen Canada 88.*

RELATIVISM WITHOUT REFLECTION

Our educational system is probably the major source of "mindless relativism." The problem is not that students have been exposed to the concept of relativism and know how to make use of it, but that relativism has been taken as some kind of "a given": students are taught that "everything's relative." Few, however, seem to know why.

Here Bloom's critique is devastating. Relativism, he writes, "is the virtue, the only virtue, which all primary education for more than fifty years has dedicated itself to inculcating. The students, of course, cannot defend their opinion," Bloom stresses, because relativism is the result of indoctrination. "The best they can do is point out all the opinions and cultures there are and have been," and question the right of anyone "to say one is better than the others." Says Bloom, "The purpose of their education is not to make them scholars but to provide them with a moral virtue — openness."[8]

Here we see an important paradox. The school and university teach the importance of open-mindedness. Yet, the fact of the matter is that our educational institutions are instilling closed-mindedness. Critical evaluation is essential to creativity and to progress. When relativism becomes an assumption rather than an hypothesis in need of investigation, it strangles critical thought. Before we look at the facts, we are told that everything is equal.

Our educational system should not assume that ideas and behavior are relative, but should critically explore the accuracy and efficacy of ideas and behavior. Education should stimulate people in a pluralistic society not to think less but more. Currently in Canada, the unreflective adoption of the relativistic assumption is leading us to think not more, but less. The time has come for us, like our American counterparts, to "open our closed minds."

EMPLOYMENT SKILLS WITHOUT LIFE SKILLS

Canadians are taught that education has two main purposes. First, it is a means to an end; that end includes such goals as literacy and the acquisition of skills. Second, education is an end in itself; it contributes to the development of the individual, and its curricula are aimed at expanding our knowledge and critical abilities.

But formal education does not teach people how to live. Educators put students through programs that introduce them to a large number of disciplines, and students graduate from high school with a rudimentary knowledge of everything from geometric propositions to the respiratory system of a frog. Yet most do not know how to cope with life.

An extremely important debate that has been raging among psychiatrists and sociologists over the past three decades is highly relevant. At stake is how we view personal emotional health. For much of this century, we have believed in the twin concepts of "mental illness" and "mental health." Our assumption is that people fall into one of the two categories. If people are mentally healthy, they are able to live life reasonably well. On the other hand, if they are mentally ill, they cannot. The way that people become well is to expose them to treatment that takes such forms as psychotherapy, drugs, and — even still — shock treatment. The settings, ranked in terms of current prominence, consist of private offices and clinics, psychiatric wards, and mental hospitals.

However, such a view has been seriously challenged. Two people in particular, Americans Thomas Scheff, a sociologist, and Thomas Szasz, a psychiatrist, have been questioning the merits of the concept of "mental illness." They argue that the idea was invented by the medical profession, which has treated "mental illness" as analogous to mental health. The two critics maintain that the analogy is inappropriate. Scheff, for example, says that "mental illness" diagnoses have little of the precision of physical illness diagnoses, and are typically applied indiscriminately to many kinds of behavior that deviate from our laws and even our conventions. When we don't know how else to label the different and the bizarre, says Scheff, we say that people are "mentally ill." For Scheff, "mental illness" is "residual deviance":

> The culture of the group provides a vocabulary of terms for categorizing many norm violations: crime, perversion, drunkenness, and bad manners are familiar examples. . . . After exhausting these categories of behavior, however, there is always a residue of the most diverse kinds of violations, for which the culture provides no explicit label. . . . The violations may be lumped together into a residual category: witchcraft, spirit possession, or, in our own society, mental illness.[9]

Szasz argues that mental health is not a quality that we possess, enabling us to make the right choices in life. It rather is a label that we receive after we make the right choices. People whom we regard as "healthy" are essentially those who can cope with life.[10] Following Szasz, people who can "cope" can do two things well: they can relate to other people, and they can establish goals and the means for reaching them.

Apart from when an identifiable physical factor is involved, then, "mental health" results from people learning how to live life. While it would be nice to think we could simply give people a drug that would magically "straighten them out," we all know that social skills and problem-solving abilities take years and years to acquire. Plain and simple, *they are learned*.

Such an interpretation of mental health is now becoming widespread. In 1986, as Minister of National Health and Welfare, Jake Epp released a document at the International Conference on Health Promotion. "Today, we are working with a concept which portrays health as a part of everyday living," it began, with quality of life involving "the opportunity to make choices and gain satisfaction from living. Health is thus envisaged as a resource which gives people the ability to manage and even to change their surroundings."[11] A companion "Charter" document stressed a recurring theme: health is seen not as an end-state but "as a resource for everyday life . . . emphasizing social and personal resources, as well as physical capacities."[12]

The painful fact of the matter is that large numbers of North Americans are not receiving sufficient information from our educational institutions on how to live. The tremendous market for information on how to cope with life — books, programs, workshops, seminars — attests to the difficulty many are having as they attempt to deal with relationships, career, children, and so on. They have not been taught how to relate to people or how to solve problems. Their socialization — the process by which they learn to become participant members of society — is simply incomplete.

Job-training and a liberal arts orientation are not enough. On the heels of participating in a four-day personal development program, a well-known Canadian professor suggested that he had received more insights into interpersonal life in four days than he had received in the course of obtaining four degrees. Ten months later, a psychology professor, totally unaware of his colleague's admission, told him that he had received more interpersonal insight in five days than he had received in the course of netting six degrees.

Educators are doing a good job of teaching people about life. But it's not enough. Personal and social well-being require that our schools do a much better job of teaching people how to live. We now have considerable insight into how Canadians can cope more effectively with life. It's time for educators to get the word out.

MATURATION WITHOUT MORALITY

Social life requires that individuals subscribe to some basic norms or rules that make collective existence possible. The explicit rules need to be enforced by values that people internalize: we can't police everything.

In Canada, our emphasis on the individual has not been matched by an emphasis on the necessity of such consensus. Our emphasis on relativism and the cultivation of choice for choice's sake has been socially sadistic. Bloom asks, "When there is no shared goals or vision of the public good, is the social contract any longer possible?"[13] The answer is no.

Canadian educators have played a major role in maximizing the freedom of the individual and minimizing the necessity of ethical consensus. Let there be no confusion: what is at issue here are not some optional norms that bigoted moral entrepreneurs want to "push on people" — some kind of legislating of personal morality. The concern centers around the need for values and norms that extend beyond mere laws — a necessity recognized by even the most amoral social scientist. If we are going to maintain that any behavior "this side of the law" goes, then, as a society, we are going to be in big trouble.

In a November 1989 York University lecture series presentation on corporate ethics, William Dimma, a former professor and now deputy chairman of Royal LePage, had this to say:

> . . . ethics go beyond the law. The law is ponderous; it changes too slowly to be a satisfactory standard of ethical behavior. For the most part, the law does not anticipate ways in which it can be circumvented; rather, it responds belatedly to those who exploit its loopholes. . . . At any point in time, there are practices which, though legal, are neither condonable nor ethical. . . . And it has the unfortunate side-effect of legitimizing any activity not made explicitly legal, a common problem in a legalistic society.[14]

Dimma maintains that "ethical concerns, like environmental concerns, are increasingly important and more central to our lives, both corporate and personal."[15]

Precisely because we cannot legislate and enforce everything, it is critically important that we arrive at some consensus regarding key norms and values, and then instill them. Education is obviously a pivotally important source of such socialization.

It is ironic that the English educational system, long regarded by many in Canada as the best in the world, is being called upon to do a better job of transmitting values and ethics. In a speech at Oxford in the summer of 1988, Home Secretary Douglas Hurd said that he expected the National Curriculum Council to consider how "personal responsibility, self-discipline and civic duty can best be delivered through the school curriculum." Hurd said that changes in the structure of the family have created numerous problems for children, including inadequate care and insufficient affection. The changes have also produced numerous problems for society, ranging from insubordination and juvenile deliquency to violence and "a moral brutishness which seems to make [young people] incapable of any kind of imaginative sympathy for their victims. . . . The old lady whom they mug, the housewife whom they rob, the girl whom they abuse, is just an object, a toy, with no individuality, no feelings, no purpose beyond that of giving temporary gratification to her tormentors." Hurd asserted that, for many young people, "the school represents our only chance to break into what could otherwise be a circle of bad parenting and juvenile delinquency from one generation to another." He called on educators to help counter the prevailing "moral under-achievement" and added that personal and social education should become an integral part of school life. Mainstream subjects, tutorial groups, and assemblies should incorporate moral values.[16]

Educators in Canada would be wise to listen.

The Workplace

The emphasis on individualism and relativism that has emancipated employer and employee has also brought chaos to the workplace. A hint of the problem is offered in an observation made by Dimma: "There is little doubt that, on a continuum anchored by materialism and greed at one end and by idealism and a sense of community at the other, the balance continues to shift ominously in the wrong direction."[17]

ALL FOR ONE AND NONE FOR ALL

If both employer and employee are autonomous, loyalty is precarious. In the corporate sector, for example, loyalty is increasingly hard to come by. As Toronto lawyer Brian Grosman points out, decent employees have few guarantees that their loyalty will translate into decent rewards from decent people. Employers have little reason to believe that employees will be trustworthy team players who put the organization's interests above personal interests.[18] No one should be particularly surprised. If the group cares not about individuals but only about productivity and profit, there is little reason for individuals to care about the group.

Such a situation can create instability in the lives of organizations and individuals. Guarantees of loyalty from either side might be unrealistic, but at times they would be welcome relief. The problem is that a culture that has instilled an ethic of individualism makes it difficult for one to have one's cake and still wolf it down: for either party to make a commitment is to relinquish one's freedom and flexibility. The workplace resolution is for both parties to treat the alliance as short-term and mutually self-serving. Termination is determined by self-interest on the part of one side or the other.

THE DEMISE OF TRUST

The pervasive cultural emphasis that "everything's relative" has the potential to have devastating effects on the workplace. An 1989 poll by Louis Harris of 250 Canadian office workers found that 82 percent said that their top concern was that company management be "honest, upright, and ethical" in dealings with employees and the community. Yet, only 36 percent said their bosses met that standard. Seventy-seven percent said that it is very important for management to recognize the contributions of workers, but only 42 percent thought their bosses did so. Harris suggested that such mistrust of management appears to be the result of the flurry of corporate mergers, acquisitions, and restructuring.[19]

In a symbiotic work setting, everyone wants payoffs; otherwise, the deal's off. But without mutual commitment to some basic norms, there are problems. Employers can be exploitive, guided only by the law and by labor supply. The results: inadequate salaries, the denial of benefits, verbal abuse, sexual harassment. Employees also can be exploitive, guided only by law and by the possibility of being fired. Some examples: poor effort, mediocre contributions, and supply theft.

As companies grow, the trust level between employee and employer can only be expected to decrease. Robert Reich recently wrote in the *New York Times Magazine*: "As those engaged in rearranging the slices of the pie become more numerous and far wealthier than those dedicated to enlarging the pie, trust declines." Reich adds, "Without trust, people won't dedicate themselves to common goals. They will turn their energies instead to defending their own interests."[20]

Dimma, in warning about the excesses of personal greed, somewhat facetiously adds, "Now please don't misunderstand me. Greed is essential to the proper functioning of our economic system." Disguised as hustle and ambition, or push and shove, it "powers the free enterprise engine." But, he adds, without being tempered by "something well beyond and quite different from greed," the driver of the engine will some day run off the road and over a cliff.[21]

The Family

There is no question that today we have more choices about how to structure our families, more role choices, more choices about our sexual behavior. Still, from the standpoint of personal and social well-being, there is reason to wonder how progressive our emancipation has actually been.

EMANCIPATION FOR WHAT?

The message that the availability of options sometimes seems to convey is that it makes little difference what choices one makes. But the sheer expansion of possibilities does not mean that different choices lead to the same level of well-being for individuals and for society. The presence of choices says much about a society's tolerance level; but it says little about the efficacy of the choices themselves.

An important question we need to ask is this: Do we have any vision of family life in Canada? Institutionally and individually, is tolerance our starting place, or our ending place? Do we have any "dreams," or have individualism and relativism made them obsolete?

If pluralism declares all kinds of family life to be equally desirable, we are left with two major problems. First, we are unable to explore the possibility that some family arrangements are more effective means to well-being than others; the research is decreed to be inappropriate. Second, we cannot commend to young people and others the forms and roles that seem to work the best. In attempting to be open-minded, once more we run the risk of being the opposite.

Here it would seem to be extremely important to differentiate between what we tolerate and what we advocate. For example, it is one thing to say that people who experience divorce should not be stigmatized. It is quite another thing to say that divorce is personally and socially desirable. People frequently pay a significant emotional and financial price, even when society offers "a green light." Similarly, living together may be found to be functional for some people, especially those who are younger, when educational and career factors make cohabitation essentially a premarriage reality — whether they eventually marry each other or someone else. However, there is good reason to believe that, in many instances, living together fails to provide the structural stability necessary for long-term, emotionally gratifying relationships; the presence of children often makes such instability particularly undesirable.

Our current emphasis on choice in Canada has blurred the distinction between toleration and advocation. Our major institutions — the media, the school, government, and even religion — have been saying less and less about better and best possibilities. Young Canadians especially have been among the losers.

LIVING WITH THE CHOICES

The emphasis on choice has created a strange paradox for Canadian families. People stress the importance of exercising their rights as individuals when it comes to such matters as marriage and sexuality, having children, and working outside the home. Yet many of those same people expect society to be there to cover the financial and human costs when things go wrong. Financially and emotionally, the expenditures are extremely high.

Columnist Clair Bernstein recently highlighted what some of our marital choices can mean for children. "Marriage is now a disposable contract," she wrote, with the marriage breakdown "a built-in expectation even at the moment the marriage vows are exchanged. The consequences of this option," she said, "are soon to hit us: a lost generation of youth — the victims of the breakup — whom society and its government has abandoned to a helpless life of poverty." Marriage breakup is expensive. Husbands find it difficult to maintain two households, and single mothers are left in desperate situations. At this point, the government is called in. Bernstein argues that the state should provide mothers with adequate incomes in the short run, and should also provide services for retraining and psychological preparation for reentry into the workplace, as well as new structures for bringing up children. She concludes by saying that we need to be willing to foot the bill for such programs, or "accept responsibility for a next generation of youth who have grown up in poverty, in many instances without love and caring, who will increase the ranks of drug dealers, crack addicts, skinhead groups and fill our courts and prisons." If we aren't willing "to pay the price in money," she warns, we will one day "pay the price in fear."[22]

These are sobering thoughts. What isn't as clear as the prognosis is the responsibility of individuals in all of this. Put bluntly, if they got themselves into this predicament, then why is it, to use Bernstein's words, that "*we* must accept responsibility"?

Clearly, compassion demands that we help members of our society who are having problems. But choices always carry costs. Individuals who want the freedom to choose have to be prepared to live with the consequences of their choices. Why? Because individualism does not let us have it both ways. Individualism fosters an outlook of personal gratification. If we fail, what reason do we have to expect that our individualistically minded compatriots are going to suspend their self-interests and bail us out? If the rules of the game are that individuals should win, then the players cannot be expected to come to the rescue of someone who holds a losing hand. Individualism destroys the very impulse that it tries to call forth when it fails. Individualism gone wild accelerates self-absorption and eliminates compassion. Increasingly, individualistically minded Canadians will be less and less willing to subsidize the choices of individuals.

The choices some of us make are already meeting with considerable resistance. For example, women who have chosen to marry and have children and work outside the home maintain that "society" should pay for their child care. Other women who have chosen to marry and have children and chosen to work inside the home say that society should pay them a salary. The remainder of Canadians who comprise our exchange-oriented "society" are clearly asking and asking loudly, as they are asked to reach for their chequebooks, "What's in it for us?" The widespread demand for abortion raises the same issue. Women who choose to engage in sex and choose to terminate a pregnancy also are inclined to expect that "society" pay for their abortions. While interest groups crusade for the rights of the mother, the rights of the unborn child, and even the rights of the father, very few dare suggest that all three voices need also to at least listen to a fourth voice — the rights of society. That may change.

If society pays for the consequences of choice, then society will demand input into the expenditures. Choices will have to be evaluated and the best options advocated. Otherwise, freedom of choice will not guarantee enhanced life for everyone. We don't want adults to get hurt, children to suffer, people to be impoverished or sexually exploited. We also want to cut our dollar losses. Emancipation increasingly can be expected to involve far more than merely "cheering for choices."

Religion

Religious groups, operating in a culture in which individualism and relativism have become highly pervasive, are feeling the effects. People are picking and choosing what they want from religion; they also are inclined to treat truth as a matter of personal conscience.

For their part, groups are like restaurants that find themselves serving up large numbers of appetizers but relatively few entrées. What's more, given the market conditions, they face important limitations.

CONSUMER RELIGION

In Canada, religion is not expected to be very aggressive. A pluralistic society has no place for religions that want to be overly zealous in recruiting people who are members and adherents of other faiths. Frankly, evangelism is not very Canadian; it smacks of intolerance, even bigotry. It also is a violation of privacy. And when it's directed at new arrivals, the poor, the young, and the aged, it borders on imperialism and exploitation. Some say it may even violate the Charter of Rights and Freedoms.

Most groups comply with this norm of restraint. Apart from perhaps some of the Conservative Protestants, along with Jehovah's Witnesses and Mormons, our country's religious groups don't compete with each other. Few could be accused of "stealing" another's members. They essentially service the religious needs of Canadians and maintain a posture of cooperation and respect for one another.

Religion, Canadian-style, is also not expected to be very demanding. Time and money limitations translate into a willingness of members to give only so much time and money. Moreover, as volunteer lay staff, they can be encouraged and humored and shown gratitude, but they can't be pushed too hard, chastised, or fired. If leaders upset them, they can move elsewhere — or, even worse, choose to stay, and occasionally make life difficult.

Committed members constitute a minority. Unless they can see personal payoffs — be they good feelings, benefits for their children, rites of passage, or tax writeoffs — most Canadians don't want to have much to do with religious groups. Few are mad or upset; they simply don't want much. While leaders and others who value faith ideally see religion as addressing the entirety of one's life, it has at best a marginal place in the lives of most Canadians.

The findings of the 1987 national survey of the country's fifteen- to twenty-four-year-olds are — for those concerned about religion's influence — nothing short of devastating. While 80 percent of young people identify with a religious group and over 85 percent want those groups to perform rites of passage for them, only 12 percent say that God has a great deal of influence in their life, and a mere 14 percent indicate that they highly value religion. Just 16 percent report that it is important for them to live out their faith in everyday life.[23]

TRUTHLESS RELIGION

The individualism of Canadian religion is matched by its relativism. Most groups no longer advocate truth. Accordingly, while religious identification remains stable, religious content seems largely up for grabs.

Issues that divide people seldom even carry the guise of being theological in nature. What usually is involved is concern about sheer change or lifestyle. For example, in the mid-1980s, Canadian Anglicans were up in arms about changes in liturgy. The United Church has been emotionally split over the question of the ordination of homosexuals. In both instances, theology took a back seat to the change and lifestyle issues.

To the extent that members of some groups have any aversion to other groups, the culprit tends to be culture rather than theology. Disdain for Conservative Protestants on the part of some Anglican, United Church, and Roman Catholic "Mainliners," for example, is hardly associated with differing views on the Trinity or eschatology. What typically annoys Mainliners is the apparent unenlightened piety and simplistic and rigid views of faith and life. On the other side of the fence, some Conservatives, such as Baptists and Pentecostals, while upset somewhat with the Mainliners' theology, appear to be as much troubled by their lifestyles, the absence of an evangelical vocabulary, and the presence of sacramental traditions. For most people, theology is a secondary issue.

The pervasiveness of relativism in Canadian culture has made the claims of theological truth passé. To attempt to assert truth is to break the viewpoint rule. And the standards of the pluralistic censor are effective: religious truth claims look very much "like gray cats on a dark night" — they're extremely hard to spot.

It's not that religious groups never speak out. They are quite welcome to express their views on social and economic issues, and they frequently do. However, most such expressions, regardless of whether they come from a Roman Catholic, United, Anglican, or conservative Protestant research base, hardly sound prophetic. Usually they reflect the educational and ideological backgrounds of the people who have prepared them.

But when a question cannot readily be addressed through social research and collective opinion — for example, a question pertaining to the purpose of life and what lies beyond death — religious leaders, it is clear, have little to say. Frequently they sound little different from counselors and others in offering what amount to naturalistic interpretations of life and death.

About two years ago an Anglican member of an audience asked me, "Do you think that religious groups will find themselves competing more and more with secular competitors in the area of meaning?" To which I replied, "Yes. But it seems to me that the more important question you need to ask is this: given the impact of relativism, *do religious groups even have a market entry?*"

"Imagine this scene," I suggested. "A twenty-year-old man on a plane finds out that the person beside him is a minister. 'I find that interesting,' he says quietly. 'About three months ago my sister died of leukemia. She was barely seventeen. Do you think I will ever see her again?' " In the face of such a question, do leaders and others have anything to say, anything to bring — a "meaning entry"? Sociologically speaking, if they remain speechless, or if they are merely pastoral, then — let no one be naive about the consequences — they will be beaten out by competitors, religious and otherwise, who are not lost for words.

Given religion's increasing tendency to abdicate the meaning sphere, it should surprise no one that alternatives are, indeed, being posited and adopted. "Answers" typically take the form of "add-ons," whereby a belief such as reincarnation is added like a foreign food option to one's Protestant or Roman Catholic smorgasbord. People are looking for answers; if conventional religions are silent, the vacuum will be filled by "consumer cults" and nonreligious alternatives. For example, there is perhaps no greater entry into the "meaning market" than the media. Oxford's John Carey, for example, argues that the backdrop for thought in the pre-communication age was religion. While individuals then were not necessarily religious, religion, he explains, supplied many of the ideas that enabled them to interpret their existence.[24]

In contrast to the media's important voice, Canadian Christian leaders commonly are vague about almost everything — Christian content, commitment, and consequences immediately come to mind. On a number of occasions I have told clergy that I feel I've been unfairly criticized for my measures of religious commitment. As a sociologist, I have reminded them, I don't have a vested interest in telling them what religious commitment looks like. "So let's make the corrections," I have said. "*You tell me* what commitment looks like, and I'll be happy to go out and measure it." I've also asked them to tell me what kind of consequences operationalize ideas such as justice and faithfulness and well-being, since they have also frequently taken potshots at my measures here as well. What I find is that, when religious leaders are put on the spot to verbalize the nature and consequences of commitment, they border on muteness. In such situations, the person whose views are regarded as appropriate is either one who doesn't take a clear position on anything, or one who articulates the view that "commitment is relative to the individual involved." Anyone who goes beyond no opinion or the endorsement of relativity — suggesting that belief in God or prayer, for example, are salient — is immediately stigmatized. The person who bucks the pluralistic and relativistic norms of the day and goes public with private views and beliefs pays a fairly sizable bill. They are scarcely any clearer when asked to state "what religion does" — what kind of consequences commitment has.

The country's religious leaders give evidence of being in a remarkable situation: they are telling Canadians that they need something, but cannot verbalize what "it" is. They also maintain that this unidentifiable "something" has important consequences, but are unable to articulate what they are. It doesn't take a marketing expert to realize that the prospects for such an "invisible product" are not exactly good.

INNOCUOUS RELIGION

The symbiotic relationship that has been emerging between religious consumer and religious supplier appears to have resulted in some good mutual payoffs. Individuals selectively take; groups selectively give. If that's all that religion is seen as being — something that changes its shape with the times in accordance with public demand — then the current situation represents no problem.

However, if people who value faith have a vision of religion as being more than synonymous with culture, more than a product that adjusts to ever-changing markets, then the consumer-supplier symbiosis represents a travesty. If religion is more than what individuals want or envision — if, for example, there are really gods or a God "out there" who demands one's "heart and soul and mind and strength" — then catering to individual demand represents a sell-out of outrageous proportions.

And if there is such a thing as religious truth and we do not pursue it, we are prematurely limiting what is knowable. Is there absolute truth about God and life and death and everything? We will never know unless we continue the search. For religious leaders to blaze the way in abandoning the expedition seems to be a strange combination of abdication and self-liquidation.

Religion, in unabridged form, has much to bring to our times. It addresses, the fundamental questions of existence — why we are here, where we can find our worth, how we are to relate to others, where we are going. Accordingly, religion is capable of speaking with authority to at least three themes that social scientists and futurists agree remain pervasive — the quest for meaning, for self-affirmation, for community.[25]

However, delimited by individualism and demoted by relativism, religion in Canada has ceased to be authoritative. Canadians who continue to ask questions, seek hope, and pursue community find religion to be offering only piecemeal, fragmented responses.

Sociologists have long argued that a primary function of religion is its contribution to social solidarity. Religion has created communal bonds and united individuals in groups. It has integrated entire societies, encouraged enduring friendships, called for lifelong marriages. There is no doubt that such integration has also led to collective hostility toward outsiders, to bloodshed, and to war. But, used for good or ill, religion has served to "pull people together."

Individualism and relativism, in the course of fragmenting religion, have also destroyed a major source of social integration. Peter Berger comments that theorists have argued that a society will not survive unless people are prepared, if necessary, to die for it. He recalls a widely published photograph of a few years ago showing a Princeton student demonstrator carrying a poster with the inscription, "Nothing is worth dying for." Such an outlook, suggests Berger, is widespread. He adds, "Human beings are not prepared to die for a contract based on the pragmatic accommodation of interests."[26] If alternatives to the championing of group life are not found, what many see as the victory over an oppresive institution may in reality prove to be a short-sighted exercise in social masochism. Sadly, religion, rather than decrying the excesses of individualism and relativism, has tended to embrace them. It thereby has lost both its message and its vocal chords.

Politics

Individualism and relativism have not spared politics. In turn, government leaders as of yet have been slow to take note of the excesses, let alone respond to them.

A NATION OR NATIONS?

If we lack a sense of Canadian nationalism, we show ongoing signs of making up for it in the form of provincial "nationalisms," at least at the level of government. Premiers and their cabinet sidekicks who seldom mumble about the importance of building the best country possible show a remarkable penchant for defending the interests of their provinces. People on the block may have limited interest in the neighborhood; but they do care about the upkeep of their own individual properties.

WILLINGNESS TO FIGHT FOR ONE'S COUNTRY

"Of course, we all hope that there will not be another war, but if it were to come to that, would you be willing to fight for your country?"

	Yes	Depends	No	Don't know	TOTAL
Israel	89	3	3	5	100
United States	77	7	14	2	100
Australia	60	20	18	2	100
Britain	49	17	28	5	100
CANADA	44	24	28	4	100
France	41	25	26	8	100
West Germany	15	36	33	16	100

SOURCE: *Gallup Canada, Inc.*, August 25, 1989.

A classic symbol of such cautious and conditional participation in the national enterprise is the presence, in our 1982 Constitution, of section 33, the "notwithstanding" clause. By invoking the clause, the provinces — and Parliament, for that matter — can declare any law exempt from the sections of the Constitution pertaining to fundamental freedoms, legal rights, and equality rights.

Some would argue that the Meech Lake controversy revealed Canadian "provincialism" at its best. In his presentation to the Joint Committee of the House of Commons and Senate in late 1989, Pierre Trudeau claimed that there was talk, the very day after the initial agreement in 1987, of massive decentralization with "the accord representing the greatest victory for the provinces since Confederation . . . . a triumph for provincial patriotism."[27] Former Liberal cabinet minister Donald Johnston maintained that the accord would make the federal government into "a coordination unit for the provinces." He went on to say, "Under this framework, the federal government may be likened to a condominium manager with responsibility delegated by the owners to take care of the common property, cut the grass, remove the snow and clean the lobby and hallways."[28]

Onlookers take as a given the fact that provincialism is "good politics." The media assume it, teachers transmit it, students consume it, citizens believe it. According to the propaganda, provinces have to work hard to ensure that their concerns are looked after in this "dog eat dog" Confederation of ours. Provincial politicians have their work cut out for them simply trying to stay even, let along make some gains. The stakes are high, the tension is thick, the mood is grim.

The problem with such provincial individualism is that it is out of touch with reality. It is based on a model that doesn't exist, namely, that we are a highly stationary population that stays in one place and needs to be looked after.

In fact, the vast majority of Anglophones are geographically highly mobile. We move freely from one province to another. During the three-year period of 1986 through 1988, for example, interprovincial moves totalled over one million — more than twice the 412,000 immigration figure for the same time.[29] Our loyalty to any one province is frequently questionable; heavens, we aren't even sure sometimes what province we should call home. Further, even if we tend to stay put provincially, chances are good our relatives and close friends are spread across the country.

What's more, we are fickle. We are apt to wave cheerfully at the provincial politician lying on the battlefield as we move our worldly possessions to the opposite side of the lines — lured by such noble causes as a better job offer or the prospect of more sunshine. A national poll in November 1989 found that some three in four people see themselves first as Canadians, second as citizens of a given province. Reflecting the mobility factor, those who feel most pro-province are disproportionately from Quebec and Newfoundland, as well as rural and young.[30]

For most of us, provincial tugs-of-wars are largely mythical wars. They appear to involve issues that are technical rather than practical. At the height of the Meech Lake debate in the spring of 1990, federal and provincial politicians were slinging grenades in every direction. Quebec premier Robert Bourassa insisted that

CANADIANS ON THE MOVE

% Moving Where: 1986, 1987, 1988

AREA OF ORIGIN	AREA OF DESTINATION							
	ATL	QUE	ONT	MAN	SASK	ALTA	BC	TOTAL
ATLANTIC	26	9	45	3	1	9	7	100
QUEBEC	13	—	68	2	1	6	10	100
ONTARIO	23	24	—	8	4	18	23	100
MANITOBA	6	3	35	—	12	20	24	100
SASKATCHEWAN	3	2	18	14	—	42	21	100
ALBERTA	8	4	33	6	10	—	39	100
BRITISH COLUMBIA	6	5	36	6	6	41	—	100
IN 1000'S: OUT	158	106	222	76	84	221	149	1016
IN	136	86	312	58	50	175	199	1016
NET	-22	-20	+90	-18	-34	-46	+50	0*

SOURCE: *Statistics Canada, Cat. 91-209E, 1990:92.*

*Figures rounded.

the rejection of Meech Lake would lead to separation. Nova Scotia premier John Buchanan said the Atlantic provinces would have to join the United States if Quebec left Canada.[31] Saskatchewan MP Simon deJong said the western provinces could be forced to the join the States if Meech Lake failed.[32] Alberta cabinet minister Jim Horsman said Alberta would lose its best ally if Quebec separated.[33] Newfoundland premier Clyde Wells said his province would nonetheless rescind its approval, and in early April it did so – earning him the label of "mental case" from assistant deputy Speaker Denis Pronovost, who subsequently apologized and resigned. The prime minister's Quebec lieutenant, former Parti Quebecois member Lucien Bouchard, said English Canada might be forced to decide whether it wants Quebec or Newfoundland. Quebec intergovernmental affairs minister Gil Remmilard added, "This country can easily live without Newfoundland."[34] Bouchard quit in May, declaring that René

Levesque had been right — that sovereignty association was right for Quebec.

While all of this was going on, as late as May, more than one-half of Canadians said they knew "little" or "nothing" about the accord. Moreover, the vast majority couldn't have cared less: only 27 percent outside Quebec and 26 percent within that province regarded it as a "very serious" problem.[35] Such a strange situation was reminiscent of the Constitution struggles of the early 1980s, when politicians and the media were fixated on the patriation issue, while average Canadians were concerned primarily with the economy and unemployment.[36]

Despite the claims of returning provincial conquerors, even the apparent victories primarily appear to be "triumphs over trivia." What we really want is to "stay alive and live well." Only at the point that we find our quality of life in jeopardy do we want the provinces to "go to bat for us."

And so the obvious question arises: Quebec aside, just who are the provincial politicians fighting so hard to protect? Surely not the Albertan who left last week for British Columbia, or the Newfoundlander who now lives in Toronto, or the Nova Scotian who paddled across the water to Prince Edward Island. Provincial politicians may be beautifying their townhouses; but their tenants are coming and going. In the 1990s, provincial individualism in Canadian politics is both irrelevant and unnecessary. Canadians benefit when and only when provincial politicians work together to create the best possible country.

Quebec, of course, represents a significant exception to much of what has just been said. Proportionately, population movement in and out of Quebec is the lowest in the country.[37] For the relatively stable Quebec population, the provincial government carries considerable responsibility in interprovincial negotiations.

However, if individualism has been unnecessary in the case of the other nine provinces, it frequently has been counterproductive in the case of Quebec. Throughout Canadian history, provincial politicians in Quebec invariably have raised the threat of separation when they have felt it has been in their best interests to do so. Early in 1990, Pierre Trudeau minced no words in his assessment of such tendencies: "I don't like (Quebec) nationalists because they are bad losers. . . . It is my impression that Quebec will never attain real stature so long as her political class is saddled with nationalists who are cry-babies and blackmailers."[38]

It is not an historical exaggeration to say that Quebec has been like a marriage partner who has threatened to leave if there is conflict. In fairness to Quebec, such a strategy may sometimes have been necessary in order to get the rest of the country's attention. Still, the threat of leaving makes marital life painful; it does little more for national life. Group life of any kind is only possible and productive when those involved make a decision to be involved and then proceed to problem-solve. For Quebec or any other province to go at things from the opposite direction — maintaining that they will only be involved if the problems are solved — is to cause never-ending strain. Post-Meech Lake is only the latest "marital crisis."

Worn out by the ongoing threat of separation, the other marriage partner eventually loses the will to try. The long-feared departure brings anguish, but also considerable relief. Canadians are showing signs of growing tired of Quebec's threats. After all, any province is capable of making the same murmurings. A late 1989 *Maclean's* national survey found that, should Quebec wish to separate, only half of the people in the rest of the country feel an effort should be made to persuade the province to stay. In the words of Preston Manning, leader of the Reform Party, "There is a weariness in the West, a feeling that it is time to ask Quebec to make a commitment to Canada, rather than the other way around." Yet, it's important not to lose sight of the fact that, as the 1990s began, while 33 percent of Quebec residents said they would like to see the province separate from Canada, the figure outside Quebec was only around 20 percent.[39]

Nevertheless, in a culture in which individualism is pervasive, any person and any province that is not perceived to be adding something to one's life cannot be expected to be tolerated for long. Quebec is no exception. Reciprocally, individualism in Quebec may finally lead that province to make its move — either within Confederation or outside it.

PEOPLE-LESS POLITICS

At the individual level, politics in Canada have become self-serving means to self-serving ends. The growing inclination of Canadians to support persons rather than parties and to band together to pursue common causes is indicative of the politicalization of self-interest.

The consumption mentality that is rampant in other spheres such as media, education, and religion is also pervasive in the political arena. Canadians opt for candidates who will serve them best, and think nothing of supporting different parties at the provincial and federal levels. Party platforms, priorities, and performances cannot possibly be expected to satisfy the self-interests of a diverse population. Only the party die-hards will hang in through it all – and even here a defecting recalcitrant or two is not uncommon.

Candidates frequently feel torn between carrying the party banner and hiding it, between identifying with a federal or provincial party and distancing themselves from it. Obviously the major political dilemma is how to satisfy – or at least create the illusion of satisfying – diverse, self-interested constituents. The person who succeeds, with or without the party, wins the election. At their worst, politicians become captive to constituents. Donald Johnston comments that politicians are sensitive to public opinion, and adds, "Government by polls, not principles, is a political reality."[40] Some observers saw the leadership emergence of Audrey McLaughlin, for example, as springing from less than noble party motives. The *Vancouver Province* reported that during the convention, one federal MP told an undecided male delegate that if McLaughlin was elected leader the party's support would automatically jump 5 percent because of gender. An editorial published the same day read, "That she's the first woman in North America to hold major national political office is a confirmation of opportunism rather than a deep commitment to the principles of equality." Perhaps an overstatement, but nonetheless a reminder that parties are "market sensitive."[41]

A burgeoning number of interest groups are lobbying politicians. Some people might argue that such groups are indicative of a more compassionate society, that Canadians are uniting in order that important social changes might take place. According to such an interpretation, to see groups concerned about the environment, peace, and abortion is to see people who care about others.

Clearly, some Canadians who march and lobby are altruistic, concerned about the implications of environmental destruction for future generations, of peace for people whose lives are torn apart by war and oppressive regimes, of abortion for unborn children. But it is equally clear that interest groups often exhibit little interest beyond their own close-knit circles. Many people lobby because they themselves stand to benefit directly if they are successful. The affluent typically lobby for the affluent, minorities for minorities, students for students, and on and on. Chris Wood of *Maclean's*, in reflecting on recent survey findings on the preoccupations of people born in the 1950s and 1960s, writes that "the baby boom generation is rapidly abandoning its former idealism. . . . Now, when baby boomers speak out, they are concerned about close-to-home issues: neighborhood safety, clean air and water, day care and equality in the workplace." Pollster Bruce Anderson of Decima observes, "You can get the idea that it is idealism, but below the surface it's me-oriented."[42]

These seemingly normal patterns of "voting for the person" and "lobbying for one's cause" are patently defective for social life for one obvious reason: the major goal is personal well-being, with questionable concern for the issue of social well-being. The tendency for politics to degenerate into a pathway for realizing self-interest is widespread. If optimum personal and social well-being is to be experienced in this country, such an expression of excessive individualism has to be countered.

In early 1990, columnist Carol Goar wrote that Canada is currently suffering from an acute case of self-absorption. "This is the spring we've been waiting for," she said. "The threat of nuclear war is receding, troops are being called home, repressive regimes are toppling and democracy is breaking out all over the place. Yet here in Canada we remain encased in our own pocket of gloom." Goar pointed out that our politicians had convinced us that we had until June to get our Constitution in order, or the nation would split. Interest rates were high, and ahead lay the objectionable new goods and services tax. Together, such problems seemed to make us feel that we had a right to be miserable. Goar then cut to the heart: "This is absurd. We are not victims of adversity. We are victims of too much rhetoric, too many self-imposed deadlines and too short a collective memory." The challenges facing the likes of Gorbachev in struggling to create a democratic federation, de Klerk in dismantling South African racism, Bush in scaling down the military-industrial complex central to the U.S. economy, and Kohl and Modrow in reuniting Germany are staggering, wrote Goar. She concluded, "Future generations will look back on the late 1980s and early 1990s as one of the most exciting periods in human history, as an era of hope and ferment. Then they will look at Canada, one of the richest, freest countries in the world, wandering around under its own private storm-cloud, feeling wet and cold and persecuted. And they will shake their heads in bewilderment."[43]

Our obsession with the individual and choice, our mosaic madness, is carrying considerable costs. It is affecting our everyday interactions, our most personal relationships, our institutional involvements. The madness is highly destructive, keeping us from experiencing the best possible quality of life, individually and collectively. But the recognition of its presence can mark the beginning of its demise. Social sanity is not beyond the realm of possibility.

8

Moving on to Better Things

Some people looking at Canada today would have us return to the past to recover something of our "paradise lost." But as we have seen, the problem with such a position is that the past was far from a paradise. The emphasis in the post-1950s on the individual and justice has been of critical importance. It has brought with it widespread liberation and hope.

Our social solutions, therefore, do not lie with the past and what we had, because what we had was not enough. Our solutions lie with the future, with what we might have. We need to combine the best of what has gone before with the best of what we now have, in pursuing a quality of life that surpasses anything that we have ever known.

Our problem does not lie with freedom. We need freedom in order to realize our potential as individuals; when we do, society as a whole benefits. Our problem does not lie with pluralism; the contributions of diverse groups in a climate of mutual respect can enrich the total social life. Our problem doesn't lie with individualism; social life gains from the unique contributions of individuals. Our problem doesn't lie with relativism; many things in life are relative and social life loses if we fail to have an atmosphere of exploration and openness.

Our problem in Canada lies with *excess*. Personal freedom frequently takes the form of a kind of individualism that is not accompanied by social commitment. The policy of pluralism becomes an end in itself, rather than functioning as a foundation on which the best of personal and social life can be built. And relativism of the popular variety blindly sanctions choice, discouraging discernment and prematurely eliminating evaluation.

The time has come for us to move on to better things. There is a great need in Canada for individuals and institutions to affirm some essential social and personal goals.

Clarifying What We Want

THE POINT OF IT ALL

International poll data consistently point to people worldwide wanting two things: they want to stay alive and they want to live well.[1] Canadians are no different. Our national preoccupation with coexistence, however, has taken priority over an emphasis on giving our collective energies to pursuing the best life possible. At a conference early in 1990, a federal government employee suggested to me that pluralism in Canada essentially means that "we are supposed to stay out of each other's way." It's hardly an inspiring national goal.

In settling for the goal of coexistence, we have allowed our means to bury our goals. Bilingualism was not intended merely to allow French-speaking and English-speaking Canadians to coexist; the hope was that the two dominant linguistic groups would proceed to work together to produce the best social life possible. The goal of multiculturalism was not simply to permit myriad cultural groups to coexist; the dream was that the various groups would bring the best of their heritages together and produce a nation richer because of its cultural diversity. The Charter of Rights and Freedoms was intended not only to protect individual Canadians; the expectation was that such protection would also result in an enhanced quality of life at all levels — personal, regional, national, global. Our history has made us a pluralistic society. Bilingualism, multiculturalism, and the Charter recognize that historical reality and make coexistence possible.

WHAT CANADIANS WANT MOST

% Indicating "*Very Important*"

	CANADA	BC	PR	ONT	QUE	ATL
Happiness	90	93	90	88	91	90
Freedom	89	95	91	92	81	87
Being loved	84	85	83	84	83	85
Family life	84	88	85	85	79	88
Friendship	83	85	83	82	84	84
Success	67	56	68	66	73	66
Comfortable life	66	63	66	67	65	71

SOURCE: *Project Can85.*

POLICIES WITH A PURPOSE

There is nothing wrong with bilingualism, multiculturalism, and the Charter. They are vitally important building blocks. The problem lies with the fact that the building blocks have become the sum of the building. We have stopped with coexistence. We have seen our victory in two official languages, diverse cultures, and individual rights. Coexistence has become our national obsession, and equality has become the indicator of how well we are coexisting.

Accordingly, our governments, the media, interest groups, and academics continue into the 1990s to give an inordinate amount of attention to monitoring our quest for equality. Better educated young people lead the way in being sensitive to unequal and abusive treatment. Canadians from the tip of Newfoundland through Quebec to the farthest edge of British Columbia want to stay alive and live well. It is to the goal of well-being that we so badly need to redirect our national, institutional, and personal energies.

What is being called for is not the outpouring of some kind of nationalistic fervor that will miraculously bind the country together. The point is not merely to "build a great nation." To have such a goal would be to replace one inadequate national vision with another. Coexistence is not enough; nationalism is not enough. What has the promise of both "inspiring" Canadians as well as drawing them together is the collective pursuit of the best kind of life possible, individually and socially. In the conscious collective quest for well-being, pluralism will find its cause.

Pluralism with a well-being cause is potentially a policy with a powerful outcome. It acknowledges the diversity of a society, but it does more: it guarantees a milieu of freedom and acceptance in which diverse people can work together to experience the best possible quality of life. Discrimination and inequality cannot be allowed to get in the way. Still, they are barriers to realizing the dream of well-being, not the dream itself. Bilingualism is more than learning two languages to expand one's linguistic capabilities. Multiculturalism is more than art festivals and food fairs. The Charter of Rights is more than a license for liberty.

We have a dream, and we also have a game plan. Centrally important to the pursuit of well-being is finding a balance between the individual and the group. Before we encourage viewpoints, we must discern which views are best. The individualism and relativism that make personal freedom possible need to be counterbalanced, or they will make social life impossible.

Getting There: Balance

During our first hundred years after Confederation, we gave excessive attention to the group. Since the early 1960s we have given excessive play to the individual. We must do a better balancing act. No one is saying that it will be easy. Martin Luther King, for example, argued forcefully for the necessity of blending opposites, but pointed out that such balancing is in fact very rare: "The idealists are not usually realistic, and the realists are not usually idealistic. The militants are not known to be passive, nor the passive to be militant. Seldom are the humble self-assertive, or the self-assertive humble." Nevertheless, he said, because "life at its best is a creative synthesis of opposites in fruitful harmony," balance must be pursued.[2]

This side of the border, Pierre Trudeau, for all his emphasis on the individual, has also argued for balance. He points out that, given the need to justify authority without destroying human independence, "the most useful conclusion philosophy has come to is that one must keep an equal distance from both alternatives. Too much authority, or too little, and that is the end of freedom. For oppression also arises from lack of order, from the tyranny of the masses."[3]

There is an urgent need for a better balance in Canada between the individual and the group. The balance is not a social luxury; with the passage of time, it will increasingly become a social necessity. In the face of rampant individualism, people across the country need to be reminded of an important basic fact: in order to experience well-being, Canadians need each other. Such a reality places us in good company. From the time that our ancestors took their first teetering steps on the planet, they recognized that is was easier to stay alive and live well if they stuck together. There was safety and sustenance in numbers; group life also provided emotional, sexual, and spiritual fulfillment.

Our predecessors knew what we know — that personal well-being does not take place in a social vacuum. On the contrary, it's the product of good social environments. In our day, that means good relationships, family life, schools, workplaces, communities, nations, and a good world. Those earliest people undoubtedly grasped a related reality: personal well-being is also the source of social well-being. Canadians who are happy and feel good about their lives are able to make positive contributions to group life. Upbeat, positive, enthusiastic people bring something to others. They have an energizing effect. They enhance personal relationships and enrich organizations. They make an impact.

Social groupings that work well are usually characterized by different but complementary individual contributions. Our abilities, training, and talents vary greatly. But together the diverse parts produce a sum greater than the isolated parts.

Further, human progress is dependent on the interplay of culture and individuals. Groups transmit a cumulative body of knowledge; new arrivals have the potential to build on that base, to create things that were not there before. Creativity isn't the mark of everyone. Sociologist Charles Cooley suggests that, in the give-

and-take process of living in societies, individuals for the most part take.[4]

But some people do "give." The ability of people to reflect and create has resulted in important scientific and technological strides. We have a significant understanding of our world, and even our universe. Our planet is more manageable and more accessible; our lives are much healthier and much longer; our existence is much easier and more problem-free. A few individuals reflected and created; the rest of us share in the benefits.

But we all know that there's a catch: social membership in Canada — or anywhere else — isn't free. Benefits from group life carry a personal price tag. When we enter into relationships and join groups, we have to give up some of our freedom and resources. Social life calls for rules, for guidelines that make collective life possible. Friendships call for trust, marriages for loyalty, organizations for conscientiousness, societies for obedience. Further, in order for groups at any level in Canada to accomplish what they want, people have to take on responsibilities. Canadians also have to contribute resources — from goods and services in previous eras to taxes, surtaxes, and more taxes in our day.

The need for balance between the individual and the group urgently needs to be reaffirmed. Rampant individualism will obliterate social life. It will make interaction empty and relationships tenuous, family life unstable and the workplace less productive, education custom-made and religion a consumer item, citizenship and community involvement nothing but means to self-serving ends.

It also will result in significant costs for future generations. One only needs to look at the environment for a vivid illustration. Terence Penelhum has been among those who have pointed out that our pollution of the water, for example, makes it harder for our successors to keep the water clean than it has been for us. "The effects of our actions are passed on to others," he reminds us, "so that they do not start from scratch, but further behind." If we don't act responsibly, we may reach a point where the damage is so severe that "it becomes impossible for us and our successors to restore it."[5]

Balance between the individual and the group will be associated with a number of characteristics. I want to touch briefly on four – opting in, problem-solving, communication, and accountability.

OPTING IN

Canadians are notorious fence-sitters. Our political involvement has been conditional and tenuous. Canadians of English origin exhibited a nostalgic reluctance to cut ties with Britain and assert national autonomy. Quebec's relationship to the rest of the country continues to be highly conditional. The remaining provinces relate to each other and the federal government with a cautiousness that is seen as becoming of federalism.

Such a political style has spilled over into the culture as a whole. Many Canadians are conservative and cautious, reluctant to take chances, wanting to keep their options open. Our national obsession with tentativeness is a major obstacle to social and personal well-being. If we don't decide what we want, we have no goals to which we can direct our collective and individual energies. The clichés that sum up the dilemma are innumerable: "If we don't know where we're going, we're never going to get there"; and perhaps more telling in the Canadian instance, "If we don't know where we're going, it doesn't matter which road we take."

By now the principle has been so fully supported that it is virtually lawlike: social ties work when we decide we want them to work. Similarly, there is no mystery as to when they end: they end when we decide we want them to end. Internationally, wars have started when nations have chosen to start them. When nations are at peace with one another, it is because they have opted for peace; they take steps to get along. Nationally, states and provinces work well together when they decide to do so.

The same is true of good relationships: people have good ties when they decide to have them. Psychiatrist Scott Peck, for example, goes so far as to say that love is a decision. He defines love as "the *will* to extend one's self for the purpose of nurturing one's own or another's spiritual growth." As such, he writes, love is not a good feeling, or dependence, or self-serving sacrifice. "Genuine love is volitional rather than emotional. The person who truly loves does so because of a decision to love." Love requires a decision because it takes considerable energy and therefore cannot be given to many. To be able to build genuinely loving relationships with a spouse and children, he maintains, is more than most people accomplish in a lifetime.[6]

Earlier, in discussing relationships, I was critical of both the old "fusion model" that often obliterated women, as well as the new "autonomy model" that frequently makes relationships highly self-serving. Following Peck's thinking, relationships in Canada often are in trouble because, when we speak about being in love, what many of us have in mind is *being loved*. The people we choose are people who make us feel happy and good, who are interesting and stimulating — all traits reflecting what they bring to us. Rarely do we think in terms of what we might be able to bring to *them*. Marriage Canadian-style tends to symbolize a decision to receive each other's love, rather than a decision to love each other.

And when the promised goods are not forthcoming, relationships based on mutual self-interest are doomed to fail. When we no longer feel "loved" — that is, happy, good, stimulated — we no longer want the relationship. In contrast, when two people decide that they want to love each other in the manner that Peck describes relationships do not come and go. A problem-solving outlook kicks in. Social ties work when we decide we want them to work.

The same principle holds for problems within societies. In 1936, American sociologist Willard Waller wrote a stimulating essay on social problems. He argued that if we really wanted to solve social problems — including poverty and housing shortages — we could. But we don't — because it is not in the best interests of everyone to do so.[7] One person's problem is another person's opportunity. As a commodities trading instructor in the film *Limit Up* put it, "The problem is not a shortage of food but a shortage of money. If poor people had money, we'd be happy to feed them."

We can have national unity — if we want it. We can have good relationships and gratifying institutional experiences — if we want them. To decide we want the best in personal and social life is the first step in making it happen.

Life beyond coexistence is possible. If we are to approximate optimum living, globally, nationally, institutionally, and individually, the starting place is to decide that we want it.

PROBLEM-SOLVING

When we decide that we want group life "to work," it becomes possible to give our energies to bringing it about. Of central importance to that process is a problem-solving outlook. A person with such an outlook recognizes that problems are inevitable but solvable.

Here again, Peck is helpful. He begins his *The Road Less Traveled* with the words, "Life is difficult."[8] He suggests that, once we see problems not as aberrations but as a natural and inevitable part of life, it becomes possible to turn our energy from being surprised by them and resentful of them to dealing with them.

People with a problem-solving outlook acknowledge that to live is to encounter problems along the way. They are not unexpected blips on our daily screens that sink us into depression and despair. Rather, they arise because that's the nature of life. We will solve them as they come along. The initial response to a problem is emotional — disappointment, anger, pain, regret. But the next response, following as soon as possible, is, "What can I do about it?"

Productive personal and group life is characterized by such a mentality. Canadians at every level of social life — ranging from everyday interaction through family life, friendships, relationships, and organizational involvement to the provincial and national arenas of political life — are in need of problem-solving outlooks. To some extent, it obviously exists. Often it does not.

Large numbers of people in service occupations, for example, are adept at focusing on problems rather than solutions — "Your motor is shot." "You probably will miss the plane." "You don't have the right pieces of I.D. to cash the cheque." "If you can't find it on the shelf, we don't have it." They excel at reminding us that we do, indeed, have a problem.

Professionals also are hardly exempt. Teachers and professors occasionally respond to a student's distress over grades with indifference and detachment. Physicians often maintain a demeaning posture toward patients' time schedules, routinely overbooking and making people wait for long periods in penlike areas aptly dubbed "waiting rooms."

In sharp contrast to such people is the individual who recognizes that we have a problem and sets out to see what can be done about it. "The car has some problems, but we can fix it." "I'll call the gate and let them know you're trying to catch the plane." "I'll check with my supervisor and see if there's any way we can cash the cheque." "If there's none on the shelf I'll check in the back." "Let's see if we can turn that grade around." At minimum, the person with a problem-solving mentality says, "I don't know if I can work this out, but I'll do the best I can."

The reason such a decision to "make life work" is so important is that it switches us into a problem-solving mode. The positive posture exists because of our choice. As a father or mother, for example, we don't take the position, "If my infant son or daughter is good or happy, I will look after them." Rather, we take the stance, "Because they are my children, I will look after them." Two statesmen could readily stomp away from the negotiation table. But they won't if they have decided that, no matter what, they are going to find a solution to a difficult political matter.

On the other hand, when we have a falling out with a parent, for example, it never is because of an event or a series of events. It is because of how we decide to respond to events. The relationship fails because at some point we decide to stop problem-solving and let the relationship fail. If we both chose to reaffirm our decision to have a good tie, then the relationship would continue to be mutually gratifying.

In Canada, wherever there is dissent and hostility — between provinces, cultural groups, men and women, abortion groups, and so on — the major question is not, "Can the problems be resolved?" but, "Do we want to resolve the problems?" If we decide in favor of resolution, we will solve our problems. There are no exceptions to the rule.

Canada is a nervous nation. We are constantly on guard for signs of conflict, for claims of unequal treatment. Such a posture is largely the product of having no national dreams beyond getting along. Consequently, we give much of our energy to rooting out any semblance of racism, sexism, intolerance, or bigotry. Problems of equity represent "news" in Canada and are given considerable attention by our media. We are a country that constantly worries about itself. We are like the couple that continually focuses on their relationship, rather than living out life together.

We also have a tendency to take polar positions. Categories of Canadians line up on different sides of fences: women vs. men, minorities vs. majorities, region vs. region, labor vs. management, pro-lifers vs. pro-choicers, alleged haters vs. alleged haters of haters. Such a win-lose mentality makes social life unenjoyable to unbearable. It results in winners and losers — producing an outcome in the name of equality that is no different from that which was produced in the name of elitism.

From the time we tried to form a nation, we have been inclined to focus on our national problems rather than our solutions, to nurture getting along rather than getting on with good living. What's more, it shows. American sociologist Seymour Lipset, after examining our literature, suggests that we have something of what he calls "a loser mentality." He cites Canadian writer J. M. S. Careless who writes that, in contrast, Americans "cannot conceive of losing unless there is a conspiracy somewhere." Lipset notes that our monthly magazine, *Saturday Night*, in its New Year's issue of 1986, had as its front-cover title, "Beautiful Losers — A Canadian Tradition."

Nationally and individually, we are in need of a problem-solving outlook. For too long we have been content to keep the country together. Many of us have acted victimized by our own personal problems. We need to do a better job of instilling a problem-solving mentality. People from the west coast to the east coast have to be taught that "we are all in this together." A better Canada requires that we no longer pit ourselves against each other and demand our individual rights. The appeal of student union president Alain Perreault at the funeral of the Montreal students needs to be heard far beyond the halls of Notre Dame Cathedral and beyond only the sexism issue: "Let us work together, let us come together . . . let us together find hope."

It is extremely important for us to instill in Canadians the basic idea that social and personal problems are inevitable, but that by working together, we can solve them. Upon his election as prime minister of Poland in August 1989, Solidarity acitivist Tadeusz Mazowiecki shook hands with members of the former Communist government and said: "I am counting on cooperation. The principle of struggle, aimed at eliminating one's opponent, must be replaced by cooperation. Otherwise we will not move from a totalitarian system to democracy."[9] Upon his landslide victory in February 1990, which produced the first NDP federal seat in Quebec, Phil Edmonston said: "What better proof of the tolerance of Quebeckers. We as Canadians, French Canadians and English Canadians, have much more in common than what separates us, so let's build a great Canada."[10]

In human interaction that ranges from the immediate through the local, regional, and national to the global, a problem-solving outlook is urgently needed.

A Distinct Illustration: Quebec Few issues generate more emotion in Canadian life than the possibility of Quebec's separation. The very thought sets off alarms in English Canada, with the media leading the way in declaring that separation is synonymous with crisis. Many politicians and their constituents in Quebec approach the idea triumphantly. The late June 1990 announcement that Quebec's future would be debated by a special nonpartisan commission was greeted with enthusiasm by many Quebeckers. The rest of the country appeared to play the role of anxious and helpless onlookers. Quebec MPs — who seemed to be resigning daily from both the Liberal and Conservative parties — did so with declarations of newfound liberty. The short-term result? Momentum in French Canada, paralysis in English Canada.

In the midst of the hoopla and gnashing of teeth, it's time that someone got the message out: *there is no crisis.* The only crisis is one that we have created.

At this point in history, Quebec is again reviewing its options.

Every other province has the same prerogative. There is no need for Quebec to be particularly triumphant or obnoxious, to use separation as a threat, to be rude to a visiting monarch. There also is no need for the rest of Canada to play the role of over-dependent, sniveling siblings, frantically trying to encourage one of their older sisters not to leave home.

No, Quebec's reflections on its future do not represent a crisis for Canada. Despite the irresponsible declarations of the alarmists, Canada will continue to exist, regardless of what Quebec decides to do.

A problem-solving outlook calls for Quebec to carefully consider what is best for Quebec — to find solutions to its cultural and demographic problems. In the meantime, the rest of Canada needs to back off. To the extent that it is appropriate, of course, the country needs to assert its desire not to lose Quebec. But in order for Quebec to experience what it wants, it might have to "leave home." The rest of Canada has to be prepared to accept that.

Quebec needs time to decide what is best for Quebec. Once that decision is made, the rest of the country needs likewise to problem-solve, developing the most positive and productive relationship possible with "the new Quebec."

The situation in Quebec does not represent a crisis for Canada. What will create a crisis is our failure to treat the situation as solvable. In that case, our obsession with a fictitious "coming disaster" will be self-fulfilling, creating anxiety and distress. It doesn't have to happen.

COMMUNICATION

In order for problem-solving to take place, the communication lines have to be up. The importance of communication appears to be well understood. We know that groups cannot function well unless people talk to each other and listen to each other. Beyond face-to-face conversations, groups draw on an extensive range of print and electronic methods in their attempts to communicate and coordinate. The necessity of good communication is a reality that appears to be fairly well understood in a wide variety of social situations — husbands and wives, parents and teens, employers and employees, politicians and constituents.

Precisely because two-way communication is stressed in so many group situations, it's puzzling why communication is so conspicuous by its absence in one critically important area. We might call it the National Exception. When majorities and minorities deal with each other, the communication ideal is suspended. It sounds strange to say it but it's time it was said: In Canada, we can't talk. The rules of communication are well understood: minorities who feel disadvantaged are allowed to speak out, but majorities are not.

Let's get down to specifics.

A major reason Elijah Harper could succeed in stalling the passing of the Meech Lake accord by the Manitoba legislature was that no one could "bad mouth" a Native. Let's not fool ourselves. A significant number of people were mad; had a pro-youth or pro-abortion or pro-religious member of the legislature used the same tactics to promote his or her cause, they would have faced incredible abuse. But in Canada, officially at least, minorities cannot be attacked. One syndicated columnist noted that the Anglo-Canadian majority was reduced to the role of virtual spectators, with even the most rabid Quebec nationalists suddenly left speechless. "It's one thing to level accusations about being kicked around by the English-speaking majority," he wrote, but "it's not easy to switch in midsentence to make the same accusations against one modest Cree."[11]

In keeping with the communication rules, if Natives feel they are being discriminated against when they are trying to obtain housing, they can call a news conference to register their concern. If a Jewish organization believes that anti-Semitism is on the increase, it can issue a press release. If women feel they are experiencing discrimination in the workplace, they can hold a press conference. If Sikhs want to wear turbans in the workplace, they can turn to the media to express their concern over the opposition they encounter.

However, the communication is all one-way. If the majorities involved do not agree with the claims of the minorities, they are labeled racists or bigots. Imagine a mayor who maintains that Natives are not being discriminated against, a Catholic priest who says that anti-Semitism has not increased, a man who suggests that women are receiving equal treatment in the workplace, a chief of police who does not favor turbans in the city force.

Canadians do not allow majorities to speak out. And we don't encourage minorities and majorities to speak to each other. The norm is not positive communication between groups. Rather, people *speak out* throught the media.

Beyond civil liberties, the social health of our nation requires that all Canadians be given the chance to voice their perceptions. If the rules of the game allow only those who are feeling abused to talk, we won't solve our problems. Instead, what we will cultivate is growing hostility on the part of the majorities who have been instructed to remain silent.

Take the issue of turbans beings worn in the RCMP. Western Canadians or others who took exception to the proposal were labeled as racists by everyone from the Prime Minister to the editors of the *Lethbridge Herald*. They weren't allowed to speak up. Contrary to the critics, there was more than racism involved. Thompson columnist Stewart MacLeod, for example, wrote shortly after the decision was made that he personally didn't have "any overpowering feelings" about the outcome. "But what strikes me as grossly unfair," he said, "is the growing tendency to associate all opposition to the change as a form of racism." Racism may have been a factor with some opponents, MacLeod continued, but "to tar everyone with the same, broad brush is not only doing a great disservice to those who feel strongly about traditions . . . it may even encourage a new, underground form of racism." Those who wrote letters felt obliged to give paragraphs to stressing they were not racially motivated; for many there was an obvious reluctance to even raise the issue for fear they would be misunderstood.

MacLeod suggested that most people outside the West have never understood the special feeling that westerners have had for the RCMP and its traditions. He recalled John Diefenbaker's opposition to a Liberal proposal to replace "RCMP" on Mountie vehicles with "police." "This government," Mr. Diefenbaker thundered, "with its preponderance of ministers from Ontario and Quebec, where there are provincial police forces, knows nothing about how we in the West regard the RCMP — absolutely nothing." The change never went through. MacLeod made a very incisive point: the Solicitor General said the Charter of Rights would force the change because the dress code discriminates against certain religious groups. If so, then "it seems to me that . . . those tradition-minded, and well-meaning, opponents should not have to fear racial accusations when they ask legitimate questions."[12]

There's another important issue that largely has been lost. One reason that it's so important that we talk is that we don't really know each other as well as we think we do. Stereotypes abound. Sociologist Jean Burnet has pointed out, for example, that minority groups are not in fact a homogeneous, integrated group making up of one-third of the population. They are extremely varied, and not necessarily positively disposed toward one another — or toward the majority. Conversely, Burnet reminds us, historically *all* people of British origin were not hostile toward newcomers, nor were *all* newcomers receptive and kind to Anglo-Saxons. Because we are so different, we have to talk.[13]

To the extent that we have decided that we want to pursue optimum social ties in Canada and are committed to a posture of problem-solving, we can talk, and talk openly — knowing that our tie is already in place and is not dependent on what we say and hear.

Such breaking of the "we're not supposed to raise that" norm can be both surprising and, I'd like to think, refreshing and valuable. A simple illustration. For years I have taught a section on intergroup relations as part of my Introductory Sociology course. I have presented material on prejudice and discrimination in Canada in a detached manner. Students, a fair number of whom have been Native, Asian, and Black, typically sit back and passively take down the notes and feed them back on the exams. In the past two years, I have been interrupting this rotelike process by interjecting some pointed statements and questions. "We need to talk about these things. Are the claims about discrimination in housing and service valid? Do those of you who are members of cultural minorities find that this is happening to you? And the rest of you — you who form the majority — are you or your parents or friends doing the kinds of discriminatory things researchers say you are? You are walking pieces of data. What about it?" I have sometimes brought in some well-known members of minorities to get the conversation started. Student reaction at first has been surprise and uneasiness. To be so direct — well, it's not the Canadian way. My view? We have got to talk to each other about these things. If we don't, then we'll remain polarized with problems that won't go away.

Calgary lawyer Ron Ghitter laid the issue out bluntly in a recent address. "Is it not time to ask honest questions with honest appraisals and honest evaluation," he said, "rather than this continual walking-on-eggshells approach where everyone is afraid to say what they really mean unless it's among their closest friends? We must stop operating behind the facade of fairness and our legislation. We must speak to the issues honestly or we will never make any progress."[14]

If western Canadians and Quebeckers are ever going to begin to understand each other, then we've got to be able to talk. Westerners have lots of questions they want to ask — but seldom if ever are allowed to. They also badly need to hear what average people living in Quebec have to say. Canadian men and women need to talk more to each other. In too many settings, men oppress women and women sit back and say little. In other instances, women have power and men sit back with mouths closed for fear of saying something wrong. It's not a good situation. We need to talk to each other.

John Trent, a political science professor at the University of Ottawa, seems to feel the same way. In July, 1990, Trent held the founding meeting of Dialogue Canada, a group that wants to bring Canadians together to talk, in order that they might deal with ignorance and misunderstanding. Regional chapters and an eventual national organization are planned. It's a step in the right direction.

ACCOUNTABILITY

A fourth basic principle essential to well-being is accountability. Our ancestors knew well that social life was impossible unless individuals were willing to be responsible for their behavior — to own up to what they had done. Our criminal justice system, for example, is based on the assumption that people are responsible for what they do or say. If group life is to be fair and just, individuals must take responsibility for their actions.

Unfortunately, individualism and relativism have the potential to reduce one's sense of accountability. On some occasions some Canadians can hide within their roles, claiming that because of their position — in medicine or education, law enforcement or the judiciary — they are not accountable to anyone. In April 1990, for example, a judge was being investigated by the Manitoba Judicial Council. The judge's lawyer challenged the council's right to hear the complaints against the judge, who allegedly had made disparaging comments about women. His lawyer argued that judges have absolute immunity when making remarks in the course of rendering verdicts.[15]

Beyond people occupying seemingly exempted roles, excessive individualism in the life of anyone can lead people to say that they are simply expressing themselves freely; if other people cannot handle what they express, then, "tough — I have my rights." Relativism chimes in: "No behavior is any better than any other behavior."

Such thinking is socially castastrophic. In relationships, when conflict takes place, individualism leads to an impasse. She is upset because he had an unannounced dinner with a female friend. He insists that it was quite innocent, and if it bothers her, then "that's her problem." Accountability, on the other hand, brings different rules to the situation. If his behavior bothered her, then it is not merely "her problem." He *did*, after all, have dinner with this other person. He doesn't have to accept her interpretation, but he does have to "own" his behavior. The incident did take place. What is up for grabs is the meaning of the incident.

Accountability is badly needed in a Canada where we are maximizing the right to individual behavior. Otherwise we can say goodbye to our aspirations of approximating "a just society." Individuals and groups have to be willing to be accountable for their performances. What's more, when they are not, accountability needs to be called for.

Members of minorities who fail to achieve their goals can readily blame their failures on injustice. They can say that almost anything they don't like is due to their gender, their race, their ethnic tie, their age, their disability, or their appearance. Members of majority groups likewise can deny the role that they themselves play in what takes place. They can blame their problems on the fact that they are *not* female, not French, not bilingual, not young, and so on.

Some quick examples. An Ontario professor says that he is not being hired because he is a male. The school has introduced a policy of affirmative action; it intends to hire only females for the next ten years. Accountability means that the professor is willing to consider the possibility that he may not be the best candidate for the job, and that the college acknowledge that it is engaging in a policy of reverse discrimination as a way to correct past wrongs against women applicants.

A feminist leader points out that there is backlash against women from men, reflecting resentment over the economic and occupational gains women have been experiencing. Accountability would involve women considering that it may be a backlash to gains, but that it also may reflect a reaction to the interaction styles of some of the feminists themselves. Men, in being accountable, would reflect on the extent to which they themselves have made such behavior necessary, by being so slow to respond to the past and present inequities to women.

Southern Alberta Natives called a press conference in late 1989 to report that they are experiencing discrimination in renting houses and apartments. The chairman of the Alberta Human Rights Commission agreed and warned the region that it needed to correct its practices. Accountability means that the Native community would acknowledge that Native tenants have not had a good record in the care and upkeep of rental units in the area, but stressing that every effort is being made to improve the situation, and new arrivals to the city need to be given a chance. Accountability would also mean that landlords acknowledge that, yes, they are wary about Native tenants in the light of past experiences, but that they are willing to work with the Native community in trying to resolve their mutual concerns.

Social life involves interaction — stimulus and response. In a society such as ours, where premier attention is given to equality, allegations that groups and individuals are not being treated justly will be common. And so they should be. People who are victims of racism and sexism, bigotry and prejudice, exploitation and abuse have cause to speak out. In a just society, unjust treatment must be decried. But there is no virtue in individuals and organizations being falsely accused. Clearly, justice and fairness call for all actors in the social drama to be accountable.

For example, nonpersonal descriptions of behavior — racism, closed-mindedness, child abuse — can readily be transformed into personal ascriptions — racist, bigot, child molester. Such labels carry considerable weight, and once assigned to individuals and organizations, have significant social implications. Unfortunately, labels are incredibly self-sufficient creatures. They produce personal and social consequences whether they are factually sound or the product of someone's fertile imagination.

In the light of the ease with which labels can be applied and the damage which they can do, it is imperative that those who label be accountable. To "cry wolf" is not merely to get no help when the wolf arrives; it also leads to wolf-hunts. In a just society, labeling has to be done carefully and responsibly. Otherwise labels can become weapons that can be indiscriminately used on individuals and organizations that are not to one's liking. Those who label have to be held accountable.

Freedom of speech has to have limits this side of character assassination. Three junior high school girls accused a Canadian school teacher of fondling them. In late 1989, the court found him innocent. The label nonetheless will remain. The teacher's career in the community and perhaps anywhere is over. And the girls? To the best of my knowledge, nothing was done to address the issue that their charge was contrived. Presumably because of their ages, they were not held accountable for their allegations.

During the 1989 NDP convention, one delegate was asked why she didn't want to support Dave Barrett. "Because he's a sexist," replied the delegate. When the reporter asked, "What do you mean?" the delegate responded, "He behaves like a prima donna, not like an ordinary person."[16] If operational definitions of terms like "sexist," "racist," and "bigot" are allowed that kind of range, virtually no one in Canada is going to be safe. In writing about the inclination of people to assign inappropriate, inflammatory political labels, the counsel for the Canadian Civil Liberties Association, Alan Borovoy, notes, "Inevitably, there will be a temptation to dismiss as academic these admonitions about language. . . . We cannot afford to blur the distinctions among the injustices we face. Of course, we must vigorously fight injustice in this country. But the rhetoric we use has to be tailored to the evil involved."[17]

I am hardly trying to offer an exhaustive prescription for better balance between the individual and the group. Yet the four features briefly discussed — opting in, a problem-solving outlook, communication, and accountability — are among the characteristics that experts from yesterday and today recognize as centrally important to social life at every level — the national, the regional, the organizational, the relational.

What makes excessive individualism potentially so socially dangerous is that individualism gone wild runs counter to all four of these basic principles. Opting in is dependent on personal payoffs. Problem-solving is seen as optional, based on whether it is in one's own best interests to resolve a problem area. Communication is not viewed as necessary if it is not to one's advantage either to listen or talk. Accountablity puts demands on individuals that some would just as soon avoid.

In short, excessive individualism runs contrary to all four of these essential components of productive social life. To fail to find a balance between the individual and the group is consequently to invite social chaos.

Pursuing the Best

Relativism allegedly makes a pluralistic society possible. But taken to excess, relativism can rob a society of one of its richest assets. In legitimizing diverse choices, it can stand in the way of exploring the best of available options. The danger is that we give everything an "A." We blur bad with better, mediocrity with excellence. The net result is that we do not pursue the best, either as individuals or as a nation. Personally, we settle for viewpoints.

Nationally, we settle for coexistence. Relativism leads us to misread the finish line.

ENCOURAGING VIEWS

One of the most unfortunate aspects of making bilingualism and multiculturalism ends in themselves in Canada is that we fail to give adequate emphasis to diversity as a national resource. We stress tolerance and understanding, when we should also be giving major emphasis to social strength and collective assets. Precisely because we have the resource of English and French cultures, we can be a better nation. Beyond associating multiculturalism with variations in clothes and foods and festivals, it means that we can benefit corporately from the diverse contributions of people who have come together from all parts of the world. The whole can indeed be more than merely the mosaic sum of diverse parts. Our diversity is one of our greatest resources. In Thomas Berger's words, that "diversity shouldn't terrify us: it should be our strength, not our weakness."[18]

If we view Canadian society as a group of cultures that coexist like tiles in an art piece, we have nothing but parts beside parts. Socially, such a view translates into mosaic madness. But if we have a design in mind, if we try to pool our varied resources to create a society that is more than just the sum of its diverse parts, then we can work together in pursuing optimum well-being. Here the mosaic model provides an enriched means to Pierre Trudeau's "sanctuary of sanity."

In keeping with such an ideal, we need to continue to encourage diverse expression in Canada. Precisely because we are so different, we have much to bring to every imaginable area of Canadian life – finance, science, technology, production, politics, education, family life, leisure, the arts, religion, with the list going on and on. Our heterogeneity is matched by few nations, and it will only accelerate in the future. Anxiety about our diversity needs to give way to the passionate cultivation of the expression of viewpoints.

ENCOURAGING DISCERNMENT

In the next breath, it is critically important for Canadians to evaluate those different viewpoints carefully. Specifically because we will be inclined to posit so many possibilities, discernment is indispensable to determining which options are "bad, better, and best." Everything's possible. But everything does not necessarily lead to the same end. What we need to understand better is what values and what kinds of behavior can best contribute to personal and social well-being.

If that is to happen, then the current obsession with "mindless relativism" needs to be replaced by reflective critiques of the benefits and costs of available options. Unreflective relativism needs to give way to the search for what is best. Tangibly, this means that Canadians young and old need to be encouraged to pursue the best in everything, and to make reflective choices. They need to be taught the difference between tolerating ideas and examining which ideas are the most sound, between accepting the lifestyles of others and determining which lifestyles contribute the most to personal and social well-being.

It also means that we need to be carrying out research and evaluation in order to provide Canadians with the information they require to make the best decisions. A quick example. Statistics Canada, in its 1990 publication *Report on the Demographic Situation in Canada 1988*, includes an analysis by sociologist Carl Grindstaff entitled "Long-Term Consequences of Adolescent Marriage and Fertility."[19] Grindstaff looks at what happens to Canadian females who marry in their teens, highlighting "certain consequences of early childbearing." He finds that the earlier the marriage and the earlier the childbearing, the lower the incidence of university completion, income, and location in a professional occupation. The observation of family expert Harriet Presser, he suggests, is apt: "To the extent that marriage, schooling and employment are socially advantageous to women, and women themselves have such aspirations, the data indicate that teenage motherhood has negative social consequences."

Such a report is not judgmental. But it is extremely helpful in laying out the consequences of young women choosing to marry before twenty. It has the potential to help to provide a basis that young people can use in opting for the best of available choices.

In Canada, we need to encourage diverse viewpoints. And then we need to evaluate them.

ENCOURAGING RISK-TAKING

Advancement requires the taking of chances. "Where one is" represents the known, which brings with it a measure of security and comfort – whether warranted or not. To introduce change is to introduce uncertainty and the possibility of loss.

So it is that if we as individuals are to move forward and experience more, we have to be willing to run the risk of experiencing less. Social progress, in turn, is highly dependent on creative people who are willing to risk the consequences of deviating from the majority. The irony is that creative nonconformity is frequently resisted. In Albert Einstein's oft-cited words, "Great spirits have always encountered violent oposition from mediocre minds." Precisely because society is so nonreceptive to the very innovation from which it benefits, individuals who will "take chances" are always needed.

Today, the importance of risk-taking is given considerable play. Therapists and personal growth advocates are calling on people to "push out their boundaries" and to "abandon their comfort zones." The old folk-wisdom cliché of "nothing ventured, nothing gained" has been co-opted, translated, and expanded by the experts. Canadians are being reminded that the key to realizing their goals – be they social, financial, physical, occupational, or educational – lies in their willingness to "take a risk." We need to risk being rejected when we try to resolve a relational problem, risk losing money in trying to improve our financial situation, risk losing the security of an old career in turning to one we prefer, risk failing an evening university course in initiating a return to school, risk not being comfortable in doing "something" we have put off learning until now – skiing, piano playing, public speaking, for example.

In Canadian group life, our pluralistic norms can inhibit us from taking chances for fear that we will sound too opinionated or dogmatic, or be labeled racist or sexist.

But if Canada is to be a country where freedom of expression truly exists, people must have the courage – and the integrity – to insist on their right to be heard. Too often in the past, the ideological right has suffocated the voices of the left; these days the left is inclined to suffocate the voices of the right. Religious groups are indicted in blanket fashion for contributing to racism; REAL women are condemned by the feminists. One is reminded of Woody Allen's footnote in introducing himself to a producer in *Annie Hall*: "I'm a bigot — but for the left." The corrective to right-wing bigotry is not a left-wing counterpart. In a free society, we need to be free to take chances, including ideological chances.

Just as large numbers of Canadians unthinkingly accepted the absolutism of the past, so very large numbers are unthinkingly accepting the relativism of the present. Most of us in academic, media, and religious settings, for example, play a pretty safe game. We don't stick our necks out very far. Moreover, we have the audacity to applaud ourselves for being open-minded, when the reality is that our relativism has frequently made our minds airtight.

As a country, we have done a good job of laying a pluralistic foundation. Now we need to consolidate our gains and move on. Maximum well-being requires that we find a balance between the individual and the group, and that together we pursue the best kind of life possible. Such a Canadian dream is not beyond our grasp.

9

THE KEY PLAYERS

IDEAS HAVE SOCIAL SOURCES. Our values, beliefs, and aspirations for the most part can be traced back to people, notably to family and friends, the media and the classroom, to our social experiences. If we are going to move on to better things in Canada, the twin themes of balance and pursuit of the best will have to receive greater support from our primary sources of ideas.

The tragic massacre at the University of Montreal in December 1989 clearly identified the key idea sources at this point in Canadian history. The media reported the event to the nation and also interpreted it. Education's input took the form of experts being asked by the media to provide the color commentary. Religion neither was asked for comment nor had much to say, but was called upon to perform the rites of passage. Politicians tended to play a reactive rather than a leadership role, with respect both to the event itself and to those who were calling for change. Voices from other spheres were scarcely heard.

If Canada is to find a better balance between the individual and the group and do a better job of pursuing the best in everything, the media are going to have to lead the way. Our schools are in a position to play an important if not primary role. Religion has the resources to be a key player, but has to be regarded as a long-shot contributor. Government will probably continue primarily to respond to the initiatives of these three institutions along with other interest groups.

The movement toward improved balance and pursuit of the best will be very difficult in view of the fact that all four institutions have been infiltrated; they all have been significantly shaped by excessive individualism and excessive relativism. Still, they are the key players in turning things around. They need to be awakened. And they can be. Fortunately, we have the personal and institutional resources to make it happen.

Individuals

THE STARTING PLACE

Institutions are not mysterious, monolithic entities that operate in isolation from individuals. While they shape us, they also are shaped *by* us. Institutions, after all, are run by individuals whose values and outlooks reflect those of the culture they live in. The people responsible for the content of the late news, for example, are influenced by values and views of reality, just like the rest of us. Further, institutions must be responsive to the public to stay alive. Newspapers need subscribers, schools need parents, religions need members, politicians need voters.

Consequently, the social changes that are needed in Canada will depend on institutions, particularly television, but they'll start with individuals — people like you and me. We can exert social influence in two major ways: as participants within the array of social institutions in which we find ourselves — starting with the family, and through putting pressure on the key institutional sources of ideas — the media, education, religion, and government.

The history of social change is the history of individuals working through institutions, and of individuals joining together to offer a collective voice that could not be ignored. Change will begin with individuals and spread to institutions.

FRUSTRATION IN NEED OF EXPLANATION

During the past few years, I have ventured out of the barren coulees of southern Alberta and done extensive speaking and media work across Canada. My experiences have corroborated what my surveys and those of others have been finding: large numbers of Canadians are feeling deeply frustrated with the country. The all-time low endorsement of the Conservative government in 1990 was one indication of the faintness of the nation's pulse.

It's not that Canadians are unhappy with life. But as they look at national and provincial leadership, they see politicians who are out of sync with where people are and what they want.

My sense is that large numbers of Canadians are weary and frustrated, but they aren't exactly sure why. In discussing the implications of excessive individualism and excessive relativism with audiences in various parts of the country, I have found that the analysis has been striking a responsive chord. Most Canadians are not opposed to tolerating and accepting the country's diverse groups. They see the importance of having two official languages. But in Quebec and elsewhere they want to get on with life. They want to live and live well. They want to go beyond coexistence and set their sights on a more inspiring national dream. They are tired of being told that the Canadian end in all is to tolerate choice. Many think that the federal and provincial governments are doing little to allow them to move on to better things. Their discontent comes to the surface when politicians act as though there is no point to pluralism except to tolerate and accept difference.

The national mood is ripe for constructive interpretation and positive change. That mood is readily apparent in the enthusiasm of post-Meech Quebec. But it is also apparent in the exasperation of post-Meech English Canada. As Canadians come to understand more clearly why they are upset, as the mosaic curtain is lifted, enabling them to see the quality of life that is possible, individuals and institutions will begin to feel the effects.

The Media

The fact that the media are the modern-day creators of the world should not come as bad news to anyone. Media, in a technical sense, are just "mediums" for conveying ideas. What is at issue is the content of those ideas. The phenomenal capacity of the media both to construct social reality and influence the kind of life that people think they want introduces incredible possibilities for well-being. The debate between media freedom and media irresponsibility should not obscure the much more important fact:

never before in history has an institution had the potential to make such a powerful contribution to personal and social well-being. However, if that is to happen, some important developments must take place.

A MORE SELF-CONSCIOUS MEDIA

It is not at all apparent that people involved in the media in Canada readily grasp the extent of the media's power. The ease with which programs and papers unveil stories that contribute to anxiety and fear, distrust and skepticism, seems to suggest that many people in the media are guided largely by ratings and revenues, subscriptions and profit. At their best, members of the media often underestimate their influence. They assume that viewers and readers can differentiate between what they see, read, and hear, versus what is actually happening in "the real world." At their worst, the media are simply indifferent to the possible negative social and personal consequences of focusing on the deviant, the bizarre, and the novel.

Technology has revolutionized communications and given the media unprecedented power to shape both individuals and social life. An elementary first step in ensuring that the power of the media is used to enhance well-being is for the media clearly to comprehend their accentuated ability to influence people, societies, and the world. In short, people at the controls need to know the capabilities of the glistening new mind-making machines. The shaping of individuals and society is an extremely important enterprise. It calls for a highly self-aware Canadian media.

A MORE SOCIALLY CONSCIOUS MEDIA

Unfortunately, mere awareness of their power will hardly guarantee that members of the media will contribute to well-being. There is little doubt that, for many in the communications business, primacy is given to success and profit. Nevertheless, we need media that recognize that, while they have the freedom to do virtually anything they want in the name of freedom or dollars, to do so is to inflict significant personal and social damage.

The media not only should be aware of its power to influence perception but — with due respect to ratings and profits —

should also be committed to using that power to further well-being. The media are in a position to impress on Canadians the necessity of balance between individuality and group ties. Currently the balance isn't there. Personal gratification and personal freedom are the dominant themes in programs, stories, and advertisements.

Beyond being known as the morbid and negative bearer of the latest bad news, the media are in a position to demonstrate the importance of opting in and problem-solving. Tragedies and problems and perversion will forever intrigue the public; no one is expecting the media to abandon such material. But this is not to say that such reports cannot be supplemented by a position that problems need to be resolved, as well as indications of how individuals and society might find solutions and hope. Responsible media might also provide some indication of how common and "representative" violent crimes and their locations really are, so as not to have everyone expecting to encounter violence in every small motel and underground parking lot, every shower and basement.

The media also have the potential to personify the importance of communication in making social life possible. They not only can continue to encourage the diverse voices of Canadians to be heard, but also insist that individuals and groups be accountable for their behavior. Beyond reporting backlashes to feminism and racism, for example, they can and should be asking not just the accused to respond — as is typically the case — but also the accusers, to make them accountable for their role in "the discrimination drama."

It hardly takes a cynical sociologist to point out that the media in Canada frequently contribute to social problems rather than to their alleviation. Old fires, like separatism, are fanned, and innocuous debates between individuals and groups are fueled, in order to do little more than produce an item that will be here today and gone tomorrow. We need much more.

Take immigration, for example. The media have contributed to a gross misunderstanding of the nature and extent of immigration in Canada. With their major markets in the cities that receive the largest number of immigrants — Toronto, Montreal, and Vancouver — the media create the idea that the country is experiencing phenomenal influxes of newcomers, who are frequently being met with resistance. *Maclean's*, for example, ran a July 1989 front cover story with the headline "An Angry Racial Backlash" imposed on the captioned photo of Immigration Minister Barbara McDougall.[1]

The statistical truth of the matter is that the 1988 immigration level — at about 160,000 — was almost exactly the same as twenty years ago. In fact, between 1983 and 1986, it had dropped to under 100,000 per year. Besides being somewhat lower, what has changed is the composition of those coming to Canada. In 1988, for the first time, more than half were Asians, with people from developing countries also more numerous. The more common migration phenomenon in Canada is interprovincial movement, totaling close to 350,000 people each year. In 1988, Ontario, for example, received about 90,000 immigrants — and just over 100,000 people from other provinces; in B.C., the corresponding score was about 10,000 to 25,000 in favor of people from other provinces.[2]

The media are also capable of encouraging Canadians to pursue the best in all things. They can help provide us with the kind of information we need in order to make informed choices. In recent years, at least, such educational contributions have not been readily apparent. Two of the most publicized issues have been the Free Trade Agreement and the Meech Lake Accord. Yet two Gallup polls found that, for all the media attention, only 19 percent of Canadians felt they had sufficient knowledge to assess the Free Trade Agreement by the time it had been signed with the U.S. As of May 1990, 54 percent of the populace said they knew "little" or "nothing" about the Meech Lake accord, including 52 percent of Quebec residents.[3]

In encouraging discernment, there is a need for a better alliance between the media and the academic world. At the moment, the two spheres represent Canada's two information solitudes. The media, give or take some sectors of the book publishing industry, along with the CBC's *Journal* and the *Globe and Mail*, have a high measure of aversion to academics. They draw infrequently and selectively on personnel, the occasional conference, and, on rare occasions, a professional journal. Academics, for their part, are often cynical of the media, and seldom — for lack of both inclination and ability — make their research findings available in forms that are fit for public consumption. Very few ever succeed in linking the two spheres; David Suzuki is a rare exception. The chasm is to our national and personal detriment. It needs to be bridged.

Individualism and relativism are rampant in the Canadian media. Rightly or wrongly, a measure of arrogance has come to be associated with the media's high profile and power. The times, however, call for much more than a media that insist on autonomy and then proceed to act socially irresponsible. This is not a day when the issue being contested is the freedom of the small-town newspaper publisher to have his say. We are talking about reality construction. With increasing education, it is only a matter of time until average Canadians realize that the issue of a responsible media is as important as the issue of an autonomous media.

Perhaps we need better checks and balances. Letters to editors and networks, an occasional brief chance to offer rebuttals, and complaints to press councils hardly offset the mind-making and role-modeling influence of the media. Our concern for social well-being requires the careful examination of media influence.

But that's the downside. A self-conscious and socially conscious Canadian media can be the primary source of enhanced well-being in this country. The media need to rise to the challenge.

There is an important footnote that needs to be added. Given the tremendous influence the American media have on Canadians through cable television, motion pictures, music magazines, newspapers, and books, it is increasingly important that Canada exert some control over these forms in this country. As things stand, we can get our maple leaf neatly arranged, only to have it devoured by the eagle. It's a formidable, intimidating task. But it's an issue that has to be resolved. Economic concerns have led to a large number of Canadian-U.S. agreements, including Free Trade. Environmental concerns have led to agreements on such issues as acid rain. Concern for the effect that the media have on the quality of social life in both countries calls for serious talks and significant agreements.

Education

Our educational systems clearly have the potential to contribute substantially to Canadian well-being. Public schools lead the country in the respect and confidence they are accorded — outdistancing even the Supreme Court. Many people maintain that children today are getting as good or better an education as they did in the past. More young Canadians than ever before are both aspiring to go to colleges and universities and in fact doing so. Further, the growth of continuing education programs attests to the fact that education less and less is being seen as over once we enter the world of work. Education sociologist Jos. Lennards notes, "Given the rapidity of scientific and technological change, the stock of knowledge and skill we acquire between the ages of five and twenty-four will no longer suffice for a lifetime."[4]

EDUCATION GETTING BETTER OR WORSE?

"Do you think children are being better educated or worse than you were?"

	Better	Worse	Same	Don't Know	TOTAL
1989	47	34	14	5	100
1981	47	38	9	6	100
1971	63	20	12	5	100
1948	74	12	10	4	100

SOURCE: *Gallup Canada, Inc.* October 12, 1989.

To date, education in Canada has been a major proponent of both individualism and relativism. University-trained teachers and professors of the post-1950s were taught that the freedom of the individual is of paramount value and that truth is relative to people and places and points in time. These teachers in turn have been passing on to their students the virtues of individualism and relativism.

RESTORING BALANCE

The strong emphasis our schools place on the individual must be counterbalanced by a greater emphasis on the group. In large part, the idea of a group-individual balance is an outlook that colors how a teacher or professor presents material. But it also obviously has curriculum and course content implications, notably the presentation of material that assists young people and others to cope with life.

Much more emphasis needs to be given to imparting skills for living. We now know much about some of the components that are essential to personal and interpersonal well-being — features that enable people to achieve goals and relate well to others. "Reading, writing, and arithmetic" are no longer enough. Areas including "reflection, risk-taking, and relationships" also need to be given primary attention. Canadians need to learn the central importance to social life of concepts such as opting in, problem-solving, communication, and accountability.

The tremendous popularity of books, programs, and workshops aimed at helping people to cope with life — family, relationships, career, and so on — should be sending educators a message. Very large numbers don't know how to live, precisely at a period in our history when they have more formal education than ever before. Something is seriously wrong.

Educators in some parts of the country acknowledge the need for improved social and living skills. In Ontario and Alberta, for example, programs teaching values and interpersonal development have been expanded. In other provinces, similar programs either have been initiated or are in the planning stages. Still, such efforts are frequently met with resistance. Educator Gordon Campbell is a former Canadian college president and professor who is currently setting up educational programs in St. Lucia and Taiwan. Recently, he described things to me this way:

> The current situation in Canada for educators is something like trying to navigate a canoe through treacherous rapids. One is simply trying to stay afloat, not tip over, not hit the rocks, not rip any holes in the craft. The hope is that the rapids will eventually give way to a serene lake. But for now, the name of the game is sheer survival.

RESUMING THE SEARCH

Our educational institutions should be leading the nation in encouraging the expression of all views and the pursuit of the best views. Expression, discernment, and risk-taking should be central educational themes.

In Canada today, the norm for the academic enterprise is relativism. Having popularized the concept of cultural relativism, we stress the importance of being objective, or at least being conscious of our biases. Social scientists, and their colleagues in the humanities and the like, present viewpoints and avoid value judgments when discussing such things as lifestyles, family structures, sexual orientation, and religion.

Of considerable importance, in the words of Berkeley's Robert Bellah and his associates, many scholars "have become specialists in fields where only specialists speak to one another."[5] Kenneth Westhues of the University of Waterloo says that a major worry that hangs over social science in our time "is the inordinate priority on exchanging words among ourselves, to the neglect of communicating at all with people outside our various fields."[6] Canadian sociologists, for example, know a great deal about sociology; it is not as clear that they have been succeeding in telling people a great deal about Canadian life. Then again, if there is no such thing as "truth" and "best," perhaps there is no nobler cause to which social scientists can direct their intellectual energies.

In contrast to such closed-minded and insular styles, Canadian schools and universities need to resume the search for what is better and best. From kindergartens to graduate schools, students must be encouraged to become familiar with existing views, to evaluate them critically, and creatively posit new possibilities. Academics must lead the way.

For too long, many Canadian professors have been "talking to themselves" — engaging in esoteric debates, slaying mediocre hypotheses with sophisticated statistical missiles, and publishing their results in peer-created, peer-reviewed, and peer-read journals. They have not been telling us all that much about how our world works. Sociologist Westhues puts things this way: "The question is whether we practictioners of social science are . . . so much occupied with talking among ourselves and so isolated from evaluation by outsiders, that we constitute a kind of parasitic community."[7]

There is a great need for social research in Canada that aspires not only to enhance academic disciplines, but also to provide a better understanding of life. Such research will allow Canadians young and old to choose well from available options.

If that research is to be adequately disseminated, academics need the media. The media need to be co-opted as invaluable allies, both on and off academic turf. Better use of the media needs to be made in the school and on the campus. But the media also need to be tapped for educational purposes away from the classroom, in the living rooms and on the newsstands of the nation. If academics have anything to say to the public as a whole about how the world works, they need to do a far better job of getting the word out. To rely almost exclusively on students and in-house publications is not enough.

American academics have had considerable success in popularizing their work: names like Alfred Kinsey, Margaret Mead, Harvey Cox, David Riesmann, Peter Berger, and David Elkind come to mind. Canada has had very few counterparts, except for Suzuki and perhaps, in 1965, John Porter and his *Vertical Mosaic*. If anything, Canadian academics have tended to be critical of such "crossover" works, viewing them as "pop" books. Former Health and Welfare Minister Monique Bégin, now a University of Ottawa professor, recently summed up the situation succinctly in beginning a statement with the words, "The journalist in me, which is a disease to have in academic life . . . ."[8]

And finally, there is a need for educators to lead the way in taking more intellectual chances. Much of what is published about Canada by Canadian social scientists, for example, is characterized by accuracy and thoroughness, but little risk-taking. A few years ago, a friend and I were talking about a new book on Canada written by a colleague. "I like the book," I said. "He's been thorough — but somehow it reads like a sound encyclopedia; there seems to be something missing." My friend interjected bluntly, "He didn't take any chances." Sound and safe is the Canadian academic norm.

Educators need to do more than encourage diverse viewpoints and critical discernment: they also need to take chances, risk being wrong in the name of saying something new that will stimulate thought and growth.

Writing in the late 1950s, Arthur Lower of Queen's expressed his concern over the fact that the growth of mass education was leading Canadians toward what he called "the deadly average." Our "god of Equality," said Lower, is leading us to equate "equality of soul [with] equality of mind." He called for educators to pursue the best, noting that, while the average person throughout history has taken what the mass producers have provided, "the great cultures were built by great artists" and by people "of great taste and discernment."[9] In pursuing balance and the best, the educational sphere in Canada represents one of our major players. We need its contribution.

Religion

Religion is Canada's sleeping giant. Life in Canada today is lived with limited recourse to religion. Religion is rarely a factor in determining national and regional matters. Free Trade, Meech Lake, and tax debates have been carried out without reference to religion. And religion also has limited effects when it comes to personal matters — values, attitudes, perceptions.

A LATENT INFLUENCE

Religion does not lack for detractors, who — like Auguste Comte, Karl Marx, and Sigmund Freud — see it as something of a relic. But its historical record is impressive. Religion has had staying power. Few societies have managed to live without it for long. Further, religion's relationship to human history and specific societies has been anything but static. Its role over the centuries has been dynamic and ever-changing. Predictions of its demise have never been fulfilled.

Even as Marx could be heard calling for the death of religion and Freud was asserting that its disappearance was imminent, sociologist Max Weber was insisting that the economic system in Western society was carrying the stamp of its influence. In his classic work, *The Protestant Ethic and the Spirit of Capitalism*, Weber argued that the moral tone of capitalism in the Western world had been profoundly influenced by the Protestant Reformation. Religious ideas, he maintained, can have an important influence on attitudes and behavior.[10]

Today, religion is playing an important role in revitalizing slumbering countries, calling for democratization and justice. One has only to look to Poland, the Philippines, and Latin America to see a Roman Catholic Church that is having a noteworthy impact on social change; to South Africa to see the influence of clergy, such as Archbishop Desmond Tutu and Reverend Allan Boesak, in confronting apartheid; to East Germany and Romania to see Protestant and Catholic churches functioning as centers for public meetings aimed at addressing pressing concerns. Even from Russia, from no one less than President Mikhail Gorbachev, came the call in late 1989 for the aid of religion in nurturing the ethics and morality necessary for social life.

Religion can have a powerful influence on culture — including Canadian culture. There are two very good reasons religion in Canada is down, but anything but out.

First, the constituents are still there. Attendance, interest, and influence may be down, but identification with religious groups remains high — and stable. Although regular attendance has dropped dramatically in the past several decades, only a few Canadians — about 10 percent — claim that they never attend religious services. In Quebec, those "never" attenders actually decreased from 10 percent in 1975 to 4 percent in 1985. And most Canadians of all ages continue to look to religious groups for baptisms, weddings, and funerals.

Canada's religious groups continue to have very large constituencies. In addition, many and perhaps most are fairly powerful organizations, usually national or multinational in scope. Collectively, their strength is all the more impressive. The nation's religious groups continue to have substantial human and organizational resources.

Consequently, religion has the potential to exert much influence on individuals and the social structure — the media, education, and government.

But beyond resources, there is a second reason religion in Canada may well experience a renaissance as we move into the twenty-first century. Individualism carried to an extreme locates life's meaning in the individual — personal development, personal success, personal gratification. It is not at all clear, however, that such self-grounded meaning is adequate for most people.

Back in the 1920s, Max Weber noted that when the meaning of work could be interpreted in the context of a religious view of the world, such as being "called" to work hard and well, work took on self-transcendent meaning. However, in reflecting on the fact that, by then, the work ethic had becoming increasingly autonomous from its religious roots, Weber wondered what kind of personal significance it would continue to have, beyond being "associated with purely mundane passions, which often actually give it the character of sport."[11]

Religion has provided a frame of reference for interpreting life — our ultimate origins and purpose — and death. To replace such a framework with an emphasis on the individual is, for many people, rationally inviting but functionally inadequate.

Similarly, interpersonal experiences that leave us with feelings of joy, humor, and warmth — in contrast to those encounters that leave us feeling distraught, empty, and cold — are poignant reminders that everything is not relative. There are some things that elevate us as human beings — acts of kindness, thoughtfulness, and extension, that transcend cultural boundaries. Conversely, our planet increasingly condemns violence and injustice and suffering. It was said of the Nuremberg Laws during the famous trials, "Civilization cannot stand their being ignored because it cannot stand their being repeated." Echoing Kant,

Peter Berger writes, "Deeds that cry out to heaven also cry out to hell."[12] Like individualism, relativism is initially attractive. But it also fails in the face of human experience. Relativism's limits leave people looking for more.

Canadian society is in need of the reaffirmation both of balance between the individual and society and the need to pursue the best in everything. Such issues are anything but peripheral to religion. On the contrary, they touch its heart. The relationship between the individual and the group is an *ethical* issue; the need to pursue the best is a *truth* issue. Few, if any, institutions are in a better position than religion to speak to matters of ethics and truth.

Moreover, religion has much to say about going beyond sheer coexistence. Religious studies professor Douglas Hall of McGill makes the important point that in pluralistic cultures, Christians, for example, are called "to get beyond tolerance." While they, along with others, are required by law to tolerate other people, they are also required by the Christian faith "to recognize that tolerance is not enough." What tolerance can translate into, he notes, is simply looking past people, allowing them to have their beliefs, however "false," because we really don't care. Says Hall, "It *may* be good enough, legally and politically, for the pluralistic society; but it is not good enough . . . for the one who did *not* say "Tolerate your neighbour," but "Love your neighbour."[13]

Religion does not lack for opportunity in Canada. As Professor Harold Coward of the University of Calgary points out, the world's major religions historically have actually arisen in religiously plural environments. If anything, when the pluralistic challenges receded to the background — such as was the case with Christianity in the Middle Ages — a period of spiritual stagnation set in. The reassertion of pluralism, he maintains, "infused new life into the tradition that was confronted." Coward concludes that "although the challenge of religious pluralism is a crisis of our age, it is at the same time an opportunity for spiritual growth."[14]

A LOST MESSAGE

If religion is to awaken from its slumbering state in Canada, its first hurdle will be to get its own house in order. The devastating damage caused by individualism and relativism needs to be assessed and addressed. It has been extensive.

For the most part, Canada's religious groups have been captured by culture. They themselves have not been calling the agenda shots. There is little doubt as to the source of the directives; as Peter Berger has put it, "Relevance and timeliness are defined for the society at large," including religion, "primarily by the media." He adds the cautionary footnote that, as such, religion's attempt to be "relevant" is a fragile business.[15]

Excessive individualism hardly was turned away at the church steps. As for relativism, it has stripped religion of its clear and decisive voice. People are left wondering, notes Berger, why one should buy psychotherapy or concern for racial justice in a religious package "when the same commodities are available under purely secular labels." He adds that "the preference for the former will probably be limited to people with a sentimental nostalgia for traditional symbols – a group that . . . is steadily dwindling."[16]

Yet, the limits of individualism and relativism mark the entry point for religion. Religion, in full form, has the potential to bring much to our times. Historically, faiths have had a great deal to say about self and society, about the delicate balance between the individual and the group in the pursuit of well-being. They also have had much to say about the importance of commitment and problem-solving, communication and accountability. Religions have maintained that there are better and best ways of thinking and acting, that truth, though elusive, must be earnestly pursued.

What is therefore necessary in a pluralistic environment, notes Brian Stiller, the executive director of the Evangelical Fellowship of Canada, is for those who value faith to do two things: they need to be present, and they need to say something.[17] Aspects of pluralism might well be used to religion's advantage. For example, well-known writer and researcher Don Posterski recently wrote that Christians need to recognize that the days of the religious monopoly are over. Yet, in the course of accepting the reality of diversity and showing an appreciation for the available options, they can use the tolerance factor as an opportunity to "interact with alternatives."[18]

The resources are there: so is the opportunity. What's needed is for religion to say something clearly enough and loudly enough so that Canadians can hear.

A LOUDER VOICE

As with education, if religion is going to get its message out, it is going to have to do a far better job of co-opting the media for its own purposes. To date, religion's experiences with the media have hardly been productive. Religion frequently has found itself a media target. In the 1970s, the Canadian media gave considerable attention to new religious movements and allegations of kidnapping and brainwashing by groups such as the Moonies, while the dramatic decline in Roman Catholic attendance, for example, was largely overlooked. In the 1980s, the media in Canada took great delight in focusing on sexual and financial religious scandals in the United States. Television and radio stations, newspapers, and magazines that otherwise would scarcely mention religion were providing daily updates on the pronouncements of Oral Roberts, and the soap-operalike downfalls of Jim Bakker and Jimmy Swaggart. No regard was shown for the implications of such publicity for religious leaders and followers in Canada. In 1989 and 1990, the Roman Catholic Church, which ordinarily finds its national publicity limited to a Papal visit or an occasional Conference of Bishops' pronouncement, suddenly was in the news — a welcome respite for the United Church and its controversy over homosexual ordination. The sexual abuse of young boys by priests was widely publicized, again with the qualifiers — so essential to minimizing the destructive labeling of every priest in the country — conspicuous by their absence.

Little wonder religious leaders are shy of the media. However, unless religious groups can make their voices heard through the media, notably television, they will have a limited place in the mind-making and social-shaping that the media are carrying out.

It is one thing for religious leaders to be aware of findings such as those reported in *Fragmented Gods*, to the effect that only about 4 percent of Canadians are currently watching religious programs on television with regularity, compared with almost 30 percent in the late 1950s, and that most of these are weekly service attenders.[19] However, if such findings merely console critics of American televangelists, the major message is lost. The findings need to motivate those who value faith to come up with problem-solving strategies that will enable them to use television more effectively to converse with Canadians.

The national Vision cable channel is an admirable start. But the key is attracting an audience, which means that religious groups must also gain exposure on the commercial networks, as well as in other media. One obvious strategy is to buy air time and advertising space; that's expensive but, on occasion, possibly the best route to take. A second strategy is for individuals and organizations who value religious faith to function as interest groups that attempt to influence media content. On occasion, the media may be willing to provide some airtime or news space.

There is a third possibility. Some of the highest-profile religious figures in recent decades — Archbishop Desmond Tutu, Mother Teresa, Jesse Jackson, Terry Waite, and Martin Luther King — have been *newsmakers*. They received attention because they were doing things that were seen as making a difference. Perhaps one of the main reason religious leaders in Canada have received so little media attention is that they so seldom have been playing a prophetic role — taking chances, speaking out. One exception was the late Toronto Anglican Archbishop, Lewis Garnsworthy. He was outspoken, and not infrequently was strongly criticized. But he did take chances. And he received press.

What was amazing in the week after the Montreal massacre in 1989 was the failure of the nation's religious groups to speak up. In the midst of the polarization of the sexes, I, for one, listened to see if the United Church, the Anglican Church, the Roman Catholic Church, the Conservative Protestant churches, or any other religious group would say something — perhaps attempt to call Canadians not to be divisive but to come together and work together for the national and personal good. As the soul-searching and allegations raged on for some ten days, no such voices were heard.

The old cliché of "prophets crying in the wilderness" depicts a pre-mass-media image. There is good reason to believe that such religious individualists might well get access to the media spotlight in our day. Religious leaders who, in William Hordern's phrase, "say nothing to culture that culture is not already saying to itself,"[20] can hardly expect to get airtime. Conversely, it may well be that precisely at the point that those who value faith begin to engage Canadian culture rather than simply mirroring it, the media will be more inclined to take notice.

Religion, which prides itself on being able to speak to culture, has been remarkably silent in the face of the presence of individualism and relativism. Prophets have been scarce. Few voices can be heard criticizing the excesses or offering correctives. Ours is a day in which such voices need to be heard. Religion, as it has been known to historically, has permitted the kind of evaluation that Canadian life currently requires. In Berger's words, "The principal moral benefit of religion is that it permits a confrontation with the age in which one lives in a perspective that transcends the age and thus puts it in proportion."[21] If religion still has anything to say, "the time is at hand" to say it.

Government

Meech Lake was billed by the federal and provincial governments as a national crisis. Politicians and the media maintained a posture of tenseness and grimness. The country was expected to follow suit; to do less would have been to show irreverence for a Canada that could very well be breathing its last. This great crisis consumed our national attention and energies. It also cost us money. On May 23, Finance Minister Michael Wilson told reporters that Meech Lake "is not just a constitutional or political matter but an economic matter, and it can affect the cost of money, investment decisions, and lives of people. I think Canadians haven't appreciated the economics of Meech." The day after his speech, the *Globe and Mail* reported that "the crisis" was likely to drive up the prime lending rate to 14 percent, the highest level since the summer of 1982.[22]

Meech Lake represented an attempt to amend the Canadian Constitution in such a way as to obtain Quebec's signature. As such, it was "an internal matter"; there was no apparent necessity to rush toward finalizing the agreement. Quebec's signature after all, had been missing for eight years. There was consequently little reason to be overly concerned should the calm cleaning up of areas of disagreement take a few months, or even a few years. In many ways Meech Lake was a houskeeping matter. In world perspective, it was a matter of cosmetics.

Nonetheless, our elected representatives somehow managed to blow this relatively innocuous matter into a full-scale crisis. Lacking a real deadline, they somehow managed to convince themselves and everybody else that ratification's "D-day" was June 23, 1990. The media went along with the politicians, filling yawning pages and empty news slots with updates on the emerging crisis. The media did an outstanding job of alerting average Canadians to the very real possibility that the Canadian sky was falling.

This national strain and drain eventually ended in apparent victory, with the prime minister and premiers emerging as the players whose eleventh-hour heroics won the game for the country, and engaging in not a little mutual back-patting. Not all of us bothered to attend the post-game party. As it turned out, of course, the celebration was short-lived.

PASSÉ POLITICS

The confrontational politics that historically have characterized our federal and provincial governments are increasingly out of touch with where the world is going. Tired of wars and tension that yield few winners, more and more people in this country and elsewhere are recognizing the need to choose peace and cooperation, then work together to bring it about.

These are times when a Russian president and a Polish prime minister are talking about the need for communists and noncommunists to work together to enhance life, when a freed Black political prisoner and a president are acknowledging the need for Blacks and Whites to come together to build a new South Africa, when the United States and the Soviet Union are agreeing to dismantle huge portions of their military forces in recognition that the day is different. In such an era, it is almost embarrassing to watch Canadian politicians wrestling with each other over domestic matters. During the Meech Lake countdown, McGill professors Morton Weinfeld and Pierre Anctil asked, "Why are our political leaders allowed to play poker with the destiny of the country?" The future holds breathtaking opportunities. "Yet, as the century draws to a close . . . we remain mired in our comparatively petty squabbles. For shame."[23] Columnist Allan Fotheringham wrote, "Meech makes us all mad. The irritation at the nonsense of a nation being broken up over lawyers arguing over commas in constitutional sub-amendments makes otherwise semi-sane people do irrational things."[24]

If our federal and provincial representatives were the members of our company's board of directors, we would fire them. If our prime minister was the CEO, his days would probably be numbered. They not only didn't get the job done; in the course of failing, they tore up the country.

The dawn of the twenty-first century is issuing in an age where leaders are increasingly going to be expected to be committed to the pursuit of maximum social and personal well-being, to put aside their differences and work together to bring the best kind of life possible into being. Concepts such as opting in, problem-solving, communication, and accountability are all going to be dominant ideals. Why? Because the world is coming to realize that the alternative is at best sheer existence, at worst self-destruction.

In a Canada where people want to live well, we are looking for politicians who can transcend the mundane goal of coexistence. Strategies such as obliteration and blackmailing of one's political opponents are out. If we are to have a country that sets its sights on pursuing well-being, we need politicians who will unequivocally opt in to Canada, and work with problem-solving outlooks in resolving their differences and achieving their objectives.

We speak of providing a model for the world and point to our revered mosaic. A more noble goal would be to have no more

Meech Lakes, to aspire to being a country in which our political representatives lead the world in their commitment to well-being and to the methods that bring about its achievement.

POSITIVE POLITICS

Canada needs a positive approach to politics, whereby governments at the federal and provincial levels go beyond their self-serving jockeying for power and leverage.

Canada needs governments that are committed to well-being. What happens at government levels sets a tone for all of life, influencing the national, regional, community, interpersonal, and individual levels of our existence. If governments are warring or unstable, we feel socially and personally unsettled and troubled. Conversely, when our governments operate positively, the social and personal effects are also positive. Assured that our *social* existence is secure, we as well can give our attention to pursuing well-being.

Perhaps politicians, in the aftermath of our constitutional struggles, will be willing, as Premier Bourassa suggested in May 1990, to say, "Let's work together, let's turn the page, let's prepare the international economy, let's face other challenges."[25] If they do not, we need to remove them from office, one by one. What other countries recently have been attempting to do through revolution, we are in the privileged position of being able to accomplish through replacement. With or without the present casts, the show has to improve.

The time has come for government to move on. The importance of the bilingualism and multiculturalism building blocks in a culturally diverse Canada needs to be reaffirmed. But the government will continue to fail the nation if it stops there.

Leaders who can transcend visionless coexistence will strike a responsive chord in the hearts of Canadians who are hungry for more significant goals and dreams.

10

CONCLUSION

I'M A FAIRLY TYPICAL CANADIAN. My grandparents on my father's side were Americans from Pennsylvania and Missouri, a generation removed from England. My mother's parents were from small Welsh villages. The Welsh link has been dominant — with some regularity I venture back to Cardiff and wander around rural Wales, imagining what the past may have been like. I also feel at home in the United States. I have lived there for two stretches of three years each, and frequently visit.

But while I cherish my national heritages, I am a Canadian, which for me means much more than being a Welsh-American hybrid who attends Welsh song festivals and watches American sports on TV. Living in Canada means more than merely sharing common geographical turf with an assortment of other cultural hybirds and purebreds who are all encouraged to give preeminence to the national cultures of their origins.

Why? For one thing, I have only a slight grasp of my Welsh past, and my American heritage was never really cultivated. Moreover, what I know of both leaves me with an appreciation for the aspects of each that are positive, but with no desire to perpetuate the features that need improvement.

So where does that leave me, and thousands — no, millions — of other Canadians, in a country that tells us that our national end is to live out our cultural heritages? The answer lies in taking a closer look at our ancestral past.

The Dream That Created Diversity

The vast majority of our parents, grandparents, and great-grandparents came to Canada not to live out the old life here, but to find a new life, one much better than what they had known in the countries of their birth.

In May 1990, as I drove up the winding narrow road that leads to the village of Nasareth in northern Wales and again looked at the rolling, sheep-dotted hillsides, I thought of the risk that my grandfather — then only a young man in his early twenties — had taken embarking on that long voyage to Canada, never to return. As I walked down the narrow little main street of Corris in central Wales, where my grandmother had walked as a child, I was moved to think of the risk she had taken as a young woman heading off to the distant and unknown land of Canada. She, too, would never see her homeland again.

They and so many other hundreds of thousands of immigrants came to Canada because they had a dream of a better life. Historically, there is perhaps no single characteristic more common among those varied new arrivals than that dream. Our relatives who preceded us from Britain and France, from the rest of Europe and Asia and Africa and the Americas, came because they saw hope of better things. It is not an exaggeration to say that the dream of a better life is the very source of our cultural diversity.

That dream needs to be reemphasized in our time. We, like they, want to stay alive and live well. That's why it's so important that we resolve the issue of coexistence, so that we who have come to Canada and those who were here when we arrived together can give our energies to pursuing the best existence possible in this land.

Our cultural diversity is one of our richest assets. Our dream of well-being — along with a willingness to work for it — is a goal that brings cohesion to that diversity. Social sanity lies in refocusing on the dream that created a multinational Canada.

What It Will Take

A question of motivation emerges from this analysis: What will it take for Canadians to move on to better things? What will lead people to become more concerned about a balance between individualism and the group, more concerned about pursuing the best of available choices? What will lead institutions to encourage such emphases, when they have thought it to be in their best interests to stress individualism and relativism?

One can appeal to altruism, urging Canadians to have a greater concern for the social good. I would like to believe that there are large numbers of people from Newfoundland to British Columbia who would respond to such a plea. While individualism is rampant, there is, I believe, a growing recognition of some of its destructive results. Many of us feel a certain revulsion when individuals and organizations experience success at the expense of others. We certainly applaud winning; but little affirmation is given to those who win with callous disregard for those who lose. Many, I think, are attracted to the idea of a Canada that is committed to the goal of social and personal well-being, that values individuality while emphasizing themes like problem-solving and communication as means to better group life.

Similarly, the importance of pursuing the best of available possibilities is not "a hard sell." To call Canadians to be discerning is to ask them to think more, not less.

Many of these "reflective altruists" are, of course, already well aware of the need for balance and pursuit of the best. The hope is that they will be joined by other people who have aspired to good personal and group life, but just now are beginning to catch a glimpse of what it is going to take to make it happen.

The appeal to altruistic concern for the well-being of the entire society of course has definite limits. Philosophers provide the arguments and sociologists and psychologists the data that make the conclusion clear: significant numbers of Canadians are guided by self-interest, plain and simple. Egoism is alive and well in this country. That leaves us with the tough question: What will it take to bring these people around?

Fortunately, there is an answer: their very self-interest! As Freda Paltiel, a senior policy adviser to Health and Welfare Canada recently put it, when people who have power are asked to share it, they tend to have three typical responses. The first is, "Gee, ma, do I have to?" The second is, "Are you going to make me?" And, if the first two fail, the third is, "What happens to me if

I don't?"[1] We now are at the "what happens to me" stage. It would be preferable for Canadians to opt for balance and pursuit of the best out of concern for the society as a whole; however, the truth of the matter is that, in the long run, no one has much choice.

If we continue to insist on individualism at the expense of society as a whole, at best we are simply going to coexist and subsist, nationally, institutionally, relationally. At worst, we are going to experience ever-increasing social disintegration. Large chunks of the nation are going to be snapped off; the possible secession of Quebec, rather than being the end of a problem, will only be the beginning of many more. Other parts — the Atlantic region, the West, the Territories — could just as readily follow suit. Organizationally and interpersonally, excessive individualism and relativism will make group life and personal relationships all the more difficult.

Where does it all end? That's hard to say. Where does sanity begin? That's easy to say: it begins with Canadians, whether motivated by concern for others or concern for self, finding a balance between the individual and the group, and together pursuing the best kind of life possible. The alternatives lie before us like a divided highway that is coming up fast. One side is marked with a "proceed" arrow, the other with a circled X. I hope we will opt for sanity.

The Moral of the Canadian Story

And so we return to where we began. A world that is intent on freedom and increasingly open to individualism, pluralism, and relativism would do well to watch the drama being produced in Canada. Former British Columbia Supreme Court justice Thomas Berger goes so far as to say that "the idea of two linguistic communities living and working together is something that *has* to succeed. If we can't do it in this country," he says, "what hope do they have in countries like Israel, Ireland or Pakistan? We have an educated population, a tolerant population and we have a high standard of living. If we can't make it work, who can?"[2]

We may well see not only Canada but our *world* slip increasingly into social chaos. Still, that's the worst scenario. Many times in our history and world history, when compassion and reason have failed, a residual resource has surfaced: necessity. It's almost as if the gods let us "mess things up" close to the point of self-annihilation, and then say, "Enough's enough, the game is over; it's time to get serious and tidy up."

In Canada and elsewhere, the altruist and egoist alike may soon have little choice but to give up the luxury of their differences and give increased attention to balance and best. The alternative is not attractive. The times call for people to make social life work, to embark on problem-solving and the conscious pursuit of the best kind of existence possible. Whether born of virtue or expediency, there is still much hope. Nationally and globally, madness can yet give way to sanity. But it's time to make our move.

NOTES

INTRODUCTION

1 Naisbitt and Aburdene, 1990:298.
2 Naisbitt and Aburdene, 1990:311, 313.

1 OUR PREDICAMENT

1 Cited in Christiano, 1990:21.
2 Hunter and Posner, 1987:104.
3 Agòcs, 1987:187.
4 Weinfeld, 1988:600.
5 Weiner, 1985.
6 Beaujot, 1988:57.
7 Canadian Press, May 29, 1990.
8 Canadian Press, April 30, 1990.
9 *Maclean's*, January 1, 1990:2.

2 HOW WE GOT INTO ALL THIS

1 Lipset, 1989.
2 Anderson, 1988:2073.
3 Anderson, 1988:2074.
4 Cited in Prentice et al., 1988:303.
5 Grey, 1988:748.
6 Prentice et al., 1988:406.
7 Maxwell, 1987:128.
8 Prentice et al., 1988:170-171.
9 Prentice et al., 1988:172.
10 Prentice et al., 1988:172.
11 Anderson, 1988:2074.
12 Cited by Saywell in Trudeau, 1968:x.
13 Palmer, 1988:1741.
14 Palmer, 1988:1741.
15 Palmer, 1988:1741.
16 Weinfeld, 1988:591.
17 Weinfeld, 1988:591.
18 Palmer, 1988:174.
19 Weinfeld, 1988:593.
20 Palmer, 1988:1741.
21 Beaujot, 1988:55.
22 Palmer, 1988:1742.
23 Palmer, 1988:1742.
24 Palmer, 1988:1742.
25 Palmer, 1988:1742.
26 Palmer, 1988:1742.

27 Beaujot, 1988:55.
28 Schwartz, 1967:87.
29 Lower, 1958:375.
30 P. Such, cited in Lundy-Warme, 1990:263.
31 Patterson, 1988:1461.
32 Hall, 1988:1057.
33 Cited in Ponting, 1988:625.
34 Patterson, 1988:1462.
35 Patterson, 1988:1462.
36 Ponting, 1988:621.
37 Ponting, 1988:630.
38 Lundy and Warme, 1990:266.
39 Valentine, 1980:47.
40 Palmer, 1988:1743.
41 Agòcs, 1987:176.
42 See, for example, Cardinal, 1969.
43 Rutherford, 1978:39.
44 Beaujot, 1988:41.
45 Beaujot, 1988:41.

3 THE SEEDS OF TRANSFORMATION

1 Friedan. 1963.
2 In Washington, 1986:217-220.
3 Bibby, 1987a:139.
4 Fletcher, 1966.
5 Pike, 1967.
6 Bloom, 1987:25.
7 Bloom, 1987:26.

4 THE TRUE NORTH FINALLY FREE

1 Christiano, 1990:4.
2 Axworthy and Trudeau, 1990:4.
3 Lower, 1958:382.
4 Royal Commission Report on Bilingualism and Bilculturalism, 1965.
5 Latouche, 1988:1802.
6 Beaujot, 1988:56.
7 Corpus Almanac of Canada, 1974.
8 Christiano, 1990:19-20.
9 Dirks, 1988:1047.
10 Hall, 1988:1058.
11 Section 25, Canadian Charter of Rights and Freedoms, 1982.
12 Weinfeld, 1988:593.
13 *Project Can85* and *Maclean's*, January 1, 1990:20.
14 *Project Teen Canada 88*.
15 *Maclean's*, January 1, 1990:20.
16 *Project Teen Canada 88*.
17 Bibby, 1987b.
18 Bibby, 1987b and Gallup Canada, Inc., May 27, 1968.
19 Royal Commission on the Status of Women in Canada, 1970.

20 Morris, 1988:2074.
21 Morris, 1988:2074.
22 Ram, 1990:35.
23 Statistics Canada, varied publications.
24 Boyd, 1984:1.
25 Lipset, 1989:190-191.
26 Canadian Press, January 31, 1990.
27 Canadian Press, January 31, 1990.
28 Parliament, 1989:6.
29 Gallup Canada, Inc., April 20, 1990.
30 Section 15.2, Charter of Rights and Freedoms, 1982.
31 Trudeau in Johnston, 1990:46.
32 Lipset, 1989:116.
33 Gallup Canada, Inc., May 1987.
34 Canadian Press, April 6, 1990.
35 Lipset, 1989:224.
36 Ram, 1990:28.
37 Associated Press, July 5, 1989.
38 Marshall, 1951.
39 Bellah et al., 1985.
40 Steinman, 1977.
41 Peck, 1978:98, 104.
42 Spencer, 1990:327.
43 Armstrong, 1988:745.
44 Census Dictionary, 1986.
45 Ram, 1990:4-8.
46 Drawn from varied Statistics Canada publications unless otherwise noted.
47 *Project Can85*.
48 *Project Teen Canada 88*.
49 *Project Can85*.
50 *Project Canada Survey Series*.
51 Pike, 1988:267.
52 Drawn from varied Statistics Canada publications.
53 Gilbert and Gomme, 1987:214, 216.
54 Cited in Patterson and Kach, 1988:661.
55 Pike, 1988:274.
56 Provided by Don Posterski, 1990.
57 University of Lethbridge, 1990.
58 McSkimmings, 1990:21.
59 Grosman, 1988:97-98.
60 Grosman, 1988:173.
61 Gallup Canada, Inc., May 1990.
62 Cited in LeFevre, 1966:67, 74.
63 Templeton, 1983.
64 Cited in Hunter and Posner, 1987:100.
65 Canadian Almanac, 1989:552.
66 Wannel and McKie, 1986:14.
67 Canadian Almanac, 1989:279.

68 Young, 1989:14.
69 Wannel and McKie, 1986; Young, 1989.
70 Owens, 1989.
71 Strike, 1988:13-14.
72 Carey, 1988:xxxiv.
73 Patterson and Kach, 1988:662.
74 Rutherford, 1978:25.
75 Rutherford, 1978:25-26.
76 Rutherford, 1978:26.
77 Canadian Almanac, 1989:552.
78 Young, 1989:13-15.
79 Gallup Canada, Inc., March 19, 1990.
80 *Maclean's*, January 2, 1989:14.
81 *Maclean's*, January 2, 1989:15, 16.
82 See Bibby, 1987a.
83 *Project Teen Canada 88*.
84 Bibby, 1987a:43-45.
85 *Project Teen Canada 88*.
86 Penelhum, 1983:93.
87 Bibby, 1987a:126.
88 Bibby, 1987a:131.
89 Bibby, 1986.
90 Bibby, 1979.
91 Demerath, 1969.
92 *Project Can85*.
93 *Project Can85*.
94 *Maclean's*, January 1, 1990:26.
95 *Maclean's*, January 1, 1990:38.
96 Lipset, 1989:117-118. Income is in purchasing power units, standardized across countries.

5 SUCCESS IN EXCESS

1 Freud, 1928.
2 Durkheim, 1964.
3 Trudeau, 1968:xxii.
4 Christiano, 1990:20.
5 Horowitz, 1972.
6 Bellah et al., 1985:285.
7 Lipset, 1989:26.
8 Wuthnow, 1989:2.
9 Cited in Lipset, 1989:40.
10 Lipset, 1989:42.
11 Berger, 1981:xvii.
12 Christiano, 1990:25-26.
13 Levy, 1989:26.
14 Bloom, 1987:34.
15 Bloom, 1987:39.
16 Bloom, 1987:128.
17 Garnsworthy, 1986.

18 Ken McKee, *Toronto Star*, March 17, 1989.
19 Gallup Canada, Inc., May 4, 1989.
20 Stahl, 1986a: 15-16.
21 Lipset, 1989:xiii.
22 Christiano, 1990:12-13.
23 Christiano, 1990:11-12.
24 Christiano, 1990:9.
25 Cited in Christiano, 1990:14-15.
26 Christiano, 1990:3.
27 Cited in Christiano, 1990:3.
28 Christiano, 1990:22.
29 Cited in Christiano, 1990:21.
30 Axworthy and Trudeau, 1990:4.
31 Trudeau, 1968:xxii.
32 *Lethbridge Herald*, March 28, 1990.
33 Ghitter, 1990:18, 20.
34 Porter, 1965:366.
35 Canadian Press, March 22, 1990.
36 For an excellent discussion of the role of the land imagery and Canadian nationalism, see Stahl, 1986b.

6 THE INTERPERSONAL CASUALTY LIST

1 Cited in Christiano, 1990:20.
2 Levy, 1989:27.
3 *Maclean's*, January 1, 1990:42 and Canadian Press, April 10, 1990.
4 *Maclean's*, January 2, 1989:36.
5 In Wolff, 1950.
6 Associated Press, December 5, 1989.
7 Cited in Vic Parsons, Thomson News Service, March 31, 1989.
8 Canadian World Almanac, 1989:336.
9 Vic Parsons, Thomson News Service, March 31, 1989.
10 Alberta Association of Registered Nurses, *Lethbridge Herald*, May 1989.
11 Wuthnow, 1989:6.
12 *Maclean's*, January 2, 1989:36.
13 Associated Press, March 3, 1990.
14 Context Training Seminar, Edmonton, December 1988.
15 See, for example, Posterski and Bibby, 1988:12-13.

7 THE INSTITUTIONAL CASUALTY LIST

1 Naisbitt and Aburdene, 1990:139.
2 See, for example, Bibby, 1978.
3 Thomas, 1928.
4 Canadian Press, December 13, 1989.
5 *Toronto Star*, February 23, 1990:A5.
6 *Edmonton Journal*, April, 1986.
7 Wannel and McKie, 1986:18.
8 Bloom, 1987:26-27.
9 Scheff, 1966:33-34.

10 Szasz, 1960.
11 Epp, 1986:20.
12 Ottawa Charter, 1986:1.
13 Bloom, 1987:27.
14 Dimma, 1989:2-3.
15 Dimma, 1989:2.
16 In Colin Hughes, *The Independent*, July 12, 1988.
17 Dimma, 1989:12.
18 Grosman, 1988.
19 *Toronto Star*, August 26, 1989:C1.
20 Cited in Dimma, 1989:4-5.
21 Dimma, 1989:8.
22 Clair Bernstein, *Toronto Star*, April 15, 1990.
23 *Project Teen Canada 88*.
24 Carey, 1988:xxxv.
25 Bibby, 1987a:259ff.
26 Berger, 1986:44.
27 Trudeau in Johnston, 1990:25.
28 Johnston, 1990:107.
29 Statistics Canada, cat. 91-209E, 1990:92.
30 *Maclean's*, January 1, 1990:13-14.
31 Canadian Press, April 18, 1990.
32 *Lethbridge Herald*, March 28, 1990.
33 Canadian Press, March 30, 1990.
34 Canadian Press, April 6, 1990.
35 Gallup Canada, Inc., May 18, 1990, and February 5, 1990.
36 *Project Can85*.
37 *Maclean's*, January 1, 1990:13.
38 Johnston, 1990:138.
39 *Maclean's*, January 1, 1990:16.
40 Johnston, 1990:vi.
41 *Vancouver Province*, December 4, 1989:A7, A10.
42 *Maclean's*, January 2, 1989:36.
43 Goar, *Toronto Star*, March 19, 1990.

8 MOVING ON TO BETTER THINGS

1 Nettler, 1976:10.
2 In Washington, 1986:491.
3 Trudeau, 1968:xxii.
4 Cooley, 1964.
5 Penelhum, 1983:91.
6 Peck, 1978:82ff.
7 Waller, 1936.
8 Peck, 1978:15.
9 *London Evening Standard*, August 24, 1989:1.
10 Canadian Press, February 12, 1990.
11 Stewart MacLeod, Thomson News Services, June 20, 1990.
12 Stewart MacLeod, Thomson News Services, March 26, 1990.
13 Burnet, 1987:79.

14 Ghitter, 1990:21.
15 Canadian Press, April 2, 1990.
16 *Vancouver Province*, December 4, 1989.
17 Borovoy, 1988:309.
18 Berger, 1981:xvii.
19 Dumas, 1990.

9 THE KEY PLAYERS

1 *Maclean's*, July 10, 1989.
2 Gallup Canada, Inc., November 16, 1987.
3 Gallup Canada, Inc., May 18, 1990.
4 Lennards, 1990:429.
5 Bellah et al., 1985:238.
6 Westhues, 1987:9.
7 Westhues, 1987:10.
8 Begin, 1990.
9 Lower, 1958:431-434.
10 Weber, 1958.
11 Weber, 1958:182.
12 Berger, 1969:84.
13 Hall, 1989:57.
14 Coward, 1985:94-95.
15 Berger 1969:29.
16 Berger 1969:26.
17 Stiller, 1988.
18 Posterski, 1989:168-169.
19 Bibby, 1987a:32-34.
20 Hordern, 1966:46.
21 Berger, 1969:121.
22 *Globe and Mail*, May 24, 1990:B1.
23 *Globe and Mail*, May 31, 1990:A7.
24 Fotheringham, *Halifax Daily News*, June 16, 1990.
25 *Toronto Sun*, May 23, 1990:4.

10 CONCLUSION

1 Paltiel, 1990.
2 *Vancouver Sun*, May 26, 1990:B1.

REFERENCES

Agòcs, Carol
1987 "Ethnic Group Relations." In James Teevan (ed.) *Basic Sociology: A Canadian Introduction*. Second Edition. Scarborough: Prentice-Hall. Pp. 161-193.

Ainlay, Stephen C.
1990 "Communal Commitment and Individualism." In Leo Driedger and Leland Harder (eds.) *Anabaptist-Mennonite Identities in Ferment*. Occasional papers no. 14. Elkart, Ind: Institute of Mennonite Studies.

Anderson, Doris
1988 "Status of Women." In *The Canadian Encyclopedia*. Edmonton: Hurtig. Pp. 2072-2074.

Armstrong, Pat
1988 "The Family." In *The Canadian Engyclopedia*. Edmonton: Hurtig. Pp. 743-744.

Axworthy, Thomas S. and Pierre Elliott Trudeau (eds.)
1990 *Towards a Just Society: The Trudeau Years*. Toronto: Viking.

Badgley, Robin
1984 *Sexual Offences Against Children*. Ottawa: Minister of Supply and Services.

Beaujot, Roderic
1987 "The Family." In James Teevan (ed.) *Basic Sociology: A Canadian Introduction*. Second edition. Scarborough: Prentice-Hall. Pp. 197-231.

1988 "Canada's Demographic Profile." In James Curtis and Lorne Tepperman (eds.) *Understanding Canadian Society*. Toronto: McGraw-Hill Ryerson. Pp. 39-70.

Begin, Monique
1990 "Rewriting the Report for the 1990s." Paper presented at the annual meeting of the Canadian Sociology and Anthropology Association, Victoria, May.

Bellah, Robert, Richard Madsen, William Sullivan, Ann Swidler, and Steven Tipton
1985 *Habits of the Heart*. New York: Harper and Row.

Berger, Peter L.
1969 *A Rumor of Angels.* Garden City: Doubleday.
1986 "Religion in Post-Protestant America." *Commentary* 81:41-46.

Berger, Thomas R.
1981 *Fragile Freedoms: Human Rights and Dissent in Canada.* Toronto: Clarke, Irwin.

Berry, John W.
1987 "Finding Identity: Separation, Integration, Assimilation, or Marginality?" In Leo Driedger (ed.) *Ethnic Canada: Identities and Inequalities.* Toronto: Copp Clark Pitman. Pp. 223-239.

Bibby, Reginald W.
1979a "Consensus in Diversity: An Examination of Canadian Problem Perception. *International Journal of Comparative Sciology* 20:274-282.
1979b "The State of Collective Religiosity in Canada." *Canadian Review of Sociology and Anthropology 16:105-116.*
1986 *Anglitrends: A Profile and Prognosis.* Toronto: Anglican Diocese of Toronto.
1987a *Fragmented Gods: The Poverty and Potential of Religion in Canada.* Toronto: Irwin.
1987b *"Bilingualism and Multiculturalism: A National Reading."* In Leo Driedger (ed.) *Ethnic Canada.* Toronto: Copp Clark Pitman. Pp. 158-169.

Bibby, Reginald W. and Donald C. Posterski
1985 *The Emerging Generation: An Inside Look at Canada's Teenagers.* Toronto: Irwin.

Bloom, Allan
1987 *The Closing of the American Mind.* New York: Simon and Schuster.

Borovoy, A. Alan
1988 *When Freedoms Collide: The Case for Our Civil Liberties.* Toronto: Lester and Orpen Dennys.

Boyd, Monica and Edward T. Pryor
1989 "Young Adults Living in their Parents' Home." *Canadian Social Trends,* Summer, 17-20.

Burke, Mary Anne
1986 "Immigration." *Canadian Social Trends,* Autumn, 23-27.

Burnet, Jean
1987 "Multiculturalism in Canada." In Leo Driedger (ed.) *Ethnic Canada: Identities and Inequalities.* Toronto: Copp Clark Pitman. Pp. 65-79.

Cardinal, Harold
1969 *The Unjust Society: The Tragedy of Canada's Indians.* Edmonton: Hurtig.

Carey, John
1988 *Eyewitness to History.* Cambridge: Harvard University Press.

Census Dictionary
1986 Cat. 99-901. Ottawa: Statistics Canada.

Christiano, Kevin J.
1990 "Federalism as a Canadian National Ideal: The Civic Rationalism of Pierre Elliott Trudeau." Unpublished paper.

Cooley, Charles Horton
1964 *Human Nature and the Social Order.* New York: Schocken Books.

Corpus Almanac of Canada
1974 Don Mills, Corpus Information Services.

Coward, Harold
1985 *Pluralism: Challenge to World Religions.* Maryknoll, New York: Orbis Books.

Curtis, James and Lorne Tepperman (eds.)
1988 *Understanding Canadian Society.* Toronto: McGraw-Hill Ryerson.

Demerath, N. J.
1969 "Irreligion, A-Religion, and the Rise of the Religionless Church." *Sociological Analysis* 30:191-203.

Dewey, John
1964 *Democracy and Education: An Introduction to the Philosophy of Education.* New York: Macmillan.

Dirks, Gerald E.
1988 "Immigration Policy." In *The Canadian Encyclopedia.* Edmonton: Hurtig. Pp. 1047-1048.

Driedger, Leo
1989 *The Ethnic Factor: Identity in Diversity.* Toronto: McGraw-Hill.

Driedger, Leo (ed.)
1987 *Ethnic Canada: Identities and Inequalities.* Toronto: Copp Clark Pitman.

Dumas, Jean
1990 *Report on the Demographic Situation in Canada 1988.* Cat. 91-209E. Ottawa: Minister of Supply and Services.

Durkheim, Emile
1964 *The Division of Labor in Society.* Glencoe: Free Press.
1965 *The Elementary Forms of the Religious Life.* New York: Free Press.

Eaman, Ross A.
1987 *The Media Society: Basic Issues and Controversies.* Toronto: Butterworths.

Epp, The Honourable Jake
1986 *Achieving Health for All: A Framework for Health Promotion.* Presented at the International Conference on Health Promotion. Ottawa: November.

Fletcher, Joseph
1966 *Situation Ethics.* Philadelphia: Westminster Press.

Friedan, Betty
1963 *The Feminine Mystique.* New York: Dell.

Frum, Linda
1990 "Broadcast News." *Saturday Night,* May:27-35.

Frye, Northrop
1982 *Divisions on a Ground: Essays on Canadian Culture.* Toronto: Anansi Press.

Garnsworthy, Lewis S.
1986 *The Archbishop's Charge to the 134th Synod.* Toronto: Anglican Diocese.

Gee, Ellen M.
1990 "The Family." In Robert Hagedorn (ed.) *Sociology.* Fourth edition. Toronto: Holt, Rinehart and Winston. Pp. 315-341.

Ghitter, Ron
1990 Presentation to Edmonton Multicultural Communications Foundation. March 21.

Gilbert, Sid N. and Ian M. Gomme
1987 "Education in the Canadian Mosaic." In Michael M. Rosenberg, William B. Shaffir, Allan Turowetz, and Morton Weinfeld (eds.) *An Introduction to Sociology.* Toronto: Methuen. Pp. 197-234.

Grey, Julian
1988 "Family Law, Quebec." In *The Canadian Encyclopedia.* Edmonton: Hurtig. P. 278.

Grindstaff, Carl
1990 "Long-Term Consequences of Adolescent Marriage and Fertility." In Jean Dumas, *Report on the Demographic Situation in Canada 1988.* Cat. 91-209E. Ottawa: Statistics Canada.

Grosman, Brian A.
1988 *Corporate Loyalty: A Trust Betrayed.* Toronto: Viking.

Hall, Anthony J.
1988 "Indian Treaties." In *The Canadian Encyclopedia.* Edmonton: Hurtig. Pp. 1056-1059.

Hall, Douglas John
1989 *The Future of the Church: Where Are We Headed?* Toronto: The United Church Publishing House.

Hiller, Harry H.
1986 *Canadian Society: A Macro Analysis.* Scarborough: Prentice-Hall.

Hordern, William
1966 *New Directions in Theology Today,* Vol. 1, Introduction. Philadelphia: Westminster Press.

Horowitz, Gad
1972 "Mosaics and Identity." In Bryan Finnigan and Cy Gonick (eds.) *Making It: the Canadian Dream.* Toronto: McCelland and Stewart. Pp. 465-473.

Hunter, Linda and Judith Posner
1987 "Culture as Popular Culture." In Michael M. Rosenberg, William B. Shaffir, Allan Turowetz, and Morton Weinfeld (eds.) *An Introduction to Sociology.* Second edition. Toronto: Methuen. Pp. 79-107.

Johnson, Holly
1988 "Wife Abuse." *Canadian Social Trends,* Spring, 17-20.

Johnston, Donald (ed.)
1990 *Pierre Trudeau Speaks Out on Meech Lake.* Toronto: General Paperbacks.

Kallen, Evelyn
1987 "Ethnicity and Collective Rights in Canada." In Leo Driedger (ed.) *Ethnic Canada: Identities and Inequalities.* Toronto: Copp Clark Pitman. Pp. 318-336.

Lasch, Christopher
1979 *The Culture of Narcissism.* New York: Warner Books.
1984 *The Minimal Self.* New York: W. W. Norton and Company.

Latouche, Daniel
1988 "Quebec." In *The Canadian Encyclopedia.* Edmonton Hurtig. Pp. 1793-1802.

LeFevre, Perry
1966 *Understandings of Man.* Philadelphia: The Westminster Press.

Lennards, Jos. L.
1990 "Education." In Robert Hagedorn (ed.) *Sociology*. Fourth edition. Toronto: Holt, Rinehart and Winston. Pp. 399-432.

Lindsay, Colin
1989 "The Service Sector in the 1980s." *Canadian Social Trends,* Spring, 20-23.

Lipset, Seymour Martin
1989 *Continental Divide: The Values and Institutions of the United States and Canada.* Toronto: C. D. Howe Institute.

Levy, Joseph
1989 "Are Well Off Grays Too Materialistic and Self-Centered?" *Foresight,* March-April, 26-27.

Lorimer, Rowland and Jean McNulty
1987 *Mass Communication in Canada.* Toronto: McClelland and Stewart.

Lower, Arthúr R.
1958 *Canadians in the Making.* Toronto: Longmans, Green & Company.

Lundy, Katherine L. P. and Barbara D. Warme
1990 *Sociology: A Window on the World.* Toronto: Nelson.

Lupri, Eugen
1989 "Male Violence in the Home." *Canadian Social Trends,* Autumn, 19-21.

Mackie, Marlene
1987 *Constructing Women and Men: Gender Socialization*. In Robert Hagedorn (ed.) *Sociology.* Toronto: Holt, Rinehart and Winston.

MacLeod, Linda
1980 *Wife Battering in Canada: The Vicious Circle.* Prepared for the Advisory Council on the Status of Women. Ottawa: Minister of Supply and Services.

Mandel, Eli and David Taras (eds.)
1988 *A Passion for Identity: An Introduction to Canadian Studies.* Toronto: Nelson.

Marshall, Catherine
1951 *A Man Called Peter.* New York: McGraw-Hill.

Marshall, Katherine
1989 "Women in Professional Occupations: Progress in the 1980s." *Canadian Social Trends,* Spring, 13-16.

Matthews, Robin
1988 *Canadian Identity.* Ottawa: Steel Rail.

Maxwell, L. E.
1987 *Women in Ministry*. Wheaton, Ill.: Victor Books.

McSkimmings, Judie
1990 "The Farm Community." *Canadian Social Trends,* Spring, 20-23.

Moore, Maureen
1988 "Female Lone Parenthood: The Duration of Episodes." *Canadian Social Trends,* Autumn, 40-42.

Morris, Cerise
1988 "Royal Commission on the Status of Women in Canada." In *The Canadian Encyclopedia.* Edmonton: Hurtig. P. 2074.
1989 "Dual-earner Families: The New Norm." *Canadian Social Trends,* Spring 24-26.

Naisbitt, John and Patricia Aburdene
1990 *Megatrends 2000.* New York: William Morrow.

Nagel, Joane
1987 *The Ethnic Revolution: Emergence of Ethnic Nationalism.* In Leo Driedger (ed.) *Ethnic Canada: Identities and Inequalities.* Toronto: Copp Clark Pitman. Pp. 28-43.

Nettler, Gwynn
1976 *Social Concerns.* Toronto: McGraw-Hill.

Newman, Jay
1982 *Foundations of Religious Tolerance.* Toronto: University of Toronto Press.

Ottawa Charter for Health Promotion
1986 An International Conference on Health Promotion. November.

Owens, Donna
1989 "Public Libraries." *Canadian Social Trends,* Winter, 15-16.

Palmer, Howard
1988 "Prejudice and Discrimination." In *The Canadian Encyclopedia.* Edmonton: Hurtig. Pp. 1740-1743.

Parliament, Jo-Anne B.
1989 "Women Employed Outside the Home." *Canadian Social Trends,* Summer, 2-6.
1989 "How Canadians Spend Their Day." *Canadian Social Trends,* Winter, 23-27.

Paltiel, Freda L.
1990 "Status of Women in Canada: Zeitgeist, Process, and Personalities." Paper presented at the annual meeting of the Canadian Sociology and Anthropology Association, Victoria, May.

Patterson, E. P.
1988 "Native-White Relations." In *The Canadian Encyclopedia.* Edmonton: Hurtig. Pp. 1461-1462.

Patterson, R. S. and K. Kach
1988 "Education." In *The Canadian Encyclopedia.* Edmonton: Hurtig. Pp. 660-662.

Penelhum, Terence
1983 "Faith, Reason, and Secularity." In Eugene Combs (ed.) *Modernity and Responsibility: Essays for George Grant.* Toronto: University of Toronto Press.

Pike, James A.
1967 *You and the New Morality.* New York: Harper and Row.

Pike, Robert
1988 "Education and the Schools." In James Curtis and Lorne Tepperman (eds.) *Understanding Canadian Society.* Toronto: McGraw-Hill Ryerson. Pp. 255-286.

Ponting, Rick
1988 "Native-White Relations." In James Curtis and Lorne Tepperman (eds.) *Understanding Canadian Society.* Toronto: McGraw-Hill Ryerson. Pp. 619-644.

Porter, John
1965 *The Vertical Mosaic.* Toronto: University of Toronto Press.
1967 *Canadian Social Structure: A Statistical Profile.* Toronto: McClelland and Stewart.

Posterski, Donald C.
1989 *Reinventing Evangelism.* Markham, Ontario: Intervarsity Press.

Posterski, Donald C. and Reginald W. Bibby
1988 *Canada's Youth: Ready for Today.* Ottawa: Canadian Youth Foundation.

Potts, Margaret
1989 "University Enrolment in the 1980s." *Canadian Social Trends,* Winter, 28-30.

Prentice, Alison, Paula Bourne, Gail Brandt, Beth Light, Wendy Mitchinson, and Naomi Black
1988 *Canadian Women: A History.* Toronto: Harcourt, Brace & Jovanovich.

Ram, Bali
1990 *New Trends in the Family: Demographic Facts and Features.* Catalogue No. 91-535E. Ottawa: Statistics Canada.

Reisman, David
1950 *The Lonely Crowd.* New Haven: Yale University Press.

Robbins, Linda
1989 "Eating Out." *Canadian Social Trends,* Summer, 7-9.

Rosenberg, Michael M., William B. Shaffir, Allan Turowetz, and Morton Weinfeld.
1987 *An Introduction to Sociology.* Second edition. Toronto: Methuen.

Royal Commission on Bilingualism and Biculturalism.
1965 Ottawa: Queen's Printer.

Royal Commission on the Status of Women in Canada.
1970 Ottawa: Information Canada.

Scheff, Thomas J. (ed.)
1966 *Mental Illness and Social Process.* New York: Harper and Row.

Schwartz, Mildred
1967 *Public Opinion and Canadian Identity.* Berkeley: University of California Press.

Singer, Benjamin D. (ed.)
1983 *Communications in Canadian Society.* Don Mills: Addision-Wesley.

Spencer, Metta
1990 *Foundations of Modern Sociology.* Fifth edition. Scarborough: Prentice-Hall.

Stahl, William
1986a " 'May He Have Dominion': Civil Religion and the Legitimacy of Canadian Confederation." Presented at the annual meeting of the Canadian Sociology and Anthropology Association, Winnipeg, June.
1986b "The Land that God Gave Cain: Nature and Civil Religion in Canada." Presented at the annual meeting of the Society for the Scientific Study of Religion, Washington, D.C., November.

Steiner, George
1974 *Nostalgia for the Absolute.* CBC Massey Lectures, 1974. Toronto: Canadian Broadcasting Corporation.

Steinman, Jim
1977 "Two Out of Three Ain't Bad." Performed by *Meatloaf.* Epic Records.

Stiller, Brian C.
1988 "Understanding Our Times" seminar.
1990 "The Feminist Critique: Hype or Reality?" *Sundial,* First Quarter, 1-2. Willowdale: Evangelical Fellowship of Canada.

Strike, Carol
1988 "The Film Industry in Canada." *Canadian Social Trends,* Summer, 14-16.

Szasz, Thomas
1960 "The Myth of Mental Illness." *The American Psychologist.* 15:113-118.
1970 *The Manufacture of Madness.* New York: Dell.

Symone, Thomas H.B. and James E. Page
1984 *Some Questions of Balance: Human Resources, Higher Education and Canadian Studies.* Ottawa: Association of Universities and Colleges of Canada.

Templeton, Charles
1983 *Charles Templeton: An Anecdotal Memoir.* Toronto: McClelland and Stewart.

The Canadian World Almanac and Book of Facts
1989 Toronto: Global Press

Thomas, W. I.
1928 *The Child in America.* New York: Knopf.

Trudeau, Pierre Elliott
1968 *Federalism and the French Canadians.* Toronto: Macmillan.

Valentine, Victor
1980 "Native Peoples and Canadians: A Profile of Issues and Trends." In Raymond Breton et al. (eds.) *Cultural Boundaries and the Cohesion of Canada,* Part 2. Montreal: Institute for Research on Public Policy.

Wannel, Ted, and Craig McKie
1986 "Expanding the Choices." *Canadian Social Trends,* Summer, 13-18.

Washington, James Melvin
1986 *A Testament of Hope: The Essential Writings of Martin Luther King, Jr.* New York: Harper and Row.

Waller, Willard
1936 "Social Problems and the Mores." *American Sociological Review* 1:line 22-933.

Weber, Max
1958 *The Protestant Ethic and the Spirit of Capitalism.* New York: Charles Scribner's Sons.

Weinfeld, Morton
1987 "Ethnic and Race Relations." In James Curtis and Lorne Tepperman (eds.) *Understanding Canadian Society.* Toronto: McGraw-Hill Ryerson. Pp. 587-616.

Weiner, Myron
1985 "International Migration and International Relations." *Population and Development Review* 11:441-455.

Westhues, Kenneth (ed.)
1987 *Basic Principles for Social Science in Our Time.* Waterloo: University of St. Jerome's College Press.

White, Pamela M.
1989 "Ethnic Origins of the Canadian Population." *Canadian Social Trends,* Summer, 13-16.

Wilson, S. J.
1988 "Gender Inequality." In James Curtis and Lorne Tepperman (eds.) *Understanding Canadian Society.* Toronto: McGraw-Hill Ryerson.

Wuthnow, Robert
1989 "Individualism, Altruism, and Religious Tradition." Presented at the Spring Research Forum, Independent Sector, Washington, D.C.

Young, Anthony
1989 "Television Viewing." *Canadian Social Trends,* Autumn, 13-15.

INDEX

ENVIRONMENTAL CHOICE · CHOIX ENVIRONNEMENTAL ·

Printed on paper
containing over 50%
recycled paper including
5% post-consumer fibre.

Printed in Canada